Dalit in Rural India: Challenges and Opportunities

Dalit in Rural India: Challenges and Opportunities

D.K. Kaul

2008

CYBER TECH PUBLICATIONS
4264/3, Ansari Road, Daryaganj, New Delhi-110002 (India)
Ph.: 011-23244078. Fax: 011-23280028
E-Mail: cyberpublicationsdelhi@yahoo.com

DALIT IN RURAL INDIA: CHALLENGES AND OPPORTUNITIES

D.K. Kaul

First Edition 2008

Published by :

G.S. Rawat for **Cyber Tech Publications**
4264/3, Ansari Road, Daryaganj, New Delhi-110002 (India)
Ph.: 011-23244078. Fax: 011-23280028
E-Mail: cyberpublicationsdelhi@yahoo.com

Printed at : **Amit Enterprises**, Maujpur, Delhi, (9810878184)

Preface

The proportion of dalits landless labourers to the total labourers has shown a steady rising trend. In urban areas, they work mainly in the unorganised sector where the exploitation compares well with that of a feudal rural setting. Out of the total Dalit population of 138 million, the number of dalits in services falling in the domain of reservations does not exceed 1. 3 million including sweepers; less than even a percent. And this too would be grossly misleading, as out of this 1. 3 million the relatively well-off group A and B officers (in which most of the clerical staff of the PSUs also come), count only 72, 212 as against 131, 841, sweepers.

With the new politico-economic order emerging in the world, the grammar of the Dalit liberation struggle is going to be totally different from that familiar to dalits. The onslaught of the adversarial forces is being felt world over by all the oppressed people and it would be folly for dalits not to feel a part of the latter. Their objective situation as a social block is not represented by the minuscule minority that managed to find themselves in the organised sectors of economy, but by the vast majority who are left behind in the villages or the numbers who toil in the unorganised sectors in towns and cities. They need the weaponry for battling out their salvation. This battle is to be waged simultaneously on two fronts, marked by the caste and class.

—*Author*

Contents

1

WHAT CASTE SYSTEM MEANS?

Caste system as discussed here includes untouchability too, but wherever necessary it will be referred to separately. As we shall note, untouchability came into the caste system much later. The following features are generally taken as essential in characterising caste system.

It means not simply a division of labour, with each 'varna' associated with a type of occupation, but also a division of labour determined by birth permitting no occupational/social mobility. This is what distinguishes caste from class. While the former is hereditary, the latter is not-at least in principle.

It is a rigid system, separating caste from caste, with restrictions on inter-dining and intermarriage, due to a morbid fear of 'varna-sankara' (mixture of varnas). 'Caste' corresponds to jatis, and each varna is supposed to be a cluster of jatis, though there is sometimes ambiguity about which jati belongs to which varna. It is varnas that are cited in canon, not jatis. Restrictions on inter-dining and intermarriage pertained not merely to varnas but also to jatis.

It is a hierarchical system, one below the other in ritual (or purity) status, with several disabilities imposed on the fourth varna of shudras and even more on the untouchables known as 'antyajas'. It was not, however, hierarchical in power and wealth at least as between the upper castes. Dumont thought that the distinction between status and power is basic to understanding caste system (Dumont 1999:65-91).

The system is associated with a notion of purity vis-a-vis pollution, with utmost purity at the level of brahmins declining successively with Kshatriyas, Vaishyas, and then Sudras. At the other end, untouchables are treated as most impure or polluted. A touch of them is supposed to pollute others including shudras. A gradation of hierarchy and pollution was found among untouchables too, for example, bhangis (scavengers) considered as more polluted than say, mahars (agricultural labourers). Initially the notion of purity vs pollution may have been based on the need to maintain cleanliness, but it soon developed into an institutionalised form where pollution was associated with birth. The upper castes when polluted could, however, get rid of their pollution through ritual bath and such other expiatory measures. The notion of purity and pollution developed into a powerful instrument to discourage and prevent Varnasankara.

The whole system along with its taboos and restrictions is authenticated by religion or canon, giving it a religious sanctity.

At the foundation of the whole system there is a production system, which is subsistence-oriented and locally based rather than oriented to larger market, and production relations being of patron-client type, based on mutual dependence. Such a system is not necessarily geared for the generation of economic surplus and its appropriation, as it was not oriented to the larger market but to local needs.

OUR APPROACH TO THE DEMOLITION OF THE MYTH

I reject totally the myth that caste system, as defined by these features either collectively or singly, forms an integral part of Hinduism. Why Hinduism is not Varna Dharma understood as jati or birth based, will become clear in the course of this paper. Hinduism can be defined, as Gandhiji did, as search for truth, nonviolence, compassion for all beings and tolerance. Consistent with its commitment to search for truth, it is also marked by liberalism. Hinduism is a dynamic religion, not fixed or revealed once for all, and hence cannot be identified exclusively with the religion of the Vedas and Upanishads, nor with the religion expounded by 'Dharmashastras', nor with the Hinduism of the three eminent Acharyas-Shankara, Ramanuja and Madhva, nor also exclusively with medieval Hinduism and modern Hinduism.

All these phases represent Hinduism, and have contributed to its development. Moreover, there is no disjointedness between different phases of Hinduism, each deriving its inspiration from the previous ones. In that sense, there is both change and continuity in Hinduism. Since however, it is accepted by all as beyond controversy that medieval Bhakti movement was a protest against caste system and since it is equally well known that modern Hinduism as explained by Swami Vivekananda, Aurobindo and others also has rejected caste system, the focus of this paper is on previous or classical phases of Hinduism. It is this earlier Hinduism, which may be termed as classical Hinduism, that is taken as supportive to the caste system, and it is this myth that is being demolished by this paper. Our greater attention to the previous phases of Hinduism is thus not because Hinduism is defined in terms of these phases, but simply because the contention concerns these phases.

The myth is demolished in the following way:

(i) by showing that there is no strong correlation between Hinduism and caste system, either spatially or temporally;

(ii) by showing that even after the caste system emerged in Hindu society, there was considerable social and occupational mobility, and that none of the defining features of caste system listed above were strictly observed in practice particularly in the classical period;

(iii) by showing that far from supporting the caste system, Hindu canon and philosophy were actually against caste system based on birth;

(iv) by showing that, in addition, Hinduism created legends to impress the popular mind that the caste system is immoral and invalid;

(v) by showing that within the framework of Hinduism, there took place several movements against caste, starting from Bhakti movements continuing to more modern movements;

(vi) by showing that caste system emerged and survived in spite of Hindu canon and philosophy, because of factors which had nothing to do with Hindu religion.

No Correlation between Hinduism and Caste System

The statement that there is no correlation between Hinduism and caste may sound surprising to many. If not in exactly the same words, this is the sum and substance of what Dumont, the most highly regarded authority on caste system, and later even Gail Omvedt-not known to be an admirer of Hinduism-had to say (Dumont Omvedt 1994:31-32). Dumont refers to caste distinctions including even untouchable castes, among Christians in India in different regions. The discrimination against untouchable Christians is reflected in the form of their separate seating in churches, and even separate burial grounds. Even today, one can see advertisements in newspapers seeking 'Catholic Brahmin' spouses for Catholic brahmins.

Islam, supposed to be an egalitarian religion, is not free from castes at least in south Asia. Dumont himself refers to different communities within 'ashrafs', who are supposed to be high caste, and also 'non-ashrafs' who have a lower status. Among the non-ashrafs also, there are three levels of status: '(1) the converts of superior caste, who are mainly Rajputs-except for those who have been admitted into the ashraf; (2) a large number of professional groups corresponding to the artisan castes of the Hindus, (3) converted untouchables who have preserved their functions. These groups indeed seem to be endogamous' (Dumont 1999:208). There is no commensality also between ashrafs and non-ashrafs, due to difference in their status. There is caste system among Buddhists of Sri Lanka also. Some lingayats claim that they are non-Hindus because they do not accept the Vedas and the Varna Dharma, and yet they too are not free from castes and ritual gradation.

Basaveshwara (Basavanna), who led the Bhakti movement whose followers became known as Veerashaiva or Lingayats in Karnataka, was truly against caste system. But unfortunately, he could not succeed in preventing caste system among his latter-day 'followers'. On the other hand, Gail Omvedt points out that among Hindus settled for many generations in Surinam, West Indies, Mauritius, Bali, Fiji and other centres outside India, caste system was weak, almost non-existent. There took place inter-mixture more freely, including inter-dining and intermarriage, and no one took varna-based castes seriously, though identities in terms of regional jatis (such as Marvaris and Gujaratis) have not disappeared. Gail Omvedt, therefore, says significantly that caste is more a feature of south Asia than of Hinduism per se, taking root in this region because of its peculiar social and economic characteristics.

Now we may examine correlation between Hinduism and caste system over time. The first reference to the four varnas comes in the tenth mandala of Rig Veda, in two verses of Purusha Sukta (quoted in another section below). According to several scholars who have made deep research on the theme, the tenth mandala was chronologically the last to be composed. There is a good consensus on the point that previous to this, there was no varna system in vedic society. Mahabharata and Bhagavad Purana also mention that in Krita yuga, there was no caste, but only one varna of human beings-that of the children of Vivaswata Manu (Arvind Sharma 2000:136). Hence, the word manava, popular in all Indian languages. Puranas and other Hindu scriptures have preserved the racial memory of a golden age in the past when there was no caste.

According to B R Ambedkar, there were only three varnas in vedic society, and no fourth varna of shudras. He says, the economy had advanced enough to give rise to a division of labour but there was no hierarchy. He refers to other cosmologies in Hindu texts, but they are all secular, without hint of a hierarchy and without hint of a divine origin. He feels therefore that the two verses in Purusha Sukta are an interpolation, added much later after the caste system was established. According to him shudras as an ethnic group were a part of Kshatriyas, and a part of Aryan society itself. He does not accept the theory of western scholars according to which shudras and untouchables were originally non-Aryans who were defeated by Aryans, and taken into the vedic society giving them a lower status. On the other hand, shudras were very much a part of the ruling society, several of them being kings. As per Ambedkar, they fell from grace and became the fourth varna when brahmins stopped performing the rite of 'Upanayana' for them as a revenge against harassment and insults suffered by them at the hands of some shudra kings. He also says that untouchability is a post-Buddhist phenomenon, which emerged as a result of Hindus giving up sacrifice of animals and beef-eating under the influence of Buddhism, but they went to such an extreme that those who continued to eat beef were regarded as untouchables.

Whether or not one accepts Ambedkar's theory of origin of shudras and untouchables, scholars are agreed that varna-system based on birth is very much a post-vedic feature, and untouchability is a post-Buddhist phenomenon. This means that at some time, maybe for about first half of the long history of Hinduism since 4000 BC to the present day, there was Hinduism but no caste system. This is so even according to Ambedkar himself. And, as we shall see in the concluding part of this paper, Hinduism can survive after the collapse of caste system.

SOCIAL AND OCCUPATIONAL MOBILITY NOT INSIGNIFICANT

The model of caste system as defined in terms of features listed in the first section here hardly ever worked in practice. There have always been exceptions to each of these features and to each of the caste rules and restrictions. Actual occupations have since centuries deviated from the varna theoretical model. Dharmashastras themselves allowed exceptions under 'apaddharma', whereby persons who could not make their livelihood under the occupations of their own varna, could take to other occupations. Brahmins by birth have taken not only to priesthood, which is their varna based occupation, but also to several others, including manual labour. It is not unusual to find Brahmin cooks in the service of scheduled caste (formerly 'untouchables') and scheduled tribe ministers and officials. Havyaka brahmins in Karnataka have not only owned garden lands but also have been doing manual labour in them. Sudras, apart from doing manual labour and artisan jobs, which is their varna based occupation, have traditionally served as soldiers too, making the distinction between Kshatriyas and shudras quite blurred.

Ambedkar himself has given several examples of social and occupational mobility during the vedic and upanishadic period. Raikva, Janashruti and Kavasa Ailusha were admitted to Ashrams for vedic learning even after revealing their low caste status. Chhandogya Upanishad has a significant story of Satyakama Jabala. He sought admission to the Ashram (hermitage) of Gautama Rishi (not Gautam Buddha) for vedic learning. On being asked from what family he comes, Jabala frankly tells the Rishi: 'I do not know this, sir, of what family I am. I asked my mother. She answered me, "In my youth, when I went about a great deal as a maid servant, I got you. So I do not know of what family you are. I am Jabala by name and you are Satyakama by name". So I am Satyakama Jabala, sir'. The Rishi was so pleased with his truthfulness, he promptly initiated him as his pupil (Radhakrishnan 1994:406-07). So many Rishis came from obscure origin themselves, that there is a proverb which says that one should not ask about 'Rishi-Moola' (origin or birth of a Rishi). Sage Parasara was born of a Shvapaka woman, Kapinjala of a Chandala woman, and Madanapala of a boat woman. Rishis had a much higher ritual status than brahmins who were mere priests. Valmiki (author of Ramayana) and Vyasa (author of Mahabharata, and editor and compiler of vedas) and even the great Vasistha belonged to the class of the so-called low birth. Kalidasa, the greatest of great poets in Sanskrit also came from a very humble and obscure origin.

Even as late as 12th century, Vijnaneshwara in his commentary (Mitakshara) on Yajnavalkya Smriti said '*nrin pati iti nripah, na tu kshatriyah iti nemah*' (whosoever protects people is fit to be a king; he need not as a rule be a kshatriya').

The Bhakti movement, both in the south and north of India, saw many saint poets coming from the so-called lower castes. They were more prominent than Brahmin and upper castes in the movement. There were so many Sharanas (male saints) and Sharanes (female saints) in Basavanna's Bhakti movement in Karnataka that M. N. Javaraiah (1997) has written a whole book of more than 300 pages on them. It is thus evident that there was considerable social mobility in the post-vedic society too, not to mention the vedic society where it was very evident.

Because of this mobility, there was no unanimity about which caste is above which caste, because each considered itself superior to the other. They competed with others in observance of purity rules to show that they were superior to others. Thus, quite a few castes considered themselves to be Kshatriyas, while upper castes considered them to be shudras. To gain a higher rank in the caste system, they practised what the upper castes practised, like Upanayana (sacred thread ceremony), and even certain 'homas' and Pujas. Such attempts are called as sanskritisation by M N Srinivas (1977), through which eventually several castes gained in caste status. Sanskritisation as a process through which whole castes gained in caste status could not have been a purely 20th century phenomenon, though scholarly attention has been mostly confined to the modern period.

Even marriages between different varnas were not rare. It must have been because of their significant occurrence, that there is a mention of different types of marriages in Hindu texts based on which jatis were evolved. When the husband is from a higher caste than that of the wife, the marriage was called as 'anuloma'; when reverse was the case, it was called as 'pratiloma'. While the former type was tolerated, the latter was despised. There was another type of classification also; according to it, a love marriage was called as 'gandharva', and a marriage where the woman was forced into marriage was called as 'rakshasa'. The former was tolerated and the latter was despised. It is evident from literature that not all marriages were arranged by parents, and mixed marriages were not rare. It is thus not a surprise that caste distinctions are not based on racial or colour distinction, though varna meant colour. Race and colour very much cut across castes since ancient days in India so that a person's caste cannot be determined on the basis of his/her colour or racial or genetic peculiarities. Just as it is possible to find upper caste people with black complexion, it is equally possible to find persons with fair complexion among the so-called lower castes and untouchables. This could not have been so without a significant degree of inter-marriages. Both Rama and Krishna are black gods but highly adored and worshipped.

The occupational and social mobility as well as the inter mixture of castes cannot be regarded as infringements of canon or as rare exceptions. As we shall now see, even canon itself did not respect the custom of determining status and character on the basis of birth.

CANON AND CASTE

We first take up such parts of the canon that are (wrongly) interpreted to be supportive of caste system, and then take up such parts as are directly and definitively against caste system based on birth.

It is only in the dharmashastras (Dharmasutras and Smritis) that we find support to the caste system, and not in other canon. However, dharmashastras never had the same status as other canon known as Shruti (Vedas and Upanishads) and it is laid down that whenever there is a conflict between the Shruti and Smriti literature, it is the former that prevails. It is Manu Smriti, which is particularly supportive of caste system but where it conflicts with Vedas and Upanishads, the latter would prevail. Though Bhagwadgita (Gita) is not regarded as a part of Shruti, Gita is highly regarded as sacred and is very much a part of classical Hinduism. As we shall just see even the Gita is against caste system based on birth, and not supportive to it. Thus, to the extent that Dharmashastras conflict with Shruti and the Gita, the latter prevails. Apasthambha Dharmasutra may have supported untouchability, but it seems to be read more by those who like to attack Hinduism with it than by its followers! It is hardly regarded as canon, even if any Hindu has heard of it.

Though dharmashastras are supposed to support caste system, there is hardly unanimity about it among them. For example, as Ambedkar pointed out, though according to Dharmasutras, a shudra is not entitled to Upanayana, Samskara Ganapti explicitly declares shudras to be eligible for it. He also shows that according to Jaimini, the author of Purva Mimamsa, shudras could perform vedic rites.

Ambedkar refers also to Bharadwaja Srauta Sutra (V 28) and Katyayana Srauta Sutra which concede eligibility to shudras to perform vedic rites (Vasant Moon 1990:198-99). Kane points out that in spite of some other dharmashastras saying to the contrary, "Badari espoused the cause of the shudras and propounded the view that all (including shudras) were entitled to perform vedic sacrifices" (Kane 1990).

Interestingly, Manu Smriti itself shows the way to demolish its own support to the caste system based on birth. In chapter 4, verse 176 clearly states: 'Discard wealth and desire if they are contrary to Dharma, and even Dharma itself if it leads to unhappiness or arouses peoples' indignation'. Dharma here does not mean religion in the western sense, but rules of conduct. If Varna Dharma, or rules of conduct governing varnas, and caste for that matter, lead to unhappiness or to people indignation, as they certainly do, Manu Smriti itself says that such Dharma can be discarded. What then is Dharma, according to Manu Smriti? It says: "Know that to be true Dharma, which the wise and the good and those who are free from passion and hatred follow and which appeals to the heart". Mahatma Gandhi was fond of quoting this verse in his lectures. According to this verse, if the wise and the good, who are free from passion and hatred, do not accept caste system based on birth as it does not appeal to the heart, the system can be discarded according to the Manusmrti itself. So much to the support of Manu Smriti for the caste system.

Purusha Sukta in Rig Veda (X 90) has often been cited, more than Manu Smriti, as authenticating, sanctifying and glorifying the caste system. The pertinent verses are as follows:

Yatpurusham vyadadhuhu
Kritidha vyakalpàyan
Mukham kimasya kow bahu
Ka uru pada uchyete (11th verse)

When (gods) divided Purusha, into how many parts did they cut him up? What was his mouth? What arms (had he)? What (two objects) are said (to have been) his thighs and feet?

Brahmanosya mukhamasit
Bahu rajanyah kritah
Uru tadasya yadvaishyah
Padbhyam shudro ajayata (12th verse)

The brahmana was his mouth, the rajanya (king or kshatriya) was made his arms; the being called the vaishya, he was his thighs; the shudra sprang from his feet (5, 6)

As is noted above, Ambedkar considers these verses to be an interpolation on several grounds, including the fact that while the style or format of the two verses is of a question-and-answer type, the other verses in the purusha sukta are narrative in style. Even if it is taken as a genuine part of the original purusha sukta, and not an interpolation, it cannot be interpreted as supportive to caste system based on birth and hierarchy. It is essentially a metaphor taking the society to be an organic whole, of which the four varnas based on division of labour are intrinsic parts. There is nothing to indicate that they ought to be castes or jatis as presently understood.

The reference is evidently to occupations or work of respective varnas, which need not necessarily be based on birth. There is also nothing prescriptive or recommendatory about the two verses. It is only indicative of the existence of division of labour, with each varna corresponding to that part of the body of the primeval purusha with which the work or occupation of the respective varna is associated. Since vaishyas and shudras support the society through their economic or productive work, they were taken respectively as coming out of the thighs and feet of the purusha, without necessarily hinting at any lowly status of their work. Similarly since Kshatriyas' work in warfare involved mainly the use of their arms, they were taken as coming out of the arms of the purusha.

Since brahmins' work consisted of reciting mantras and preserving Vedas through oral transmission, they were taken as coming out the purusha's mouth. In a lighter vein, it could be said that this was also because brahmins are traditionally described as 'bhojanapriyah' (lovers of food)! If the intention behind the two controversial verses was to sanctify a hierarchical order, they could as well have described brahmins as coming out of the head of the purusha. It was perhaps seen by the vedic sage who composed the purusha sukta that Brahmin priests mostly used their mouth rather than their head while reciting the mantras! There is thus no need for hard feelings due to the two verses in purusha sukta.

The Gita is alleged to support the caste system on the basis of three verses. The key quotation in this context is from 13th verse in ch 4 where the Lord tells Arjuna-

Chaturvarnyam maya srishtam

Gunakarma vibhagashah

The four varnas were created by me on the basis of character and occupation.

In verse 31 of ch 2, Arjuna is cajoled into fighting on the ground that he is a kshatriya for whom there is nothing more glorious than a righteous war. Again in verse 47 of ch 18 the Lord states that one should perform one's own Dharma even if devoid of merit and not follow another's even if well-performed.

Verse 13 in ch IV holds the key to the understanding of the other two as well. Krishna refers to the four varnas, saying explicitly that they were created on the basis of Guna (nature, aptitude, character) and karma (work, action, occupation). He does not at all refer to birth as the basis for the fourfold division, which is only a division of labour where each one follows an occupation based on aptitude or natural inclination. Far from support to the caste system, K M Panikkar considers it as constituting a devastating attack on caste based on birth. 8 Kane says that if Krishna wanted to make birth as the basis of his division of labour, he could easily have said 'jati-karma-vibhagashah' or 'janma-karma-vibhagashah', instead of 'guna-karma-vibhagashah' as actually stated (Kane 1990:1635-36). He pointed out clearly to 'guna'. This is also consistent with what Krishna replied to Arjuna's specific question in Uttaragita.

Once this is clear, it follows that the Dharma referred to in the other two verses (II 31, and XVIII 47) also is based on Guna and not birth. In the Mahabharata war, persons not born as Kshatriyas also participated in the war as per their inclination, Svabhava or Guna. So there was nothing casteist in Krishna's asking Arjuna to fight like a kshatriya. Similarly, the advice to follow one's own Svadharma only means that one has to follow one's aptitude and qualities, and see where one's comparative advantage lies. A talented person may be able to perform many tasks better than others, but she cannot afford to do so, and she would achieve more by concentrating on where her comparative advantage lies. The principle of comparative advantage, instead of absolute advantage, is followed in international trade between countries. What Krishna advocated was to ask us to follow the more scientific and practical principle of comparative advantage as that would maximise social as well as individual welfare. There is nothing casteist about his advice. Comparative advantage here can also be taken in the dynamic sense, of potential that can be realised, and not in terms of present or actual Guna in a static sense.

The story of Shambuka in Ramayana is also cited as supporting caste system to an extreme extent. It is the story of a shudra who was killed on the advice of ministers by Rama as a punishment for doing penance and neglecting his caste duties. The story appears in Uttara Kanda, which is not a part of Valmiki's Ramayana which ends with Rama's return to Ayodhya in Yuddhakanda. P.V. Kane, an eminent Sanskrit scholar, is of the view that Uttara Kanda was clearly a 'work of later interpolators' (ibid: Vol 1, Part 1, p 389).

The interpolation was done at a time when varna system deteriorated and got established on the basis of birth in a rigid form. Shambuka's story is not consistent with many examples of persons of so-called low birth being initiated into Ashrams as pupils by Rishis, and becoming Rishis themselves. Matanga Rishi is mentioned in Valmiki Ramayana with high regard. He came from a caste that may be regarded as untouchable in today's parlance. Rama met him to pay his respects during his forest sojourn. Now we may take note of those parts of classical Hindu canon, which cannot co-exist caste system and have condemned the practice of determining one's character and status on the basis of birth or 'kula' (family).

Vedanta philosophy declares that there is divinity in every lecture. Krishna says in verse 30 of ch 6: 'He who sees Me in all things and sees all things in Me, never becomes departed from Me, nor am I lost to him'. The preceding and succeeding verses in the Gita also convey the same message. The lord says again: 'He who judges pleasure and pain in others by the same standard as he applies to himself, that yogi is the highest'. How can this advice be consistent or co-exist with support to caste distinctions based on birth? In the 16th chapter, the Lord narrates the virtues he looks for in human beings and says that those who possess them are divine. Among these virtues are:

nonviolence, truth, compassion to all, absence of anger and hatred, giving charity and service selflessly, forgiveness, non-covetousness and modesty. It follows that high birth is hardly relevant.

Rig Veda emphasises equality of all human beings. It goes to the extent of saying, which sounds quite modern: 'No one is superior, none inferior. All are brothers marching forward to prosperity'.

The idea that all human beings are equal before god irrespective of caste and that all are entitled to receive his light comes out clearly from the following:

Rucham no dhehi brahmaneshu
Rucham rajasu naskridhi
Rucham vishveshu shudreshu
Mayi dhehi rucha rucham
Taittiriya Samhita V 7. 6 3-4
Put light in our brahmanas, put it in our chiefs (kings), (put) light in vaishyas and shudras, put light in me by your light.

It may sound surprising to critics of Hinduism but is a fact that Hindu scriptures have backed liberalism and humanism by undermining birth, upholding character and basic worth of persons as being more important. Mahabharata makes this point very strongly, to an extent that it reflects a revolt against the caste system based on birth:

Na kulam vrittahinasya
Pramanamiti me matihi
Anteshwapij jatanam
Vrittameva vishishyate
—Mahabharata, Udyoga Parva, Ch 34, v 41.

It means:

High birth can be no certificate for a person of no character. But persons with good character can distinguish themselves irrespective of low birth.

Mahabharata emphasises the same point again elsewhere too:

Yastu Shudro dame satye
Dharme cha satatotthitah
Tam brahmanamaham manye
Vritten hi bhavet dvijah
—Mahabharata, Vanaparva, Ch 216, vs 14-15.

It means:

That shudra who is ever engaged in self-control, truth and righteousness, I regard him a Brahmin. One is a twice-born by conduct alone.

Uttaragita, which is also a dialogue between Krishna and Arjuna, makes the same point. When Arjuna specifically asks Krishna how varna is determined, he replies:

Na jatih karanam tata
gunah kalyanakaranam
Vritasthamapi chandalam
tam devah brahmanam viduh

It means:

Birth is not the cause, my friend; it is virtues, which are the cause of welfare. Even a Chandala observing the vow is considered a brahmana by the gods.

The verse above corroborates our interpretation of the three controversial verses from the Bhagavadgita quoted above. The story of Shankaracharya (8th century), prostrating before a Chandala is well known. When the latter stood in the way of the former, he was asked to move away. The Chandala asked him whether the Acharya's behaviour was consistent with his philosophy. He asked further: *Viproyam Shvapachoyam ityapi mahan koyam Vibhedabhramah* (what is this confusing distinction between a Brahmin and an untouchable?).

Shankaracharya then prostrates before him as before a guru and breaks out into five verses known as Manisha

Panchakam. He reiterates his Advaita philosophy, but in his very first verse he says that a person who knows the Supreme, whether he is a Chandala or a twice-born, is a guru for him. (Chandaloastu sa tu dvijoastu gururityesha manisha mama). 13 Ramanujacharya who came in 12th century, defied caste even more powerfully. Madhvacharya (13th century) in his Brahmasutra bhashya declares: 'Even the low born (untouchables) have the right to the name and knowledge of god if they are devoted to him.

Tirukkural, an ancient text venerated by Tamils as Tamil Veda, authored by Tiruvalluvar, says: Let him who thinks inequity be warned that ruin awaits him' (116th aphorism). Again, 'All men are born alike; the differences are due to differences in what they do.' (972nd aphorism).

There is an entire Upanishad, named Vajrasuchika, devoted to an attack on caste system based on birth. The name of the Upanishad can be translated as 'Thunderbolt suggestive', which fits its claim to blast ignorance responsible for leading to caste distinctions and away from god. It is in prose and small in size, having only nine short paragraphs. It is included as the last Upanishad in S Radhakrishnan edited The Principal Upanishads along with his translation (Radhakrishnan 1994:935-38). The following summary account is based on it. The Upanishad is argumentative in style and begins with a few questions (in second para): 'Who is verily, the brahmana (Brahmin)? Is he the individual soul (Jiva)? Is he the body? Is he class based on birth (jati)? Is he the knowledge? Is he the deeds (Karma)? Is he the performer of rites?' Then it answers the questions one by one. A Brahmin cannot be the individual soul, since soul is the same in previous births.

He cannot be the body because the body consists of physical elements, which are common to all human beings. He cannot be determined by birth, because many sages attained high rank irrespective of birth. He cannot also be determined by knowledge, as there were many Kshatriyas and others who too attained highest knowledge and wisdom, and knowledge has not been an exclusive feature of brahmins. Deeds also cannot make a Brahmin, since all human beings can do good work.

Similarly, rites and charity can also be done by all. Who then is really a Brahmin? He is the one who knows his self like an Amalaka fruit (gooseberry) on his palm, without caring for distinctions of birth, being devoid of infirmities, narrowness and ego, and who functions as the indwelling spirit of all beings. At the end, the Upanishad calls upon all to meditate on the Supreme, removing all distinctions and egoism from mind. There is no need for further proof to show that Hindu philosophy and religion are against caste system, after reading this Upanishad.

LEGENDS AS A WEAPON AGAINST CASTE SYSTEM

Apart from such direct preaching discussed above, Hinduism fought casteism and untouchability by creating legends too. Such legends appealed to popular mind directly. A legend about Shankaracharya has already been presented above.

Tiruppan Alvar (10th century BC), an untouchable devotee of Lord Ranganatha, was insulted by a priest for standing in the way to the temple. The temple doors did not open to the priest, but a voice came from within the sanctum sanctorum that unless the priest takes the Alvar on his shoulders and circumambulates the temple three times and brings him in the Lord's presence, the doors would not open. The priest had to obey, and thereafter, Tiruppan Alvar was hailed as a great saint.

A similar legend is about Kanakadasa (16th century). When he was not admitted into Udupi Shri Krishna temple by the priests, the idol is said to have turned its face around so that Kanakadasa could have the darshan (sight) of the lord through a back window. It is still known as Kanakana Kindi (Kanaka's window).

There are similar legends in other regions of India too. An interesting legend concerns working class Bhakti-saints of Maharashtra who came from low castes. The legend reflects poignantly the empathy felt by lord Vitthala for his working class devotees who struggle for their livelihood and yet are deeply devoted to him. The lord responds by deeply identifying himself with the devotees and participates in their work and toil, and brings them emotional relief.

It is also a way of raising the status of manual labour in the eyes of particularly the upper castes for the lord himself does this labour of love for his devotees. There is such a legend about several, but is particularly interesting in the case of Janabai, a woman saint from a Dalit caste. Chokhamela, a contemporary Dalit saint-poet, has immortalised this legend in one of his poems:

> *'He scours the floor and pounds the grain,*
> *sweeps rubbish from her yard,*
> *hastens to fetch water,*
> *the Lord of the wheel,*
> *and plaits hair with his own hands,*
> *sitting at peace, peering down,*
> *he quickly kills lice.*
> *Chokha says loves' labour this.*
> *He cares little for greatness.'*

MOVEMENTS AGAINST CASTE WITHIN HINDUISM

The most prominent movement within the framework of Hinduism to fight against casteism was the Bhakti movement. Though started first in Tamil Nadu as early as in 6th century BC by Shaiva saints, it found a powerful expression against caste system when Veerashaiva movement was led by Basavanna in Karnataka in 12th century. The Bhakti movement democratised, broad-based and humanised Hinduism as never before. Even if it may not have succeeded in eliminating caste system, it brought home the important fact that caste distinctions based on birth can have no sanctity in the eyes of god. The movement effectively undermined the authority of texts, which supported caste, though a false impression was also created more by upper castes than by lower castes that

Vedas supported caste. As a result, several Bhakti sects declared that they rejected the authority of the Vedas, prominent among them being the Veerashaiva movement and Sikhism.

The Bhakti movement cut across not only castes, but even religions and spread all over India. Kabir in north India, Shishunal Sharif in Karnataka, and Shirdi Sai Baba in Maharashtra were born as Muslims, but were a part of Bhakti movement and highly respected by Hindus. The movement explicitly and powerfully condemned caste system, including untouchability. Basavanna's movement in Karnataka was most aggressively against caste, and included several Dalit Sharanas and Sharanes as pointed out earlier. Basavanna went to the extent of getting a Brahmin disciple's daughter married to an untouchable disciple's son, causing a serious commotion.

Basavanna was far ahead of his time. Since the lower castes were from the working class, he preached dignity of manual labour as an important principle of his philosophy. The Bhakti movement in Maharashtra also was very similar, drawing saint-poets from the lower caste working class, though it included brahmins too. The movement in Maharashtra was started by an outcaste Brahmin, Sant Jnaneshwar, whose family lost caste because his father, a Sannyasi renounced sannyasa and got married on receiving a message from god to that effect. The movement in Maharashtra too emphasised dignity of manual labour. There is thus quite a lot of evidence to show that Hinduism constantly, deliberately and consciously fought against caste system and untouchability from time to time, even before the modern age and before the influence of western ideas.

Apart from the scattered and sporadic attacks on caste system, there were also concerted attempts to lift individual communities of untouchables as a whole and to bring them into the mainstream. These attempts started from the 19th century itself. Two glorious examples may be taken-that of Ezhavas in Kerala and Nadars in Tamil Nadu. Both examples relate to the pre-independence period of late 19th to early 20th century. These examples are of great interest as they involved two Dalit communities elevating their caste status entirely through self-efforts and very much within the framework of Hinduism. They have been much more successful than other efforts involving conversion to other faiths for the purpose of elevation in social status.

Shri Narayan Guru (1854-1928) was the chief force behind elevating the social status of Ezhavas, who is venerated by them as well as by others. He gave three slogans to his followers: "One caste, one religion, and one god for man". "Ask not, say not, think not caste." "Whatever be the religion, let man improve himself." Though a religious leader, his religion was not sectarian and emphasised that all human beings are equal before god. He wanted to totally remove all caste consciousness. When he saw that the caste Hindus did not permit the entry of Ezhavas and other dalits into temples, he first started building new temples for them into which non-dalits too could enter.

Then he started vedic schools where Dalit priests could be trained both in rituals and the philosophy of Hinduism. Next, he encouraged general and secular education for all, by starting schools and colleges. His initial temple building programme was only to mobilise his community, but his later emphasis was more on general education so that all Ezhavas and other dalits could get properly educated and seek good opportunities. He also started credit cooperative societies so that the dependence of dalits on higher castes was avoided. Thus, the guru sought all-round development of dalits. Like Gandhiji, he also tried to change the attitudes of upper castes. He did not preach hatred of upper castes to his followers, as he did not want a rift between them.

An example of his success in this regard is the support he received from progressive sections of upper castes, which resulted in a Savarna procession in support of dalits' entry in to the famous Vaikom temple during temple entry satyagraha started by Gandhiji. Narayana Guru and Gandhiji worked together in temple entry movement. Narayana Guru did not confine himself only to his own community of Ezhavas. There were other communities among untouchables in Kerala, which were even lower in social status than Ezhavas. But the guru involved them too in his attempts to elevate the status of all dalits.

Though the Nadars did not seem to have had the advantage of a charismatic and religious leader like Narayana Guru, they also did equally well under their secular leaders. The elevation of caste status came mainly through the spread of education and skills, mutual self-help by making credit available for starting enterprises, by helping caste members secure jobs by functioning as an informal employment exchange and also through Sanskritisation. 18 The members of both these communities-Ezhavas and Nadars are now highly literate and occupy important positions. Nadars have also emerged economically strong, creating a niche for themselves in industry and commerce.

The example of Ezhavas and Nadars offers important lessons for dalits. It is not enough to build their own organisation merely to spread awareness, make demands and protest against in justice, but it is also equally necessary to launch constructive programmes for the welfare of the community. The tendency to rely mainly on making demands on the government to promote social welfare among dalits is not enough. By its very nature, government bureaucracy has limitations in promoting social welfare and social mobility. The communities' own efforts at constructive programmes are also necessary.

These programmes may be to induce Dalit parents to send their children to schools, to help them in getting training and skills for jobs outside their traditional vocations, to provide guidance and help to those who wish to migrate from villages to towns and cities and help in getting jobs and houses, preventing addiction to liquor and so on. The community organisations of both Nadars and Ezhavas took care of the members of their communities like parents. Once Dalit organisations take up constructive programmes, help will come to them in a big way from private sources too like voluntary and social service organisations and philanthropic associations.

The successful example of Ezhavas and Nadars also has shown how irrelevant are conversions to other faiths to solve Dalit problem. Another important lesson, particularly from Shri Narayana Guru, is that his movement was not adversarial in character. He broke through upper caste resistance to social change, without making enemies of them. He could even enlist their cooperation and support. He was Gandhian in his approach. In Indian ethos, conciliation seems to have been far more successful in effecting change than confrontation.

A difference between Ezhava and Nadar movements, however, is that the former was not concentrated only on one community, but aimed at reaching all untouchables and lower castes which suffered social deprivation. It was a serious attempt to hit out at ritual hierarchy, which existed among dalits themselves. Success in this task, however, perhaps was not as great as in elevating the status of Ezhavas. Both Nadars' and Ezhavas' movements however, were successful in significantly reducing social deprivation among two numerically important untouchable communities, which had also a higher level of social status than others among dalits.

There have been more movements in modern Hinduism, which are not caste or community based and have helped to enrich the moral and spiritual life of their followers-such as those led by Ramakrishna Mission, Aurobindo, Brahmakumaris, ISKON, Shri Satya Sai Baba and Mata Amritanandamayi. Their main significance for this paper is that they have shown that Hinduism can very well thrive without caste system.

How then did Caste System Emerge and Survive?

If all that is contended above is true and if Hinduism as a religion and philosophy was against caste system based on birth, and even in practice, it opposed the system, how did it emerge and survive for so long? Simply because, the system performed certain functions that were valued by the society. These functions had nothing to do with religion, being entirely in the 'Aihika' (mundane) sphere. The unfortunate part of the story is that caste identities have outlived these functions. These functions may now be enumerated and explained.

A System of Checks and Balances

The varna system was not just a division of labour. It was also a system of checks and balances such that there is no concentration of power in any varna or class. It was more a system to avoid concentration of power than one meant for appropriation of economic surplus. As per the varna system, brahmins were not supposed to seek regal power. Their duty was to seek knowledge and preserve the Vedas and carry on the vedic tradition. They were not supposed to amass wealth and had to depend on other varnas for their sustenance. According to dharmashastras, 'a brahmana (Brahmin) should not hanker after gifts; he may collect them only for his livelihood, a brahmana taking more than what is required for his maintenance incurs degradation' (Kane 1990: Vol II, Part 1, p 531). As Dumont says there was a clear separation of ritual status from material power.

While the duty of Kshatriyas, particularly of kings, was to maintain law and order, protect Dharma and defend people, they too had no absolute power. It was their duty to consult their ministers and listen to people and meet their grievances. The ministry consisted of representatives of all varnas, including shudras. B. R. Ambedkar cites Shantiparva of Mahabharata, in which Bhishma advises Yudhisthira (Dharmaraja) to have four brahmins, eight Kshatriyas, 21 vaishyas and three shudras as ministers to guide him in the affairs of the state (Moon 1990:112). The relatively large allocation to vaishyas may be reflective of their numerical majority as agriculturists then, apart from their being merchants too. It is also possible that vaishyas were the largest source of revenue for the state and hence were given greater representation. If the king was unable to uphold Dharma or protect people and their property, he could even be removed by the ministers with the support of people, according to dharmashastras. A picture of harmony and perfect alliance may not always have been obtained, but it was at least the ideal.

Division of Labour-Easy Acquisition of Skills and Knowledge

Though there was significant social mobility initially, varnas became gradually hereditary and jati system evolved with increasing division of labour and specialisation. It was easier for skills and knowledge to be imparted within family from father to children as there were no trade schools or polytechnics as such. Education in skills and knowledge required in hereditary occupations began quite early right at home from childhood. As families became specialised in arts and crafts, they flourished and sought even distant markets. Kane observes that "professional castes were wealthy and well organised" as seen from dharmashastras and epigraphic records.

The organisation had reached such sophistication that there were larger professional associations called as 'gana', and village level associations called as 'sangha' (Kane 1990: Vol II, Part I, pp 66-67). Kane observes further that 'the Sudra gradually rose in social status so far as occupation was concerned and could follow all occupations except those specially reserved for the brahmana, so much so that Sudra became even kings and Manu (IV. 61) had expressly to enjoin upon brahmanas not to dwell in the kingdom of a Sudra' (ibid: 121).

Interestingly, while vaishyas and shudras were so organised in professional associations or guilds, there were no such organisations for brahmins. As Kane says, 'the Brahmanas had no organised corporate body like for Anglican church with its hierarchy of archbishops, bishops and other divines' (ibid:118). It is often argued that being at the top of the caste system brahmins designed the caste system and perpetuated it by giving religious sanctity. But they did not have an organisation to enforce it. The caste system could not have continued because of a small minority, which had neither regal nor monetary power. It continued only because all castes accepted it as in their interest.

Decentralised Democracy-Lobby Group

When the varnas transformed themselves into ethnic endogamous groups based on birth, they developed their own caste/jati panchayats to decide their own affairs, reducing their dependence on the king. The caste panchayats settled disputes within the caste in an inexpensive and prompt way. They also imparted tremendous social stability. Kings came and went, but the society remained stable in spite of all invasions, wars and political instability.

The panchayats looked after the welfare of the members of their castes in a decentralised way. The caste system provided a mechanism for decentralised democracy. Though this mechanism provided stability, it also made at least the medieval Hindu society more conservative.

The panchayats strictly discouraged inter-caste marriages and severely punished elopement in love affairs, because inter-caste marriages had the potential of weakening caste-panchayats. The separation of caste from caste was made more rigid. The hold of caste panchayats, though weakened considerably after independence, has not vanished at least in a few cases. We still hear news reports of lovers across castes intending to marry driven to suicide. This is more common in rural India, including the so-called low castes and untouchables.

The continued hold of caste panchayats is ensured by continued dependence of families on members of their caste during birth, wedding and death, and excommunication by caste panchayat is still considered a matter of terrible disgrace and shame. Caste panchayats or their more modern avatar-caste lobbies-are simply instruments to preserve caste identities or ethnic identities, to seek concessions from or make demands on the larger society or the state. In this form, they are completely disjointed from the traditional notions of ritual status, purity and pollution.

Ecological Role

There is also an ecological dimension to the caste system, brought out by Madhav Gadgil in 1983 (Gadgil 1983; Kavoori 2002). The caste system performed an important function of reducing competition for and avoiding overexploitation of natural resources. Only fishermen caste could go for fishing, and their caste panchayats evolved rules for sustainable exploitation of fisheries. Only hunters' caste could go for hunting wildlife in the forests, except the king who did it occasionally for pleasure and also to kill man-eating tigers, which intruded into villages. Only chamar or cobbler caste had the right to the dead animals and their skin. Caste panchayats evolved rules for restricting hunting in particular seasons, or particular animals so that wild life is protected and not driven to extinction. Certain forest areas known as sacred groves (known as 'devara kadu' in Kannada, or 'dev-ran' in Marathi, or 'pavithra-vana' in Sanskrit) were out of bounds for any hunting or even cutting green trees. The caste system also functioned in a way so as to control the growth of population by creating barriers for marriage. After giving several illustrations, Madhav Gadgil observes:

The caste society had thus developed two special mechanisms to regulate the exploitation of natural resources. The occupational specialisation of each caste ensured that any particular resource was primarily if not exclusively utilised by one particular caste. The intra-caste territoriality then spread the exploitation evenly over geographical regions (Gadgil 1938:282).

Gadgil points out both positive and negative ways 'of viewing this ecological steady state':

> *It may be viewed positively as a desirable state of man living in balance with nature. Alternatively, it may be viewed negatively as a state of stagnation. For if the resources are used in a balanced fashion, there would be no pressures for cultural change and technological innovation. This is no doubt what happened and the Indian society remained largely balanced (or stagnant!)*

> *freezing its caste system for perhaps two and half millennia between the time of Buddha when the agricultural colonisation of much of the subcontinent was complete and the beginning of the British rule. But value judgments apart, an important consequence of the Indian caste system was this attainment of ecological approximate steady state* (*ibid:282-83*).

Security of Livelihood and Employment.

An important feature of caste system was its localised system of production based on jatiwise division of labour for meeting local needs, rather than the needs of the larger market. As M N Srinivas explains in a posthumously published article, the base of this localised production was not necessarily a village, but a cluster of neighbouring villages, each cluster having one or more "weekly markets, where villagers and itinerant traders would gather to exchange goods, or buy paying cash. The cluster could claim a large degree of self-sufficiency as far as the production of basic needs was concerned..." (Srinivas 2003) In most parts of the India, there developed a system of making annual payments in kind or cash, as soon as harvesting was done, for services rendered by village artisans, barbers, washermen, agricultural labourers and the like.

The system of payment was not on piece-work, but involved the principle that taking care of the artisans and labourers and their basic needs was the responsibility of land owning families. Whenever there were special occasions of urgent need such as marriage, the working class families were given special help. M N Srinivas refers to different names of this system in different parts of India: "jajmani in the north, bara balute in Maharashtra, 'mirasi' in Madras, 'adade' in Mysore. The relationship between the jajman and his kamin is unequal, since the latter is regarded as inferior" (Srinivas 1980:14). The continuing tensions between land owning communities and communities which traditionally were subservient, resulting sometimes into atrocities against the latter owe their origin to this patron-client relationship and its breakdown, rather than to any canonical support to caste system. This institution in the past at least recognised the right to work and livelihood, and in the process controlled competition.

The relationship between patron and client extended beyond generations, and in the traditional system at least, it was not open to a landlord to prefer a new client merely because he charged lower for the services offered. Nor could the client seek alternative employment outside his traditional patron for a higher wage-at least not when his services were needed by his patron. It was the obligation of the patron that the client and his family did not starve. The much maligned 'Apasthambha Dharmasutra' even says that if an unexpected guest comes and there is limited food, the head of the family and his family members have to cut down their own food, but not that of the servants. The latter have to have their proper meal. The guest should not be fed at the expense of servants (Kane, Vol I, Part 1, pp 57-58).

The system was certainly not an ideal one without blemish. All the shortcomings resulting from patron-client relationship, curbing competition and subsistence oriented production followed from the system. In conditions of frequent droughts and high political instability since the medieval age, what mattered most was food security, more than growth. Yet, even under this system, arts and crafts flourished made possible by specialisation and division of labour, especially under political patronage, as happened for example under the Vijayanagara kings and Mughal emperors. It was no wonder that caste system survived under such security. Neither the Muslim rulers nor the British interfered with the system. Many Hindus may have been converted, but the caste system was imbibed into the new religions of Islam and Christianity in India, since the jajmani system and other functions of caste system had nothing to do with religion.

COLLAPSE OF CASTE AS A SYSTEM

A posthumously published paper by M N Srinivas (2003) carries the assertive title-'An Obituary on Caste as a System'.

Paradoxically, the system has expired but caste identities remain and show no sign of going. It looks, caste system is dead but its ghost remains. Caste as a system is taken to mean by Srinivas as involving mainly its localised social production base, subsistence economy, and jati (caste) based occupations. Caste as a system, however, covers all the features listed in the beginning of this paper and its functions listed in the preceding Section VIII. Srinivas refers specifically to the last function discussed here. But other functions also were no less significant in determining the structure of the system. Caste as a system has collapsed today because all its functions have collapsed. It has lost whatever relevance, role, utility and justification it may have had.

Several factors contributed to the collapse of the system-ethical, political social, economic and technological. Though the system gave some stability and even security, it lost on the side of humaneness and social justice. All kinds of indignities were imposed on lower castes, their access to learning was barred, and they were pushed to unenviable and inhuman positions. It was thus that the caste system, particularly its extreme form-untouchability, became disgraced and condemned right from Buddha's time, and again from the medieval age, and then again in the modern times.

The functional significance of the caste system also vanished, making its collapse all the more inevitable. A major factor is the emergence of the modern state as a much stronger, much more powerful and pervasive institution than it ever was with its different wings-the executive, judiciary and legislature, able to exercise powers on all. Hinduism has accepted the emergence of the modern state to enact its own laws, including personal laws, and the sphere of dharmic laws regulating the conduct of people in day-to-day life has shrunk very significantly. There is thus no need for either dharmashastras which served as de facto legislation in dharmic matters, nor for caste panchayats which acted as judiciary. To the extent that their role still continues, it is much less powerful and is superceded by the role of the state. For the same reason, the role of the varna system in providing a system of checks and balances also has vanished. The legally enacted constitution, accepted by all, provides now a system of checks and balances to maintain equilibrium and stability.

Since in the bargain, decentralised democracy of the caste system has broken down, a new type of decentralised democracy, which is village based, has taken its place. It does not need any authentication by religion, but is backed by the Constitution and state power, which is more important. For some time, the dominant castes (which are not the same as ritually upper castes) may try to hijack the village panchayats, but it is a losing battle. The system of reservation for backward castes and untouchables and also for women will gradually but definitely reduce the role of dominant castes. The secular and inclusive forces will prevail over the caste forces before long, even if they have not already done so in some areas. The political consensus against caste system and the power of adult franchise in democracy will ensure the success of democratic and secular forces and defeat caste forces.

The next factor, which worked against the caste system, was the rise of modern secular education. Education need not be and is not family-based though family education will supplement outside education. It is in schools and colleges including trade schools, professional colleges and polytechnics that skills and education are provided. Thus the need for hereditary occupation is now redundant, and social mobility will be much more.

The need for hereditary principle in occupation is now redundant also because of the rise of new occupations and the extinction of several old occupations. The dynamics of the growth of diversity of occupations is such that the hereditary principle looks totally outdated and nonsensical. The information age has thrown up an opening for new occupations, which cannot be classified into the sphere of the four traditional varnas. It is wrong to interpret that all the intellectual tasks were assigned exclusively to brahmins in the traditional varna system. Brahmins had no monopoly of intellect even if they had some monopoly to study the Vedas and officiate as priests. Even the monopoly as priests has been broken, with different jatis arranging their own priests from outside the caste of brahmins and evolving their own rituals.

The institutions started by Shri Narayana Guru and Mata Amritanandamayi have been training priests from all castes including women. The exclusive role of brahmins in conducting rituals and ceremonies is highly exaggerated. In any case, it could not have been exclusively intellectual, because every task-regal, warfare, agriculture, arts and crafts required the role of intellect. This is even more so in the modern age, particularly the information age, under which every sector demands the role of intellect and information and not one sector alone. The reason why this point is elaborated is because the new intellectual tasks of the information age cannot be mechanically interpreted as brahmanical. Can we say that the study and research in medicine fits into Brahmin varna, but practice of medicine into shudra varna? How can we separate the two?

Just as new professions and occupations emerged, quite a few old occupations have vanished. Some of them have moved right into homes and do not any longer require specialised occupations and caste groups, thanks mainly to technological change. The system of toilets has undergone a revolutionary change during the last 50 years even in rural areas, making it totally unnecessary to handle human waste and carry it on head as in the past. Toilets have moved inside the homes now, and family members themselves clean them.

Several tasks which were considered as dirty and polluting need not be done now directly by hand, and can be handled by tools and machines. It is now possible to be clean and hygienic even while handling the so-called dirty tasks. Thus any rationale for separate castes for doing dirty jobs and for isolating them is now totally lost.

Alvin Toffler (1980) in his book, The Third Wave, has pointed out to the recent phenomenon of what he calls the 'prosuming' or 'prosumer', occasioned by the blurring line between producing and consuming. This refers to 'do-it-yourself' kits and self-service, which is becoming more prominent. From furniture pieces to cars to computers, several things are supplied with step-by-step instructions for assembling them at homes. This has reduced the cost to producer and the price to consumers. What is more, the consumer enjoys the thrill of doing it oneself, of creating some thing. This phenomenon is not limited to commodities and has invaded services too. Thus, we do the daily shave ourselves with safety razor, taking over a part of the task of barber. Many of us, with or without washing machines, wash our clothes ourselves and iron them too. The social significance of all this is that the old wall of distinction between artisans and arm-chair consumer is falling apart. The old division of labour separating manual tasks from the intellectual is losing its meaning.

In this context, Arvind Sharma's reinterpretation of the purusha sukta in the 10th mandala of Rig Veda is of interest. According to Sharma, the reference here need not be to social structure as such, but to combining in the same individual different duties one has to perform during one's life, -learning, helping in the management or governance of the community and the country as in a democracy (voter being the king) including offering militancy service when needed, participation in economic or professional activities and service to society including manual labour (for one's own benefit and for the society). In his words: 'The idea is that all varnas are contained in every individual from now on instead of every individual being comprised within one of the varnas' (Sharma 1996).

M N Srinivas (2003) refers to a combination of new forces in operation, responsible for the destruction of the caste system. These forces have led to the breakdown of the caste-based mode of social production in turn leading to the collapse of the caste system. The new forces are breakdown of the Jajmani System, emergence of the larger market and decline of the village based subsistence production, urbanisation, and above all the rise of democracy based on adult franchise. Along with these, there is widespread acceptance of new values-equality, self-respect, and human dignity.

He cites several instances of how village artisan based production has given place to factory production-mass produced edible oil replacing the oil-seed pressing caste, factory produced plastic and aluminum vessels replacing the village potter caste, urban textiles replacing the village weaver and so on. Srinivas observes significantly: "The moral is that ideological attacks on hierarchy and brahmanical claims to supremacy failed to create an egalitarian social order since at the local level the production of basic needs was intrinsically bound up with jati".

Last, the caste system has also lost its ecological role and relevance, as observed by Madhav Gadgil himself in the same paper in which he pointed out this role of the caste system. The resources under the control of local communities have been depleted significantly, thanks to their take over by the state and their exploitation by the larger market forces. "Thus alienated from their ecological resource base which was depleting rapidly, the Indian caste society was rudely thrown out of the ecological steady state maintained perhaps for more than a hundred generations" (Gadgil 1983:283). The recent attempts at regeneration of local natural resources through local committees under schemes like Joint Forest Management, are not based on caste but are secular. Moreover, with the breakdown of social base of production, it is doubtful if the caste-based occupations will ever get a new lease of life.

It is evident from the above analysis that the emergence as well as survival of the caste system had nothing to do with Hinduism as a religion. The caste system was purely social phenomenon, very much in the mundane sphere. It is Aihika sphere (mundane), and not Paramarthika or Adhyatmika (spiritual). Being in Aihika sphere, rules of conduct and custom are liable to change from time to time, and not eternally fixed, as Hindu texts themselves concede.

The support to it given by dharmashastras including Manusmrti could be only a result of the social significance and role of the caste system of the time, and not the cause of it. Dharmashastras reflected what is already there in the society. They also approved rejection of it like when Manusmrti (IV 176) indicated clearly that any dharmic rule could be rejected if it led to people's unhappiness and indignation. There can be no ground for fear that dharmashastras would give a new lease of life to the caste system inspite of its being redundant and irrelevant in the modern age. Most of the verses in dharmashastras have themselves become irrelevant, at least those parts supporting caste system.

On the other hand, the collapse of the caste system would also pose no threat to the continuation and survival of Hinduism. Hinduism has been thriving with renewed vigour thanks to such leaders as Satya Sai Baba, Mata Amritanandamayi and Sri Sri Ravishankar, and institutions like Ramakrishna Mission, Brahmakumaris and ISKON on an entirely non-caste basis. This is because caste is not intrinsic to basic principles and tenets of Hinduism as enshrined in Hindu canon. Hinduism itself has fought and is still fighting against casteism in a significant way. If caste system were intrinsic to Hinduism, Shri Narayana Guru and Mata Amritanandamayi would not have worked within the framework of Hinduism.

SOCIAL DEMORALIZATION

How does the living dialogue become a religious issue or a theological issue? It is because a breakdown of this dialogue results in the spread of demoralization within society. Ambedkar's work is a great study of the colossal effects or the tremendous ill effects that flow from the absence of a living dialogue within a given society.

Ambedkar saw the widespread poverty in India as linked to the lack of a spiritual framework capable of generating enthusiasm among the people to attempt to better themselves.

Thus, like Hayek, who saw the possibility of a movement within society as a necessary component of its life and growth Ambedkar saw that the presence of enthusiasm in the population as a necessary condition of growth, including economic growth. Ambedkar attributed the reason for the lack of enthusiasm as the realization that the possibilities for movement within society did not in fact exist.

The caste system of India was in fact a system that outlawed such movement. It was not just a question of lack of opportunity that the caste system had created but the lack of any possibility for hope. The ideologies of inequality and injustice leave no room for the development of enthusiasm, he said. He demonstrated this view with an example. "As soon as a Brahmin women conceives, she thinks of the High Court whether any post of Judge has fallen vacant but when a Dalit woman becomes pregnant she cannot think of any thing better than a sweeper's post under the municipal committee."

He spoke of such lack of enthusiasm as a disease.

> *"Now, what saps the enthusiasm in man? If there is no enthusiasm, life becomes a drudgery-a mere burden to be dragged. Nothing can be achieved if there is no enthusiasm. Why does one lose enthusiasm? Main reason for this lack of enthusiasm on the part of a man is that an individual loses hope to get an opportunity to elevate oneself. Hopelessness leads to lack of enthusiasm. The mind in such cases becomes diseased."*

In fact, in all his writings and work, Ambedkar treated Indian society as a diseased society (he often used the word sick), due to thousands of years of the practice of the caste system.

This astute politician who held the Law Minister's post in Nehru's Cabinet and contributed a great deal to the discussion of all vital political issues of his time did not hesitate to state that India's loss of freedom time and again which resulted in

India being subject to foreign domination was caused by this diseased condition of the Indian mind, and due to the operation of the caste system:

> *"It is because our country as a whole never stood against the enemy. It was always a small section of the society and whoever over-powered it became the victor. This was mainly due to the pernicious caste system of the Hindus."*

This analysis differs greatly from the analysis of many nationalists in India, and outside of the causes of the paralysis of the Indian mind. No one really argues seriously that there is no such paralysis. The differences of opinion relate to the reasons causing this paralysis. The nationalists argue that the paralysis was due to foreign invasion and foreign domination. Ambedkar's position is that the foreign domination itself became possible due to the deep division among the people who are humanly divided, without any hope of coming together. There was no source to draw from when fighting a foreign element. Caste, notionally accepted as the foundation of society nullified the possibility of a common front to fight against outsiders' invasions and domination.

The invaders once in power used this deep internal division to maintain their power and to exploit India's resources. The group that had the natural leadership of the country was the Brahmins and they could not call the low castes to a common fight. Any physical act of solidarity would require holding common meetings and discourses. However, such physical contact would pollute the higher caste and make them impure. How could any strategy be developed or carried out without physical contact? Castes distanced groups of people physically. In this, caste was worse than slavery. The slaves often lived in the houses of their masters and helped in the household work. Slaves were sometimes even allowed to get some education, so that they could be more useful to the master. This is not so within the caste system. Low caste persons were to be kept in their low positions and not allowed to participate in any social activity. The low castes had to be avoided and not be touched in any way. That is how the terms such as touchable and untouchable came into use.

Ambedkar demonstrated the depth of this physical aspect of caste:

> *"I would like to tell you some of the reminiscence of my childhood. There was a Maratha women employed in my school. She was herself quite illiterate but observed untouchability and avoided touching me. One day, I remember, I was very thirsty. I was not allowed to touch the water tap. I told my master that I wanted to drink water. He called the peon and asked him to turn on the tap and I drank water. Whenever the peon was absent I had to go without water. Thirsty, I had to return home and then only I could quench my thirst."*

Ambedkar thus provided a tremendous study of how a society and the individuals within it go through a fundamental metamorphosis when it become organically incapable of what Grundtvig would have called a living dialogue. Ambedkar did not see caste as the only source from which such a negative change can take place; The same result can happen when the concentration in society is making wealth or getting enriched.

He wrote:

> *"You know the proprietors of mills. They appoint managers in the mills who extract work from labour. The proprietors remain so much engrossed in their work that they have little time to develop their minds. While they accumulate wealth and become economic giants they remain mental dwarfs." Perhaps this aspect may apply to the situation of the West in present times. Perhaps, the West too needs to wake up from decadence of this type and address its own spiritual crisis."*

It is also a well known fact of the contemporary situation in most Third World countries that the impact of international relationships combined with internal factors have created a situation of destitution, which in turn has increased demoralization within many societies. Such demoralization often leads to internal warfare or ethnic, tribal and local conflicts. In fact, the area of conflict has now shifted from the international arena to local theatres of horror. Can these be resolved purely by physical rebuilding only? Are not the issues relating to internal inspiration irrelevant, when objective conditions prevent internal communication?

The related matter is about debt renunciation. Should not the first world countries consult their own internal sources of inspiration when considering these matters? Are policies that are followed on these matters based on the traditions of enlightenment of their countries or are they based on narrow considerations unworthy of great peoples? Should these matters be left purely to bureaucrats or must they become matters of living dialogue based on the inspirational sources of the Western traditions?

Grundtvig's writings on the issues relating to neighbouring countries of his time showed enlightened views. He often opposed actions which would lead to loss of freedom or enslavement of peoples. Such deprivation of freedom and enslavement contradicted the Christian "Anskuelse." If the Economic policies pursued by the West create conditions of deep poverty and demoralization among the Third World countries is that not a matter of fundamental importance to the peoples of First World Countries?

It is in this context that Grundtvig's theology of the human as the precondition for the Christian needs to be looked at. Hinduism has created a conception of gods and a conception of holy life at the cost of destroying the human foundation of their society. This destruction was not only seen as irrelevant but also as necessary for Brahmins to achieve oneness with god. It was a conception of holiness and perfection which demanded deprivation of the humanity of most of the human beings living in Indian society. It was the inhumanity that was implied in adherence to caste that made Ambedkar look for outside inspiration. This he found in Buddhism. Buddha, Ambedhar said, was the only person who had the courage not only to condemn caste but also to espouse a promote new religious principles on the basis of the common humanity of everyone. Ambedkar wrote "The fundamental principle of Buddhism is equality. Of all Bhikkhus who joined the order in the time of Lord Buddha, about 75% of the Bhikkus belonged to the Brahmin caste and the remaining 25% were Sudra. Even then Buddhism was called the religion of the Sudra."

Here Ambedkar quotes from Buddha.

> *"O Bhikkhus, you belong to different castes and have come from various lands. Just as the great rivers when they have fallen into the great ocean lose their identity, just so brethren, O, brethren, do these four castes, Brahmins, Kshatriyas, Vaishyas, Sudra when they begin to follow the doctrine and discipline as propounded by the Tathagatta, they renounce different names of castes and rank and become members of one and same society."*

To have a common identity it was necessary to lose caste identity, which was an identity based on the superiority of some and the inferiority of others. Ambedkar's attempt to rediscover a basis to end the disease of the Indian mind led him to Buddhism which was once a powerful tradition in India. Grundtvig found the source of inspiration for democratic ideals in a reinterpretation of the local Lutheran tradition and bringing in the radical idea that the human, or the folk life was the precondition for spirituality. If the precondition was absent, the other had no ground to grow. Ambedkar was pointing to an historical example where the precondition had been killed. His was an attempt to indicate a way to recreate a similar precondition.

Grundtvig's conceptions about Nordic mythology and Christian "Anskuelse" may be compared with Ambedkar's views on the original tradition of Buddhism as a source of inspiration. In describing the work on Buddhism he said, "We have started this movement to develop and educate our minds."

Explaining the need for religion among the poor as a need arising for hope, Ambedkar referred to a German professor of his, Professor Winternitz.

> *"The Watergang Rabelan Depth, was the book which he recommended and by which I was much inspired. 'It is only the poor, he said who need religion. 'Hope is the spring of action in life. Religion affords hope. Therefore, mankind finds solace in the religion, and that is why the poor cling to religion."*

Here it must be noted that Buddhism is not a religion but the reference here is to Dhamma. The term poor is more to the term ordinary people used by Grundtvig and religion more to "Anskuelse," used by Grundtvig.

To those who had not turned to Buddhism, but remained within Hinduism but wanted Hinduism to change, Ambedkar made the following suggestion:

> *"You must give a new doctrinal basis to your Religion-a basis that will be in consonance with Liberty, Equality and Fraternity, in short, with Democracy."*

Though he said this to a group of Hindus who considered themselves to be enlightened and wanted a fundamental change, he himself did not seem to have believed in this option. A few months before this meeting he had announced that though he was born a Hindu he would not die a Hindu. In this very text of the prepared speech-Annilation of Caste-for this meeting where the above mentioned words were to be spoken, he mentioned, "I shall not be in your fold for long." He spent the subsequent 20 years, the last years of his life, in a very extensive historical studies of India's past and preparing his people to look in a different direction for inspiration.

Dalit Panthers: The Sparklet that was not to be

The degeneration that set in continued unabated till the birth of Dalit Panthers in early 1970s. There could be varied explanations for the paradigm shift in Dalit politics (movement) marked by Dalit Panthers. Remarkably, they spoke the language of defiance and militancy, which created waves. These waves had shaken the foundations of the established order in the country and in essence demonstrated what the wrath of the wretched could be! It provided a valuable insight that was pathetically missing in the Dalit politics. Going by their manifesto, Dalit panthers had broken many new grounds in terms of radicalising the political space for the Dalit movement.

They imparted the proletarian-radical class identity to dalits and linked their struggles to the struggles of all oppressed people over the globe. The clear cut leftist stand reflected by this document undoubtedly ran counter to the accepted legacy of Ambedkar as projected by the various icons, although it was sold in his name as an awkward tactic.

It reflected a historical dilemma characteristic of the Indian situation. The pathos of casteism integral with the Dalit experience essentially brought in Ambedkar, as his was the only articulate framework that took cognisance of it. But, for the other contemporary problems of depravations Marxism provided a scientific framework to bring about a revolutionary change.

Although, have-nots from both dalits and non-dalits craved for a fundamental change, the former adhered to what appeared to be Ambedkarian methods of sociopolitical change and the latter to what came to be the Marxian method which tended to see every social process as the reflection of the material reality. Both caused erroneous interpretations. It is to the credit of Panthers that the assimilation of these two ideologies was attempted for the first time in the country but unfortunately it proved abortive in absence of the efforts to rid each of them of its obfuscating influence and stress their noncontradictory essence.

Neither, there was theoretical effort to integrate these two ideologies, nor was there any practice combining social aspects of caste with say, the land question in the village setting.

Essentially, it remained an emotional and a poetic negation of the status quo, craving for the broad revolutionary change and on ideological plane inevitably reflected an amalgam of Ambedkar and Marx. This ideological amalgam could not be acceptable to those under the spell of the prevailing Ambedkar-icons and therefore this revolutionary seedling in the Dalit movement died a still death.

The possibility of the radical shift in the paradigm of Dalit politics indicated by the manifesto was totally submerged by the reactionary upsurge of the new version of orthodox Ambedkarism. The reactionaries objected to the radical content of the programme alleging that the manifesto was doctored by the radicals-the Naxalites. There is no denying the fact that the Naxalite movement which had erupted quite like the Dalit Panther, as a disenchantment with and negation of the established politics, saw a potential ally in the Panthers and tried to forge a bond right at the level of formulation of policies and programme of the latter.

But even if the Panthers had chosen to pattern their programme on the ten-point programme of the Black Panther Party (BPP) in the USA, which had been the basic inspiration for their formation, it would not have been any less radical. The amount of emphasis on the material aspects of life that one finds in the party programme of the BPP could still have been inimical to the established icon of Ambedkar. Radicalism was the premise for the very existence of the Dalit Panther and hence the quarrel over its programme basically reflected the clash between the established icon of Ambedkar and his radical version proposed in the programme. The fact that for the first time the Dalit Panther exposed dalits to a radical Ambedkar and brought a section of Dalit youth nearer to accepting it certainly marks its positive contribution to the Dalit movement.

There were material reasons for the emergence of Dalit Panthers, as there are for any episode or event. Children of the Ambedkarian movement had started coming out of universities in large numbers in the later part of 1960s, just to face the blank future staring at them. The much-publicised Constitutional provisions for them turned out to be a mirage. Their political vehicle was getting deeper and deeper into the marsh of parliamentarism. It ceased to see the real problems of people. The air of militant insurgency that had blown all over the world during those days also provided them the source material to articulate their anger.

Unfortunately, quite like the BPP, they lacked the suitable ideology to channel this anger for achieving their goal. Interestingly, as they reflected the positive aspects of the BPP's contributions in terms of self-defence, mass organising techniques, propaganda techniques and radical orientation, they did so in the case of BPP's negative aspects too. Like Black Panthers they also reflected 'TV mentality' (to think of a revolutionary struggle like a quick-paced TV programme), dogmatism, neglect of economic foundation needed for the organisation, lumpen tendencies, rhetoric outstripping capabilities, lack of clarity about the form of struggle and eventually corruptibility of the leadership.

The Panthers' militancy by and large remained confined to their speeches and writings. One of the reasons for its stagnation was certainly its incapability to escape the petit bourgeois ideological trap built up with the icons of Ambedkar. It would not get over the ideological ambivalence represented by them.

Eventually, the petit-bourgeoise 'icon' of Ambedkar prevailed and extinguished the sparklet of new revolutionary challenge. It was completely sapped of its rebellious image and its vitality and soon got corrupted with a ridiculous prefix 'Bharatiya' to it. It survived as another living monument to the ideological bankruptcy and the degeneration of the Dalit leadership. It went the RPI way and what remained of it were the numerous fractions engaged in internecine squabbles under the sly hands of the ruling classes. The Dalit Panther phase represented the clash of two icons: one, that of a radical 'Ambedkar', as a committed rationalist, perpetually striving for the deliverance of the most oppressed people in the world. He granted all the freedom to his followers to search out the truth using the rationalist methodology as he did. He abhorred all kinds of humbug and hated to be bound by any dogma. He desired his followers to do the same. Like his mentor, the Buddha, he would exhort his followers not to take any thing for granted until their own experience corroborated it or their intellect supported it.

The other is of the 'Ambedkar' who has forbidden the violent methods and advocated the constitutional ways for his followers, who was a staunch anti-Communist, ardent Buddhist, nay, Bodhisatva, who has given a permanent doctrine that was infallible. As it turned out, the radical icon of Ambedkar was projected without adequate conviction. It was implanted in an alien soil. There was no one committed to propagating such an image of Ambedkar, neither communists nor dalits. Eventually it remained as a veritable hodgepodge compared to the familiar set of icons coming from the other camp.

Phenomenon of Kanshiram: A Culmination of a Kind

The movement of Kanshiram markedly reflected a different strategy, which coined the 'Bahujan' identity encompassing all the SCs, STs, BCs, OBCs and religious minorities than 'Dalit', which practically represented only the scheduled castes. Kanshiram started off with an avowedly apolitical organisation of government employees belonging to Bahujana, identifying them to be the main resource of these communities. It later catalysed the formation of an agitating political group creatively coined as DS4-the Dalit Shoshit Samaj Sangharsh Samiti, which eventually became a full-fledged political party-the Bahujan Samaj Party (BSP).

Purely, in terms of electoral politics, which has some how become a major obsession with all the Dalit parties, Kanshiram's strategy has proved quite effective, though in only certain parts of the country. He has given a qualitative impetus to the moribund Dalit politics, locating itself into a wider space peopled by all the downtrodden of India. But he identified these people only in terms of their castes and communities. It may be said to his credit that he reflected the culmination of what common place icon of Ambedkar stood for. Kanshiram shrewdly grasped the political efficacy of this icon that sanctioned the pursuit of power in the name of downtrodden castes.

The religious minorities which potentially rears the sense of suffering marginalisation from the majority community could be easily added to it to make a formidable constituency in parliamentary parlance. Every one knew it but none did how to implement. Kanshiram has seemingly succeeded in this task at least in certain pockets. The careful analysis will show that the combination of certain historical developments and situational factors has been behind this success. As Kanshiram has amply experienced, it is not replicable elsewhere. It is bound to be short-lived and illusory unless this success is utilised to implement a revolutionary programme to forge a class identity among its constituents. If not, one will have to constantly exert to recreate the compulsions for their togetherness and allegiance. In absence of any class-agenda, which is certainly the case of BSP, these compulsions could only be created through manipulative politics for which political power is an essential resource.

BSP's unprincipled pursuit of power is basically driven by this exigency. It is futile to see in this game a process of empowerment of the subject people as could be seen (although not conclusively) from the statistical evidence of the cases of atrocities, and of overall situation of the poor people under its rule. There should be no lament over this as essentially it is where any kind of political acrobatics is destined to end in the prevailing system. The imperatives of this kind of strategy necessarily catapult the movement into the camp of the ruling classes as has exactly happened with BSP. BSP's electoral parleys with Congress, BJP, Akali Dal (Mann) that reached the stage of directly sharing State power in UP recently, essentially reflect this process of degeneration and expose its class characteristics today.

It seems to have sustaining support from the icon that BSP itself created, where Ambedkar was painted as the intelligent strategist who could turn any situation to his advantage, who used every opportunity to grab political power to achieve his objective. He is the person who saw in political power, a key to the woes of dalits and therefore exhorted them to grab it at any cost. He did not think highly of mass struggles except for tactical reasons to demonstrate the might of the leaders. For him, there existed only means not the values for securing one's goals. He did not see any permanent friend or foe in politics and joined even the Congress whom he had once declared as the enemy. He is seen as the person endowed with State authority (as a member of the Viceroy's Executive Council, Law Minister, and Chairman of the Drafting Committee for the Indian Constitution)-the sole source of his power to benefit his people. He was the sole arbiter of the interests of his people. Of course, he had disdain for all shades of communism.

Kanshiram's reading of Ambedkar ignores the fact that Ambedkar had to carve out space for his movement in the crevices left by the contradictions between various Indian political parties and groups on one side and the colonial power on the other. For most of his time, he sought maximisation of this space from the contending Muslim League and Congress, to name the predominant players, and eventually brought Dalit issue to the national political agenda. Kanshiram stuffs his Ambedkar icon entirely with such kind of superfluity that it would look credible to the gullible Dalit masses. This icon approves of his sole ideology that political power to his party (read him) could solve all Dalit problems. His strategy till then has been to be in vantage position to decide who would be the king and thereby leverage his bargaining power.

He did not care for democracy. To some extent this non-democratic stance spells his compulsions to have unitary command over his party structure as without it, his adversaries would gobble it up. He did not have any utility for any programme or manifesto, no concern for any issue howsoever burning, no qualms about policy or principles because, his sole obsession is to maximise his power by whatever means. In the rhetoric of empowering Bahujans, he does not even feel it necessary to demonstrate what exactly this empowering means and what benefits it would entail them. He never even spelt out what precisely ails his Bahujans except for highlighting their prejudiced social identities in worn-out casteist phraseology. That explains his entries into and exits from political alliances with any one with the same alacrity. The obsession with capturing power robbed him of certain fundamental values that Ambedkar never compromised.

The underlying value of the movement of Ambedkar was represented by liberty, equality and fraternity. Kanshiram does not seem to respect any value than the political and money power. In Ambedkar, one cannot miss an overflowing concern for the oppressed and wrath against the perpetrators of oppression. Kanshiram's concern scarcely transcended his speeches in his electoral rallies. It was with this concern and commitment that Ambedkar kept on referring to Marx and Marxism till his end, something as a touchstone to test his alternatives. Kanshiram simply abhorred it. Ambedkar struggled to formulate the Dalit problem. Kanshiram either took it for granted or did not care for it at all. He never tried to articulate the nature of his Bahujanas' ailment except for the rhetorical reference to their subordination by the minority upper caste Hindus. For Ambedkar certain values, moral code etc. were paramount, Kanshiram never seemed to be bothered by these issues. Ambedkar always foresaw plans and programmes; visualised appropriate structures for the downtrodden. Kanshiram expressed clear disdain for such things. For Ambedkar political power was a means, to Kanshiram it appears to be the end. Notwithstanding these broad differences, he has succeeded in luring the Dalit masses in certain pockets of the country by projecting an Ambedkar icon that sanctioned his unscrupulous pursuits of power.

The crux of Kanshiram can be traced to his superfluous attempt to replicate Ambedkar's movement of 1920s as if the times had stood still for the bygone five decades. Ambedkar's mobilisation of Dalit masses through struggles is vulgarised by him as the 'agit-prop' tool to collect people behind him. When Ambedkar realised the potency of political power, he launched his Indian Labour Party that reflected his urge to bring together the working class, transcending the caste lines. It is only when the political polarisation took communal turn that he abandoned his ILP project and launched the Scheduled Caste Federation. For Kanshiram, the talk sans caste and communities is perhaps an anathema.

His casteist platform as such appears preordained by his ambition for power. Ambedkar joined hands with a few political parties-one the communists (while joining the strike of mill workers) and the other is the Praja Samajwadi Party of Ashok Mehta in the 1952 elections. Although, he accepted the Congress support and offered to work in their government, he never tied up his political outfit to the Congress. It always appeared a politically expedient step for him as an individual without any organisational implication. Kanshiram's record so far clearly shows that he is ready to join hands with any one promising him the share of political power.

Declaredly he would avoid the leftists of all hues and accept the friendship of the rank reactionaries of every kind. Ambedkar pointed at the capitalism and Brahmanism as the twin enemy for his movement but Kanshiram enthusiastically embraced them without any pinch to his conscience. Ambedkar, in his own way, has been in search of suitable ideological carrier for the Dalit movement. Kanshiram has no utility for such a thing.

MULTIPLICITY OF BRANDS, LITTLE DIFFERENTIATION

Apart from these broad political trends, there are many regional outfits like Dalit Mahasabha in Andhra Pradesh, Mass Movement in Maharashtra, Dalit Sena in Bihar and elsewhere, etc., some of which dabble directly into electoral politics and some of them do not. So far, none of them have a radically different icon of Ambedkar from the ones described above. They offer some proprietary ware claiming to be a shade better than that of others.

HINDUISED BUDDHISM: TURNING THE WHEEL BACKWARD

Another trend in the Dalit movement emphasises the spread of Buddhism as its goal. As in politics, there are numerous organisations devoted to this task. According to them, Buddhism was the culmination of Ambedkar's mission and hence, the true Ambedkarite not only had to be a Buddhist but also had to work for the spread of Buddhism. Ambedkar's declared vision of making India a Buddhist country spells a mission statement to them. Their activities revolve around building Buddhist viharas, becoming Shramners and Bhikkus; imbibing religious mode of living and engaging in quasi-studious pursuits like learning Pali, reading Buddhist scriptures, rewriting the episodes in history. At the renaissance some amount of excava ion of skeletons is inevitable but it had become an obsession with the Dalit intellectuals, who squandered considerable energies in desecting the Hindu mythology to expose its cunning and rediscovering the Buddhist glories as their own legacy. One of the underlying motives in this enterprise was to project superiority of Buddhism and in turn their own as they believed that they were the original Buddhists. Paradoxically, all of them quibble over the distinction between 'Dharma' and 'Dhamma', claiming that Buddhism is Dhamma whereas others are the Dharmas. Unlike other religions, Buddhism does not have any place for rituals, gods or any permanent entity like soul, and is just a practicable moral code for living.

However, in practice, all kinds of mumbo jumbo that some times appears to be exceeding the familiar but on-the-wane rituals of Hinduism, are followed, so much so that not only Buddha but even Ambedkar is not spared from the godhood (Bhim Bhagawan). Of late, the relatively upwardly mobile (middle class) among dalits are increasingly getting attracted towards 'Vipasyana'-a kind of meditation that is said to have been practised by Buddha himself to get his enlightenment and so is 'prescribed' in Buddhism to be a good Buddhist. Many of them lately claim that it is the essence of Buddhism. It is amusing to see this mind-centric trend growing among dalits.

In all this, Ambedkar's attempts at rationalisation and redefinition of Buddhism are completely forgotten. What rather is remembered is that he himself had given them the 'vidhi' for marriage and for such other occasions; that he himself had devotedly said the three precepts and five oaths and stood through the long winding Gathas in the language of antiquity, that how he got into spiritual trance in front of the Buddha's statue when he visited Sarnath.

The icon they follow is that of a man incarnate of Buddha who analysed the problem of humanity and ultimately prescribed nirvana-a indescribable State marked by the extinction of all kind of craving. One who after Ashoka made greatest contributions to the revival and spread of Buddhism. It shows Ambedkar as a spiritual person who ultimately finds the roots of all the problems in the world within oneself and therefore preaches the virtue of moral rearmament and inner purity. The essence of being was to attain nirvana, the State of total contentment. It implied the futility of struggling against the material exploitation of dalits as their real salvation. It lay rather in extinguishing their own craving. It tended to internalise all their problems to themselves and stressed the need to cleanse their minds. Inevitably, it envisaged typica religious conduct from the followers with the highly pitched religious benchmarks available anywhere.

The sphere of religions abounds in such paradoxes. Its idiom basically promotes them. Buddhism could very well be conceived as the rebellion against the predominant creed of the establishment that prevailed more than 25 centuries ago, quite like Marxism in our times. Buddha was the first philosopher who forsook the futility of sterile philosophising and stressed the need to change the world. It is interesting to see in him as the first dialectician, some one in the same lineage as Hegel and Marx.

It is ahistorical to expect Buddha to give a solution to the problems of our times but it is important to appreciate the underscoring rational approach followed by him in his search. His conclusions are not important, as they are essentially constrained by the State of knowledge and overall development of the physical sciences during his times. What is important is to see the expanse of positive things that he could postulate at that time. Significantly, Buddha discarded the concept of God and soul and spoke against all kinds of rituals; he asked people to accept things only if it corresponded with their own experience or passed the test of their own intellect. He gave complete freedom to people to make amends to the Dhamma as per the needs of time. But, it could not escape the pressures of institutionalisation, which transformed it into a religion. They made him a God, wove stories that well competed with any mythology, built elaborate rituals to be followed and sapped it of its essential zeal of changing the world.

The paradox would be better illustrated by the responses of ardent Ambedkarites to the recent news about one Islamic Taliban commander threatening to dynamite two fourth-century monuments-1500-years-old statues of Buddha in central Afghanistan. The response came from highly educated non-resident Indian Ambedkarites. It was interesting inasmuch as they reveal what havoc the religious mindset that owes allegiance to Buddhism can play with even its human-centric tenets. They said that the dalits in India should immediately take out a massive procession to the consulate of Afghanistan and threaten them that no Afghan would be spared in India if they carried out destruction of the Buddha statues in Afghanistan.

It was a burst of anger at the first hearing of the news and was not to be meant but nonetheless it revealed the consciousness, the consciousness of Khomini or of any Hindu fundamentalist at work. It is one thing to speak against the fundamentalist vandalism and condemn it or even punish the responsible people in whatever way but it is quite another to don reverse fundamentalism to kill innocents to save dead stone statues in some distant land. It is important to realise the fact that even the Buddha's Dhamma whose roots are firmly in the soil of rationality and whose sole raison d'etre is the human suffering, could be mutilated to be its exact opposite by the very followers of Ambedkar who consciously cleansed it of the dust of irrationality and mysticism gathered over millennia.

SC/ST Associations: Facing a Dead End Ahead

One more significant trend in the Dalit movement has its source in the policy of reservations in services of the State. Apart from the central and State governments, the large number of public sector undertakings that were floated by them, and other institutions established and promoted with public money, also came to be the State, attracting the constitutional provisions regarding reservations for the SCs and STs in services. The dalits in these sectors represented the collective investment and achievements of the Dalit community, as reservations were the only hope for them to secure material well being. Although, they found themselves catapulted to modern sectors of economy, they found there were newer traps already in place, which clearly communicated the caste code for the modern organisations.

The dalits had to conform their behaviour to this code for their survival. It reflected all the familiar prejudices against them. Their experience of the blatant violations of these provisions generally manifested in terms of backlogs in filling reservation posts, denial of promotions and general discriminatory treatment meted out in postings, transfers and other aspects of organisational life. The trade unions and management associations would not address their woes because they involved a contradiction between the interests of dalits and non-dalits. Thus were born the SC/ST associations. Even after their countrywide proliferation, these associations do not have any locus standi with managements except for the ritualistic interviews during the annual visits of parliamentary committees on the welfare of SCs and STs.

It is a sad commentary on the functioning of the Constitution that over the last four decades it has driven these collectives to a State of hopelessness. The constitutional provisions regarding the reservations flow in the form of various circulars issued by the Government of India that are supposed to be implemented by its executive machinery. Over the years there has been a plethora of these circulars each written in such a convoluted language that even the highest court of law also felt it an arduous task to interpret them. One of the deliberate lacunae that exist in this scheme is that there is no effective onus on any one for the implementation of these provisions.

The executive can blatantly refuse to implement them under the plea of variant interpretation and drive the SC/ST employee or his association to the courts of law. Even if the poor employee or the SC/ST association could last the long winding court process over the years and succeed in getting the favourable verdict (a remote possibility though) the employer can still persist with his negative attitude. There are scores of cases of this kind where the petitioner employee or his association had to launch contempt proceeding against the employers and end up being bankrupt in the process. The helplessness of Dalit employees in the services, in a way is the reflection of the sorry State of Dalit politics. Since, there was no way these associations could effectively struggle, they landed up seeking petty favours from managements and in return being a black sheep during anti-management struggles.

The typical activities of these associations comprise celebration of the birth anniversaries of Ambedkar, representing Dalit employees to the management or administration, and doing certain philanthropic and community service, depending upon the degree of their own organisation and resources. The icon that they seem to be following is that of a saviour, emancipator, to whom they need to pay their obeisance, to obey his commandments. Their community service for instance could be easily traced to Ambedkar's call to dalits to contribute 20 % of their earnings to the cause of the community. Although, rarely any Dalit (save the poorest ones) goes so far as to sacrifice one fifth of his income over the cause of the community, none seem to refuse some symbolic contribution. Some better organised associations distribute notebooks, text books among slum children, run coaching and career counselling classes, organise relief works in the wake of calamities, open eateries in the Dalit congregations like the ones at the Dikshyabhumi in Nagpur and Chaityabhumi in Mumbai. These are the gestures of repayment of the social debt.

They see in Ambedkar as the one who struggled to get them so many facilities and it is their bounden duty to take fullest advantage of the same. It was their sacred duty to occupy positions of power in bureaucracy. It is assumed, as Ambedkar appears to have assumed himself, that the educated dalits with bureaucratic authorities will serve the cause of their community in direct proportion to their relative position. The myth is still sustained in spite of heaps of evidence to the contrary. Ambedkar's exhortation to 'agitate' is reduced down to making appeals to various authorities, having meetings with managements submitting memoranda and at the maximum, to filing the writ petitions in the courts-in short all that in the feasible range of the public service-rules. However, the constraints soon constitute the conscience. Ambedkar is reduced to a deity that imparts an identity. It is therefore that one curiously finds dalits celebrating the joint birth anniversaries of Babasaheb Ambedkar and Shivaji along with the Shiv Sena in the so-called den of Ambedkarism-the State of Maharashtra.

GENDER EQUALITY: MORE NOISE, LITTLE SUBSTANCE

It is expected of the people who avowedly fought against their unequal status, to have a congenial attitude towards the victims of other inequalities. Women are one social group who despite constituting half of the human population and contributing equally to the sustenance of human society are being discriminated against all over the world in varying degrees of severity. Gender inequality should have been the foremost issue in the Dalit movement. At least this problem could have been approached with the demonstration of a paradigm shift towards a radical culture. But unfortunately, with the rise of petty-bourgeoisie consciousness in dalits, they have adopted the more regressive culture of the forward castes. Traditionally, Dalit women had equality of sorts in so far as they worked with their men folk for managing their homestead. But now the cultural preference of relegating them to the background to do the household chores and / or to look after children is increasingly evident in Dalit homes. It is a matter of pride that right from the days of Ambedkar, women have played a major role in the Dalit movement. Among the poorer folks they still continue to do so. But this historical legacy also could not thwart the onslaught of the regressive culture.

In the din of what Ambedkar did for women, the icon that guides action is of the exponent of legal and coded equality of women, something like equality on the statutes (a la Hindu Code Bill). Culturally, dalits have not transcended the boundaries of sanskritisation, in the sense that their women folk have been given the worn out role model of a Brahmin woman; just because Ambedkar had once exhorted them to emulate her in the manner of donning their saris and other ornaments. At other times, he had reminded em of the importance of their role in community developm nt as mothers or wives and advised them to perform it better.

Thus, it may be said that the approach towards women even in the glorious days of the struggle also had not gone beyond the men-centric traditional role women donned. Similar observation can be made against Buddhism, that its meta-ideals also could not so much as grant them the absolute equality with men. It is a well known fact that Buddha had granted his tacit approval for the ladies to enter the Buddhist order as the 'Bhikkunies', at the instance of Anand-one of his close and favourite disciples, but had prescribed that they will always bow in reverence to a Bhikku irrespective of their relative seniority in the order. Although, it is said that the Dalit movement scarcely reflected the current shift in favour of equality of women, it would be erroneous to judge the events of the past by present standards.

It is not to be forgotten that Ambedkar had to communicate with dalits in their familiar idiom. The cultural change, moreover is an invisible process. What Ambedkar said or did had the limitation of historical possibilities; he would not say anything for the sake of postulating. He craved for change and strove to bring it about with a practicable approach. In relation to women, his approach needs to be understood from this perspective. Unfortunately, dalits seem to have frozen it into an icon and raised fences around themselves from the concept of radical gender equality.

Suicidal Anti-Materialism

It is a sad paradox of history that the movement of dalits, who are undisputedly the biggest sufferer of material depravation, should show an utter disregard for things material in an era characterised by stark materialism. It smacks of its distaste for the real issues of life while displaying excessive enthusiasm for the emotional issues. After the massive movement of landless labourers led by Dadasaheb Gaikwad, incidence of the material questions that afflict most of the people, could be seen as just notional (*e.g.*, the agitation for fallow lands by Samyak Samata Andolan). Even the Panthers could not escape this trend. There have been massive displays of strength of Dalit unity but it all has been for emotional issues. The examples abound.

The glorious movements for 'Namantar', against the ban on the Riddles of Rama and Krishna, and many others representing the Dalit-anger towards the attempts of castiest elements to denigrate and desecrate the statues of Babasaheb Ambedkar, certainly demonstrated potential force of dalits. The material reality that surfaced in the wake of each of these movements in terms of inhuman atrocities perpetrated in vengeance of their assertion, at the same time could not awaken them. In the Namantar case, in response to the Long March by dalits, the local Dalit hamlets were burnt down, many people got lynched, many women were raped, and all were ostracised and boycotted. Every time this heinous episode recurs and dalits bear the brunt!

With regard to the neglect of material aspects of living in the Dalit movement, the inspiring icon is made up of Ambedkar's much publicised opposition to the vulgar materialism propagated by the then communists. It is stuffed with his thoughts that reflect not necessarily disdain for the material things but a leaning towards a belief that the societal phenomena could well be shaped by the non-material things or processes. It is coloured by the fact that the tone of the struggles he launched has always been in the realm of codes, norms, traditions, and institutional practices that he aimed his struggle against for bringing about the sociocultural change, a social revolution.

The culmination of his mission, as it is seen by dalits, in Buddhism, that predominantly taught the virtue of extinguishing the thirst for material things and reaching indefinable State of mental peace called Nirvana, has certainly lent strength to this icon. Dalits always defined their struggle to be for prestige-for 'Asmita', for self-respect. The questions of land, remunerative wages, working conditions, government's economic policies etc. never interested them. In the history of four decades at no time any of their leaders or any intellectual cared to look at how the government policies or international happenings influenced the lives of average dalits in villages. Even in the face of atrocities that dalits suffer day in and day out, never does the realisation dawn on them that much of it could be traced to their State of material depravation. The fact that they cannot organise defence is also related with their material wherewithal. It does not seem to be a question of violence or nonviolence. Fortunately, Ambedkar's own stand on violence, as he often declared it in order to expose the futility of Gandhi's obsession with nonviolence in the long polemics is well known to dalits.

It reflected what according to him, the Buddha said 'to the extent possible, nonviolence; if necessary, violence". But the icon of Ambedkar that came before people was conveniently shorn of this practical attribute. This icon seems to obfuscate even Buddha as the impracticable proponent of unqualified compassion and nonviolence. It emphasises constitutionalism even in the wake of perpetration of heinous atrocities.

Elections: The incurable Obsession

Barring emotional issues, the Dalit movement has been hijacked by the petty warring factions of incompetent leaders whose sole obsession appears to be elections of whatever kind. As roosters wake up crowing at the dawn or frogs surface out of nowhere around water pools formed with the first showers of monsoon, they all surface out of their slumber with any election announcement. Then follow the talks for alliances, allegations and counter allegations of money transactions, threats of splits and actual splits. This process could be preceded by the talks of unification of various factions, if they were not together, essentially engineered by the electoral strategies of some ruling class party.

The masses however land up emotionally supporting such unity moves and ultimately fall prey to the machinations of big money. This cycle is seen repeated a number of times at least in Maharashtra, which has historically been assumed as the hub of Dalit politics even after losing its provincial relevance. This Dalit electioneering has been so shorn of reality and devoid of any political perspective as to seem end in itself, serving the personal interests of leaders. They would not have any manifesto, no strategy, no agenda or plan; no realistic assessment of their strength and weakness. Participating in elections however was their sacred duty.

The Ambedkar-icon that appears to back this strange phenomenon derives its material from the fact that Ambedkar himself relied upon elections for securing power despite his own bitter experiences, that he tended to think of the popular mandate gained through periodical elections as the only legitimate political process in the Constitutional regime and denounce other modes of mass struggle. It is additionally imbued with a hope that despite several defeats Ambedkar rose to occupy seats of power through the electoral process.

Now the people are increasingly getting dejected with the games of Dalit leaders and are found to be straying over to other parliamentary parties, even of Brahminical hues. Many of the latter have already co-opted Ambedkar. Some have lent him their veneration by including his name into their list of the 'Pratah Smaraniya'-the memorables at the dawn. They have launched the class assimilative drives like Rashtriya Samarasata Manch. Today, there is a sort of clamour for claiming Ambedkar's legacy among all the parliamentary parties. In the face of disintegration of the Dalit block and increasing political crises faced by these parties, they all need Ambedkar for their survival.

Essentially, the icon of Ambedkar they promote is customised to serve their own interests. Even the BJP, the party that swears by Hindu religion and glorious Hindu tradition and culture, has put up Ambedkar to serve its ideology and politics, with fairly encouraging results. The icon they project is that of a staunch nationalist, of one who was proud of 'Indian' (read Hindu) culture and tradition minus evils like untouchability and of one who was against communism.

The election mania is so deep entrenched in the minds of dalits that they ceased to think of any other alternative. There is no appreciation of the fact that they have been squarely cheated in this intoxicating game. At the first place, the resource sensitive game does not gel with the starkly resourceless players. Second, so far they do not transcend their caste confines, their constituency remains acutely constrained by the numbers of their own caste. Third, even if one succeeded overcoming these odds in the election, there may essentially lie series of compromises ahead for basic survival in the houses.

The system ensures that a true representative of dalits does not reach the portals of power, and if reached, he or she is soon neutralised. It is amazing that the simple empirical evidence of the systemic failure does not get across dalits. The constant strength of Dalit representation in the Indian Parliament and legislative Assemblies by virtue of the reservation policy, has been utterly ineffective simply because the various identities in addition to the caste never let them come together. Electoral Dalit politics presupposes alliances and compromises invariably with the ruling class parties who may satisfy the thirst for power of its leaders but certainly not support the Dalit empowerment.

2

AMBEDKAR—THE MESSIHA OF DALITS

INTRODUCTION

Bhimrao Ramji Ambedkar (April 14, 1891-December 6, 1956) was a Buddhist revivalist, an Indian jurist, scholar and Bahujan political leader who is the chief architect of the Indian constitution. Born in a poor Untouchable community; he spent his life fighting against the system of Hindu untouchability and the Indian Caste System.

He is also credited for having sparked a revival of Buddhism in India, known as the Indian Buddhist movement. He has been honoured with Bharat Ratna, India's highest civilian award, awarded for the highest degrees of national service.

Overcoming numerous social and financial obstacles, Ambedkar became one of the first untouchables to obtain college education in India. He went on to pursue higher studies in the United States and England, where he earned law degrees and multiple doctorates for his studies and works in law, economics and political science.

A famous scholar, Ambedkar practised law for a few years before he began publishing journals advocating political rights and social freedom for India's untouchables. Leading numerous public agitations, he would become an undisputed political statesman of the Indian Oppressed classes.

A Legacy Marking Indian Sociopolitical History

Ambedkar's legacy, as a sociopolitical reformer, has been long-lasting on modern India. In post independence India his sociopolitical thought has acquired respect across political spectrum and influenced various spheres of life like socioeconomic, education and Government policies of affirmative action by socioeconomic and legal incentives.

He is widely regarded as the "father of the Indian constitution" for his role in creating the document. His political philosophy has given rise to a large number of Dalit political parties, publications and workers unions that remain active across India, especially in Maharashtra. His promotion of the Indian Buddhist Movement has rejuvenated interest in Buddhist philosophy in many parts of India. Mass conversion ceremonies have been organized by Dalit activists in modern times, emulating Ambedkar's Nagpur ceremony of 1956.

Ambedkar organized untouchable political parties and social organizations, and served in the legislative councils of British India. He would intensify his criticism of orthodox Hindu society, as well as his criticism of slavery and exclusivism in Islam.

Despite this, his reputation as a scholar led to his appointment as free India's first law minister, and chairman of the committee responsible to draft a constitution.

Ambedkar's work would guarantee political, economic and social freedoms for untouchables and other ethnic, social and religious communities of India.

His polemical condemnation of Hinduism and attacks on Islam would make him unpopular and controversial, although his conversion to Buddhism sparked a revival in interest of Buddhist philosophy in India.

Early Life: Bhimrao Ramji Ambedkar was born in the British-founded town and military cantonment of Mhow in the Central Provinces (now in Madhya Pradesh). He was the 14th and last child of Ramji Maloji Sakpal and Bhimabai Murbadkar.

His family was of Marathi background from the town of Ambavade in the Ratnagiri district of modern-day Maharashtra. They belonged to the Hindu Mahar caste, who were treated as untouchables and subjected to intense socioeconomic discrimination. Ambedkar's ancestors had for long been in the employment of the army of the British East India Company, and his father served in the Indian Army at the Mhow cantonment, rising to the rank of Subedar. He had received a degree of formal education in Marathi and English, and encouraged his children to learn and work hard at school.

Belonging to the Kabir Panth, Ramji Sakpal encouraged his children to read the Hindu classics, especially the Mahabharata and the Ramayana. He used his position in the army to lobby for his children to study at the government school, as they faced resistance owing to their caste. Although able to attend school, Ambedkar and other Untouchable children were segregated and given no attention or assistance from the teachers. Also they were not allowed to sit inside the class. They used to sit outside the class and even if they want to drink water somebody from higher caste would pour that water from the top as they were not allowed to touch the water also.

Ramji Sakpal retired in 1894 and the family moved to Satara two years later. Shortly after their move, Ambedkar's mother died. The children were cared for by their paternal aunt, and lived in difficult circumstances. Only three sons-Balaram, Anandrao and Bhimrao-and two daughters-Manjula and Tulasa-of the Ambedkars would go on to survive them. Of his brothers and sisters, only Ambedkar succeeded in passing his examinations and graduate to a bigger school. His native village name was "Ambavade" in Ratnagiri District so he changed his name from "Sakpal" to "Ambedkar" with the recommendation and faith of a Brahmin teacher that believed in Bhimrao.

Ramji Sakpal remarried in 1898, and the family moved to Mumbai (then Bombay), where Ambedkar became the first untouchable student at the Government High School near

Elphinstone Road. Although excelling in his studies, Ambedkar was increasingly disturbed by his segregation and discrimination. In 1907, he passed his matriculation examination and entered the University of Mumbai, becoming one of the first persons of untouchable origin to enter college in India. This success provoked celebrations amongst his community, and after a public ceremony, he was given a biography of the Buddha by his teacher Krishnaji Arjun Keluskar also known as Dada Keluskar a Maratha caste scholar. Ambedkar's marriage had been arranged the previous year as per Hindu custom, to Ramabai, a nine-year old girl from Dapoli. In 1908, he entered the Elphinstone College and obtained a scholarship of Rs. 25 a month from the Gaikwad ruler of Baroda, Sahyaji Rao III for higher studies in USA. By 1912, he obtained his degree in economics and political science, and prepared to take up employment with the Baroda state government. His wife gave birth to his first son, Yashwant in the same year. Ambedkar had just moved his young family and started work, when he dashed back to Mumbai to see his ailing father, who died on February 2, 1913.

Pursuit of Education

A few months later, Ambedkar was selected by the Gaikwad ruler to travel to the United States and enrol at Columbia University, with a scholarship of $11.5 pounds per month. Arriving in New York City, Ambedkar was admitted for graduate studies at the political science department. After a brief stay at the dormitory, he moved to a housing club run by Indian students and took up rooms with a Parsi friend, Naval Bhathena. In 1916, he was awarded a Ph. D. for a thesis which he eventually published in book form as The Evolution of Provincial Finance in British India.

His first published work, however, was a paper on Castes in India: Their Mechanism, Genesis and Development. Winning his degree and doctorate, he travelled to London and enrolled at Gray's Inn and the London School of Economics, studying law and preparing a doctoral thesis in economics. The expiration of his scholarship the following year forced him to temporarily abandon his studies and return to India amidst World War I.

Returning to work as military secretary for Baroda state, Ambedkar was distressed by the sudden reappearance of discrimination in his life, and left his job to work as a private tutor and accountant, even starting his own consultancy business that failed owing to his social status. With the help of an English acquaintance, the former Bombay Governor Lord Syndenham, he won a post as professor of political economy at the Sydenham College of Commerce and Economics in Mumbai. He was able to return to England in 1920 with the support of the Maharaja of Kolhapur, his Parsi friend and his own savings. By 1923 he completed a thesis on The Problem of the Rupee. He was awarded a D. Sc. by the University of London, and finishing his law studies, he was simultaneously admitted to British Bar as a barrister. On his way back to India, Ambedkar spent three months in Germany, where he conducted further studies in economics at the University of Bonn. He would be formally awarded a Ph. D. by the Columbia University on June 8, 1927.

FIGHT AGAINST UNTOUCHABILITY

As a leading Dalit scholar, Ambedkar had been invited to testify before the Southborough Committee, which was preparing the Government of India Act 1919. At this hearing, Ambedkar argued for creating separate electorates and reservations for Dalits and different religious communities. In 1920, he began the publication of the weekly Mooknayak (Leader of the Dumb) in Mumbai. Attaining popularity, Ambedkar used this journal to criticize orthodox Hindu politicians and a perceived reticence in the Indian political community to fight caste discrimination.

His speech at a Depressed Classes Conference in Kolhapur impressed the local state ruler Shahu IV, who shocked orthodox society by dining with Ambekdar and his untouchable colleagues. Ambedkar exhorted his Mahar community to abandon the idea of sub-castes, and held a joint communal dinner in which the principle of segregation was abandoned. Upon his return from Europe, Ambedkar established a successful legal practise, and also organised the Bahishkrit Hitakarini Sabha (Group for the Wellbeing of the Excluded) to promote education and socioeconomic upliftment of the depressed classes.

In the same vein, he was highly critical of the practice of untouchability in Indian Muslim Society, lending credence to the view that he was not exclusively against Hindus or Hinduism, but was speaking of reforming social evils. In his illustrious publication "Pakistan and the Partition of India", he writes that, while Islam speaks of "brotherhood", the practice of slavery and caste discrimination were rampant in Muslim society in South Asia, such as the Ashraf/Ajlaf caste divide and the severe discrimination against the Arzal castes or Dalit Muslim untouchables.

In 1926, he became a nominated member of the Bombay Legislative Council. By 1927 Dr. Ambedkar decided to launch active movements against untouchability. He did begin with public movements and marches to open up & share public drinking water resources to which until then untouchable communities had no access; also he put up a struggle for entry in Hindu Temples which was not allowed by upper caste communities. Led a satyagraha-non-violent protest and civil disobedience-in Mahad to fight for the right of the untouchable community to draw water from the main water tank of the town. There he held a conference and drew parallels between his movement and events that convened Estates-General in Versailles on 5 May 1789, during French Revolution which forced Roman Catholic Church to undergo a radical restructuring.

On January 1, 1927 Ambedkar organised a ceremony at the Koregaon Victory Memorial near Pune, which commemorated the Indian soldiers who died during World War I. Here he inscribed the names of the soldiers from his Mahar community on a marble tablet. In a Depressed Classes Conference on

December 24, he condemned the ancient Hindu classical text, the Manu Smriti (Laws of Manu). Condemning it for justifying the system of caste discrimination and untouchability, Ambedkar and his supporters burned copies of the texts.

In 1927, he would begin his second journal, the Bahiskrit Bharat (Excluded India), later rechristened as Janata (The People). He would be appointed to the Bombay Presidency Committee to work with the all-European Simon Commission in 1928. This commission had sparked great protests across India, and while its report was ignored by most Indians, Ambedkar himself wrote a separate set of recommendations for future constitutional reforms. He was injured in an accident that occurred during a visit to Chalisgaon on October 23, 1929. Hoping to help the untouchable community, which was facing a social boycott from orthodox Hindus, he was confined in bed there till the end of the year.

Poona Pact

Ambedkar had become one of the most prominent untouchable political figures of the time. He had grown increasingly critical of mainstream Indian political parties for their perceived lack of emphasis for the elimination of the caste system. Ambedkar criticized the Indian National Congress and its leader Mahatma Gandhi, whom he accused of reducing the untouchable community to a figure of pathos. Ambedkar was also dissatisfied with the failures of British rule, and advocated a political identity for untouchables separate from both the Congress and the British. At a Depressed Classes Conference on August 8, 1930 Ambedkar outlined his political vision:

> *"Safety of the Depressed Classes hinged on their being independent of the Government and the Congress" both: "We must shape our course ourselves and by ourselves... Political power cannot be a panacea for the ills of the Depressed Classes. Their salvation lies in their social elevation. They must cleanse their evil habits. They*

> *must improve their bad ways of living.... They must be educated.... There is a great necessity to disturb their pathetic contentment and to instill into them that divine discontent which is the spring of all elevation."*

In this speech, Ambedkar criticized the Salt Satyagraha launched by Gandhi and the Congress. Ambedkar's criticisms and political work had made him very unpopular with orthodox Hindus, as well as many Congress politicians who had condemned untouchability and worked against discrimination across India. His prominence and popular support amongst the untouchable community had increased, and he was invited to attend the Second Round Table Conference in London in 1931. Here he sparred verbally with Gandhi on the question of awarding separate electorates to untouchables. A fierce opponent of separate electorates on religious and sectarian lines, Gandhi feared that separate electorates for untouchables would divide Hindu society for future generations.

When the British agreed with Ambedkar and announced the awarding of separate electorates, Gandhi began a fast-unto-death while imprisoned in the Yeravada Central Jail of Pune in 1932. Exhorting orthodox Hindu society to eliminate discrimination and untouchability, Gandhi asked for the political and social unity of Hindus.

Gandhi's fast provoked great public support across India, and orthodox Hindu leaders, Congress politicians and activists such as Madan Mohan Malaviya and Pawlankar Baloo organized joint meetings with Ambedkar and his supporters at Yeravada. Fearing a communal reprisal and killings of untouchables, had Gandhi died, Ambedkar agreed to drop the demand for separate electorates, under massive coercion from the supporters of Gandhi, and settled for a reservation of seats.

Ambedkar was to criticise the fast of Gandhi as a gimmick to deny political rights to the untouchables and the coercion he faced to give up the demand of separate electorates, in all his writings later.

POLITICAL CAREER

In 1935, Ambedkar was appointed principal of the Government Law College, a position he held for two years. Settling in Mumbai, Ambedkar oversaw the construction of a large house, and stocked his personal library with more than 50, 000 books. His wife Ramabai died after a long illness in the same year. It had been her long-standing wish to go on a pilgrimage to Pandharpur, but Ambedkar refused to let her go, telling her that he will create new Pandharpur for her instead of going to Hinduism's Pandharpur which treated them as untouchable.

His own views and attitudes had hardened against orthodox Hindus, despite a significant increase in momentum across India for the fight against untouchability and he began criticizing them even as he was criticized himself by large numbers of Hindu activists. Speaking at the Yeola Conversion Conference on October 13 near Nasik, Ambedkar announced his intention to convert to a different religion and exhorted his followers to leave Hinduism. He would repeat his message at numerous public meetings across India.

In 1936, Ambedkar founded the Independent Labour Party, which won 15 seats in the 1937 elections to the Central Legislative Assembly. He published his book The Annihilation of Caste in the same year, based on the thesis he had written in New York. Attaining immense popular success, Ambedkar s work strongly criticized Hindu religious leaders and the caste system in general. He protested the Congress decision to call the untouchable community Harijans (Children of God), a moniker coined by Gandhi. . Ambedkar would be named to serve on the Defence Advisory Committee and the Viceroy's Executive Council as minister for labour.

Between 1941 and 1945, he published a large number of highly controversial books and pamphlets, including Thoughts on Pakistan, in which he criticized the Muslim League's demand for a separate Muslims state of Pakistan. With What Congress and Gandhi have Done to the Untouchables, Ambedkar intensified his attacks on Gandhi and the Congress, charging them with hypocrisy. In his work Who were the Sudras?, Ambedkar attempted to explain the formation of the Sudras *i.e.* the lowest caste in hierarchy of Hindu caste system. He also emphasised that how Sudras are separate from Untouchables. Ambedkar oversaw the transition of his political party into the All India Scheduled Castes Federation, although it performed poorly in the elections held in 1946 for the Constituent Assembly of India. In writing a sequel to Who were the Sudras? in 1948, Ambedkar lambasted Hinduism in the untouchables: a Thesis on the Origins of Untouchability:

> *"The Hindu Civilisation.... is a diabolical contrivance to suppress and enslave humanity. Its proper name would be infamy. What else can be said of a civilisation which has produced a mass of people... who are treated as an entity beyond human intercourse and whose mere touch is enough to cause pollution?"*

Ambedkar was also critical of Islam and its practices in South Asia. While justifying the Partition of India, he condemned practices of Child-Marriage in Muslim society, as well as the mistreatment of women. He also condemned the Caste practices carried out by Muslims in South Asia. He was also critical of slavery in Muslim communities. He said:

> *"No words can adequately express the great and many evils of polygamy and concubinage, and especially as a source of misery to a Muslim woman." "Take the caste system. Everybody infers that Islam must be free from slavery and caste. (While slavery existed), much of its support was derived from Islam and Islamic countries. While the prescriptions by the Prophet regarding the just and humane treatment of slaves contained in the Koran are praiseworthy, there is nothing whatever in Islam that lends support to the abolition of this curse. But if slavery has gone, caste among Musalmans (Muslims) has remained."*

He wrote that Muslim Society is "even more full of social evils than Hindu Society is" and criticized Muslims for sugar-coating their sectarian Caste System with euphemisms like "brotherhood". He also criticized the discrimination against the Arzal classes among Muslims who were regarded as "degraded", as well as the oppression of women in Muslim society through the oppressive purdah system. He alleged that while Purdah was also practiced among Hindus, only in Muslims was it sanctioned by religion. He criticized their fanaticism to Islam on the grounds that their literalist interpretations of Islamic doctrine made their society very rigid and impermeable to change. He further wrote that Indian Muslims have failed to reform their society unlike Muslims in other countries like Turkey.

In a "communal malaise," both groups (Hindus and Muslims) ignore the urgent claims of social justice.

While he was extremely critical of Muhammad Ali Jinnah and the communally divisive strategies of the Muslim League, he argued that Hindus and Muslims should segregate and the State of Pakistan be formed, as ethnic nationalism within the same country would only lead to more violence. He cited precedent with historical events like the dissolution of the Ottoman Empire and Czechoslovakia to bolster his views regarding the Hindu-Muslim communal divide.

However, he questioned as to whether the need for Pakistan was sufficient and it might be possible to resolve Hindu-Muslim differences in a less drastic way. He wrote that Pakistan must "justify its existence" accordingly. Since other countries such as Canada also have had communal issues with the French and English and have lived together, it may not be impossible for Hindus and Muslims to live together.

He warned that the actual implementation of a two state solution would be extremely problematic with massive population transfers and border disputes. This claim was almost prophetic in its realization with the violent Partition of India after independence.

ARCHITECT OF INDIA'S CONSTITUTION

Despite his increasing unpopularity, controversial views and intense criticism of Gandhi and the Congress, Ambedkar was by reputation an exemplary jurist and scholar. Upon India's independence on August 15, 1947, the new Congress-led government invited Ambedkar to serve as the nation's first law minister, which he accepted. On August 29, Ambedkar was appointed chairman of the constitution drafting committee, charged by the Assembly to write free India's constitution. Ambedkar won great praise from his colleagues and contemporary observers for his drafting work.

The text prepared by Ambedkar provided constitutional guarantees and protections for a wide range of civil liberties for individual citizens, including freedom of religion, the abolition of untouchability and the outlawing of all forms of discrimination. Ambedkar argued for extensive economic and social rights for women, and also won the Assembly's support for introducing a system of reservations of jobs in the civil services, schools and colleges for members of scheduled castes and scheduled tribes, a system akin to affirmative action. India's lawmakers hoped to eradicate the socioeconomic inequalities and lack of opportunities for India's depressed classes through this measure, which had been originally envisioned as temporary on a need basis. The constitution was adopted on November 26, 1949 by the Constituent Assembly. Speaking after the completion of his work, Ambedkar said:

> *"I feel that the Constitution is workable; it is flexible and it is strong enough to hold the country together both in peace time and in war time. Indeed, if I may say so, if things go wrong under the new Constitution the reason will not be that we had a bad Constitution. What we will have to say is that Man was vile."*

Ambedkar resigned from the cabinet in 1951 following the stalling in parliament of his draft of the Hindu Code Bill, which sought to expound gender equality in the laws of inheritance, marriage and the economy. Although supported by Prime

Minister Nehru, the cabinet and many other Congress leaders, it received criticism from a large number of parliament members. Ambedkar independently contested an election in 1952 to the lower house of parliament, the Lok Sabha but was defeated. He was appointed to the upper house of parliament, the Rajya Sabha in March 1952 and would remain its member until his death.

CONVERSION TO BUDDHISM

In the 1950s, Ambedkar turned his attention to Buddhism and travelled to Sri Lanka (then Ceylon) to attend a convention of Buddhist scholars and monks. While dedicating a new Buddhist vihara near Pune, Ambedkar announced that he was writing a book on Buddhism, and that as soon as it was finished, he planned to make a formal conversion to Buddhism. Ambedkar twice visited Burma in 1954; the second time in order to attend the third conference of the World Fellowship of Buddhists in Rangoon. In 1955, he founded the Bharatiya Bauddha Mahasabha, or the Buddhist Society of India. He would complete his manuscript and final work The Buddha and his Dhamma to completion in 1956, although it would be published posthumously.

Ambedkar organised a formal public ceremony for himself and his supporters in Nagpur on October 14, 1956. Accepting the Three Refuges and Five Precepts from a Buddhist monk in the traditional manner, Ambedkar completed his own conversion. He then proceeded to convert an estimated 380, 000 of his supporters who were gathered around him. Administering the "22 Vows," Ambedkar and his supporters explicitly condemned and rejected Hinduism and Hindu philosophy. He would soon travel to Kathmandu in Nepal to attend the Fourth World Buddhist Conference. He completed his final manuscript, The Buddha or Karl Marx on December 2, 1956.

Death: Since 1948, Ambedkar had been suffering from diabetes. He was bedridden from June to October in 1954 owing to clinical depression and failing eyesight. He had been increasingly embittered by political issues, which took a toll on his health. His health worsened as he furiously worked through

1955. Just three days after completing his final manuscript 'Buddha And His Dhamma', it is said that Ambedkar died in his sleep on December 6, 1956 at his home in Delhi.

Some of his supporters doubt his natural death and think death may not have been natural and put forward different theories. Try to draw parallel between his and Gandhis death and blame Caste Brahmins.

A Buddhist-style cremation was organised for him at Chowpatty beach on December 7, attended by hundreds of thousands of supporters, activists and admirers.

Ambedkar was survived by his second wife Savita Ambedkar, born as a Caste Brahmin and converted to Buddhism with him. His wife's name before marriage was Sharda Kabir. Savita Ambedkar died as Buddhist in 2002. Ambedkar's grandson, Prakash Yaswant Ambedkar leads the Bharipa Bahujan Mahasangha and has served in both houses of the Indian Parliament. A number of unfinished typescripts and handwritten drafts were found among Ambedkar's notes and papers and gradually made available. Among these were Waiting for a Visa, which probably dates from 1935-36 and is an autobiographical work, and the Untouchables, or the Children of India's Ghetto, which refers to the census of 1951.

A memorial for Ambedkar was established in his Delhi house at 26 Alipur Road. His birthdate is celebrated as a public holiday known as Ambedkar Jayanti. He was posthumously awarded India's highest civilian honour, the Bharat Ratna in 1990. He is the namesake of many public institutions, such as the Dr. Babasaheb Ambedkar Open University in Ahmedabad, Gujarat.

A large official portrait of Ambedkar is on display in the Parliament building. Jabbar Patel directed the Hindi-language movie "Dr. Babasaheb Ambedkar" about the life of Ambedkar, released in 2000, starring South Indian actor Mammootty as Ambedkar. Sponsored by India's National Film Development Corporation and Ministry of Social Justice, the film was released after a long and controversial gestation period.

AMBEDKAR VS. GANDHI ON VILLAGE LIFE

Ambedkar was a fierce critic of Mahatma Gandhi (and the Indian National Congress). He was criticized by his contemporaries and modern scholars for this opposition Gandhi, who had been one of the first Indian leaders to call for the abolition of untouchability and discrimination.

Gandhi had a more positive, arguably romanticised view of traditional village life in India and approach to the untouchables calling them Harijan (children of god) and saying he was "of " them. Whereas Ambedkar had a much more negative view. Ambedkar encouraged his followers to leave their home villages, move to the cities and get an education.

LIMITATIONS, CRITICISM AND LEGACY

While the majority of contemporary sociopolitical leaders across political spectrum joined in condemnation of the social practice of untouchability, many times their priorities on the ground in eliminating these practices did not match with expectations of Ambedkar.

While in sharing of food together by different caste people became more common, practice of marriage among same caste and political voting lines based on caste achieved very little change over the years.

The situation was such that while progressive people agreed with his cause, he could not get unanimous and unequivocal support from even all depressed classes at one time. So he could not get enough milage of vote bank in actual number of parliamentary seats, in post independence era.

Reservation in India did not reach adequately to affected population due to ever growing population, practices of child labour and child marriage, discrete forms of discrimination, and casteism among even oppressed classes themselves, such as discrimination against the Bhangi undercastes by the Dalits etc.

At the same time, some economically poor sections of society got disenchanted because of affirmative action because their castes or communities were not among selected few. Above factors have been polarising Indian politics, at times, with extreme POVs. This aspect is more of reason in accusing Ambedkar as a controversial and polarizing figure in Indian politics even after his death. While Ambedkar's supporters argue that he was working to secure Dalit and Backward Caste political rights. Contemporary and modern scholars also questioned Ambedkar's research and point of view regarding origin of the caste system and racial theories.

He acquired sympathy and criticism both about his mass conversion of Buddhism as a political stunt, from his opponents. Ambedkar was also criticised for his intensely anti-Hindu views, though his supporters argue that he was only opposed to "Orthodox Brahmanism" rather than to all Hindus. He came in touch with many progressive people belonging to Bramhin and other upper classes.

Some scholars including that of affected castes took a view that Britishers are more even handed in respect of Indian caste system, and continuance of British rule can help in eradicating some of practices.

This political thought believed that let the social improvement happen first and then only we should go for political independence, and was shared by quite a number of social activists including that of Mahatma Jyotiba Phule and Ambedkar. So this earned criticism from certain quarters like writer Arun Shourie, who questioned Ambedkar's contributions to the Indian Independence struggle. His criticism about certain aspects of Islam and Islamic society in India and his favour in form of benefit of affirmative action to limited sections; limited support among many Muslims.

COST OF CHANGE

However, frequent violent clashes between Dalit groups and orthodox Hindus have occurred over the years. When in

1994 a garland of shoes was hung around a statue of Ambedkar in Mumbai, sectarian violence and strikes paralyzed the city for over a week. When the following year similar disturbances occurred, a statue of Ambedkar was destroyed. In addition, some Dalits who converted to Buddhism have rioted against Hindus and desecrated Hindu temples, often incited into doing so by anti-Hindu elements and replacing deities with pictures of Ambedkar.

IS CASTE SYSTEM INTRINSIC TO HINDUISM?

Demolishing a Myth

This paper, citing evidence from the ancient scriptures, attempts to establish that Hinduism-its vedic and classic variants-did not support the caste system; it rigorously opposed it in practice and principle. Even after the emergence of the caste system, Hindu society still saw considerable occupational and social mobility.

Moreover, Hinduism created legends to impress on the popular mind the invalidity of the caste system-a fact further reinforced by the constant efflorescence of reform movements throughout history. The caste system survived in spite of this because of factors that ranged from the socioeconomic to the ecological, which helped sustain and preserve balance among communities in a non-modern world.

M. V. Nadkarni

> *One need not despair of ever knowing the truth of one's religion, because the fundamentals of Hinduism, as of every great religion, are unchangeable, and easily understood.*
>
> *—M K Gandhi, Young India, October 6, 1921*

It is necessary to demolish the myth that caste system is an intrinsic part of Hinduism. This myth is believed by orthodox elements within Hinduism and also is propagated by elements outside Hinduism with the mischievous intent of proselytising.

Ironically both, though opposed to each other, jointly do a lot of damage.

Moreover, this myth has harmed relations between the so-called upper castes and lower castes. This paper intends to logically and with documentary proof show that Hinduism-even vedic and classical Hinduism-not only does not support the caste system, but has taken lots of pains to oppose it both in principle and practice, making it obvious that caste system is not an intrinsic part of Hindu canon, philosophy and even practice.

It will then show that the caste system emerged and survived due to totally different factors, which had nothing to do with Hindu religion.

3

CASTE SYSTEM AMONG HINDUS

The Indian caste system, prevalent also among local Muslims and Christians, exhibits some differences from those of other countries. Elsewhere, the separation between one group and the other is usually along racial lines. Within India, that is not so. Nor is there any discernable dichotomy (white/black or high/low) because the caste system forms a continuum that defies s ch ready definition. While many lower-caste people live in conditions of great poverty and social disadvantage, many upper-caste Brahmins too are poor and now disadvantaged politically. Efforts by the Indian government to emancipate the lower castes with affirmative action like reservations in education, jobs and promotions have achieved some success, although the benefits have tended to be cornered by the well-off "Creamy Layer" of lower castes.

The concept of 'upper' and 'lower' caste is therefore a matter of social standing and assimilation rather than anything based on wealth or influence. Even in this age, some castes do not allow other caste members, whom they consider to be "lower" to touch them, and would have washed themselves or their possessions if they had been touched by someone from a "lower" caste. In some parts of India, there was the practice of defining the physical distance one should keep from persons of another caste. As a result of this, children who attended a school where children of lower castes were present had to bathe in running water before returning home.

In some parts of the world, as well as in India, such discrimination still exists, though it is punishable by law and unconstitutional in India. The Indian constitution was drafted by Ambedkar, himself of low-caste origins, who is regarded as an emancipator of the Dalits.

Loss of caste could occur if individuals strayed from the norms of behaviour expected of them; for instance, if one married a person belonging to another caste. Despite the prosletysing efforts of Christian missionaries, the fact is that converts rarely achieve emancipation from the caste system to gain an equal social standing with people of privilege. Even among converts, matrimony between members of different castes is rare, although it is not unknown.

A detailed analysis of the caste system, Castes in India: Their Mechanism, Genesis and Development in India was presented by Dr. B. R. Ambedkar in his doctoral paper at the Columbia University.

Mythical Origin of Castes

This is a unique verse as it is the only one in the ancient Brahminical Veda scriptures that has a mention of Varna. This may seem rather strange, given the preponderance of caste in India. But once we recognise that the Indian society was Jati based and the Varna system was a later Brahminical interpretation of that society, this anomaly becomes understandable.

In the Puranas, it is said that the creative force of the universe, Brahma, created some humans from his mouth-they became reciters of the Veda and became the Brahmins. Then he created other humans from his arms, they became the Kshatriyas, bearers of arms, the warrior and ruling class. Brahma then created some from his abdomen, who became the Vaishyas or merchants. Finally, Brahma created humans from his feet. They served the other castes even as the feet serve the man; they came to become the Sudras (manual labourers and artisans). Thus, the whole universe is held to be one organic entity, the body of the almighty.

Most scholars are agreed that the caste system was not rigid, including in the early vedic times. Change of one's caste could be effected by all except Brahmins, by changing one's vocation and acquiring new skills, or gaining economic or political power.

Jati

Major castes were subdivided into hundreds of sub-castes or jatis. Castes were based on occupation. Endogamous marriage (including polyandry) and other association within caste was strongly enforced.

- Sub-castes within a group of jat ("birth" as opposed to varna) were called jati
- Jati members were allowed to marry only with their jati.
- People were born into their jati; this status couldn't be changed, unless through marriage or under rare circumstances.
- Each jati was part of a local system of interdependence with other groups, involving occupational specialization, and was linked in complex ways with networks that stretched across regions.

For example, in Tamil Nadu and Kerala, states of South India, castes based on occupation would include: asari (carpenters), thattar (goldsmiths), muusaari (coppersmiths), karuvar (ironsmiths), ambattar (clothes-washers), parayar (cobblers) and so on.

Modern Developments: With rapid urbanization and education of India's largely rural, agrarian population, the significance of caste has diminished, except in government mediated interventions in the form of quotas and reservations in education, jobs and promotions for the socially "lower", but numerous and thus politically important, castes.

The caste system and its attendant practices have been outlawed and declared punishable offences, but these laws are difficult to implement. There are occasional violations of human rights of Dalits (outcastes-also called untouchables) by the higher castes, including forcing Dalits into their traditional professions. Dalits in rural areas have often been victimized by other castes, many a times themselves politically powerful "Shudras" or "lower castes".

The government of India provides freeships, scholarships, reservations for government jobs and of university seats in programs of higher education (undergraduate and above) for people hailing from Scheduled castes, Scheduled tribes and Other Backward Castes; see Reservation in India. Upper caste Hindus and several secular elements counter-argue that unmeritorious Dalits, especially those from the well off "Creamy Layer" are exploiting this constitutionally obligatory discrimination to their unfair advantage and meritorious candidates are being sidelined. The site Dalitstan (presently taken down), once banned by the Indian government, is an example of anti-Brahmin and anti-Hindu rhetoric by Dalit extremists, allegedly supported by Christian missions.

Caste System among Indian Muslims

There is also several caste systems among some Muslims in India. They are broadly divided into two castes, Ashraf and Ajlaf, or oonchi jaat (high caste) and niichi Zaat (low caste). The Muslim Caste System in India was analysed by Ambedkar, who had a very dim view of the rampant discrimination of the Ajlaf castes by the Ashraf castes. In addition to the Ashraf and Ajlaf castes, there exist the Arzal under-caste or the Dalit Muslims who are regarded by the Ashraf and the Ajlaf as ritually impure and are relegated to professions regarded as "menial" such as scavenging and the carrying of night soil.

In addition, Muslims in Bengal organize their society according to social strata called "Quoms", where division of labour is granted by birth, rather than by economic status. Professions perceived as "lowly" are provided to people of certain ostracized Quoms and higher Quoms get professions perceived as superior. The Quoms are rigidly segregated with little or no intermarriage or cohabitation.

Caste System among Indian Christians

Converts to Christianity have retained the old caste practices. In particular, Dalit Christians are regarded as an undercaste by upper-caste Christian clergy and nuns and are discriminated against in society.

INDIAN CASTE SYSTEM

History: Some researchers believe that the caste system began with the Indo-Aryan migration to India. However, the theory of Indo-Aryan migration itself is a highly disputed topic. The critics claim that it was formulated to undermine the historical significance of India, and was exploited by the British to show that they had the right to invade India, as the Indians supposedly themselves were invaders.

Although many Hindu scriptures contain passages that can be interpreted to sanction the caste system, they also contain indications that the caste system is not an essential part of the Hindu religion. The Vedas place very little importance on the caste system, mentioning caste only rarely and in a cursory manner.

In the Vedic period, there also seems to no discrimination against the Sudras (which later became an ensemble of the so-called low-castes). Later scriptures such as Bhagavad Gita and Manu Smriti state that the four Varnas are created by God. A varna is a division of the society that consists of many sub-castes or Jatis. Manu Smriti and some other shastras mention four varnas: The Brahmins (teachers, scholars and priests), the Kshatriyas (kings and warriors), the Vaishyas (traders, landowners and some artisan groups), and Sudras (agriculturists, service providers, and some artisan groups). Another group of untouchables excluded from the main society was called Parjanya or Antyaja.

Passages from these scriptures suggest that the caste system was originally non-hereditary:

According to the Manu Smriti, every caste belongs to one of the four varnas. However, there have been many disputes about the varna of many castes, such as castes being considered Kshatriya by some scholars, while described as Sudra by others. While texts such as the Manu Smriti attempted to rationalize ambiguous castes by placing them in varna-sankaras (*i.e.* mixed varna), the fact remains that Indian society was, and is, composed of numerous geographically diversified but endogamous groups. With many occupational groups practising endogamy within a particular region, as well as numerous sub-d visions within the four main castes, a more complex system of sub-castes and jatis is evident. The jatis have broken up into clans like Agarwal, Iyer, etc. **The Status of Untouchables**The untouchables (now called Dalits) in Hindu society were the people wh worked in what were seen as unhealthy, disgusting or pol

ting jobs. Untouchables used to live separately within a subcultural context of their own, outside the inhabited limits of villages and townships, made pariahs in every sense of the word. No other castes could, or would, interfere with their social life since untouchables were lower in social ranking than even those of the shudras.

In the past, the Dalits suffered from social restrictions in addition to extreme poverty. They were not allowed temple worship with others, nor water from the same sources. Person of higher castes would not interact with them. Untouchables were not allowed to use the same wells as the other castes as that would "pollute" the water and indirectly the other castes who drank it. If somehow a member of a higher caste came into physical or social contact with an untouchable, the member of the higher caste was defiled, and had to bathe thoroughly to purge her/himself of the impurity. Such contact even included the shadow of an untouchable falling on the member of the higher caste. At the same time, the untouchables developed their own rich folk traditions with a lifestyle that was unhampered by the variety of restrictions on the rest of the society.

The inclusion of so-called untouchables into the mainstream was argued for by many social reformers. Mahatma Gandhi called them "Harijans" (people of God). The term Dalit (downtrodden) is used now as the term Harijan is largely felt patronising. Gandhi's contribution toward the emancipation of the untouchables is controversial. This is usually highlighted by the commentary of his contemporary Dr. B. R. Ambedkar, an untouchable himself. Ambedkar was deeply suspicious of Gandhi's motivations and frequently saw his activities as detrimental to the cause of upliftment of his people.

For instance, Gandhi, a Vaishya, was not against the caste system, but tried hard to bring untouchables into the mainstream of society and get the other castes to discard the practice of untouchability. Ambedkar, influenced by liberal thinkers like Voltaire, was interested in the elimination of the caste system and untouchability altogether. To him, Gandhi's efforts solved no problems of the untouchables as they would remain at the bottom of the hierarchy. Ambedkar suggested that the evils of the caste system would be eliminated if the upper castes (especially the Brahmins) would change their behaviour and eventually get rid of the caste system altogether.

Even among Dalits, there's discrimination. The social status of Dalit sub-castes such as Bhangi has long been a source of contention within Indian society. Upper sub-castes among Dalits like Dhobi, Nai etc. do not intearct with Bhangis, the lowest order among the dalits. They are called untouchable among the untouchables. This is an example of deep set roots of caste system in the Indian psyche.

The practice of untouchability has been formally outlawed by the Constitution of India, and has declined heavily in independent India. K. R. Narayanan, a Dalit, became the President of India in 1997.

Caste System among non-Hindus

In some parts of India, the Christians are stratified by sect, location, and the castes of their predecessors. Presently in India, more than 70% of Christians are Dalits, but the higher caste Christians (30% by estimates) control 90% of the churches administrative jobs. Out of the 156 bishops, only 6 are from lower castes. Many Dalit Catholics have spoken out against discrimination against them by the Catholic Church. Despite Islam's egalitarian tenets, units of social stratification, termed as "castes" by many, have developed among Muslims in some parts of South Asia. Various theories have been put forward regarding the development of castes among Indian Muslims. Some sources state that the castes among Muslims developed as the result of close contact with Hindu culture and Hindu converts to Islam, while others feel that these developed based on the claims of descent from the prophet Muhammad.

Ashrafs have a superior status derived from their foreign ancestry, while the Ajlafs are assumed to be converts from Hinduism, and have a lower status. In addition, there is also the Arzal caste among Muslims, who were regarded by anti-caste activists like Babasaheb Ambedkar as the equivalent of untouchables. In the Bengal region of India, some Muslims also stratify their society according to 'Quoms'. While some scholars have asserted that the Muslim Castes are not as acute in their discrimination as that among Hindus, Ambedkar argued otherwise, writing that the social evils in Muslim society were "worse than those seen in Hindu society".

Caste-related Violence

Independent India has witnessed considerable amount of violence and hate crimes motivated by caste. Ranvir Sena, a caste-supremacist fringe paramilitary group based in Bihar has committed violent acts against Dalits and other members of the scheduled caste community. Phoolan Devi, a bandit-turned-politician belonging to Mallah lower-caste was mistreated and raped by upper-caste Thakurs. She turned a bandit and carried out violent robberies against upper-caste people. In 1981, her gang massacred twenty-two Thakurs, most of whom were not involved in her kidnapping or rape.

Over the years, various incidents of violence against Dalits, such as Kherlanji Massacre have been reported from many parts of India. At the same time, many violent protests by Dalits, such as the 2006 Dalit protests in Maharashtra, have been reported as well.

Caste Politics

Mahatma Gandhi, B. R. Ambedkar and Jawaharlal Nehru had radically different approaches to caste especially over constitutional politics and the status of "untouchables". Till the mid-1970s, the politics of independent India was largely dominated by economic issues and questions of corruption. But since 1980s, caste has emerged as a major issue in the politics of India.

The Mandal Commission was established in 1979 to "identify the socially or educationally backward", and to consider the question of seat reservations and quotas for people to redress caste discrimination. In 1980, the commission's report affirmed the affirmative action practice under Indian law whereby members of lower castes were given exclusive access to a certain portion of government jobs and slots in public universities.

When V. P. Singh Government tried to implement the recommendations of Mandal Commission in 1989, massive protests were held in the country. Many alleged that the politicians were trying to cash on caste-based reservations for purely pragmatic electoral purposes.

Many political parties in India have openly indulged in caste-based votebank politics. Parties such as Bahujan Samaj Party (BSP), the Samajwadi Party and the Janata Dal claim that they are representing the backward castes, and rely primarily on OBC support, often in alliance with Dalit and Muslim support to win the elections.

Criticism: There has been strong criticism of the caste system existing in India, both within and outside India.

Gautama Buddha and Mahavira, the founders of Buddhism and Jainism respectively, were against any kind of caste structure. Many Bhakti period saints such as Kabir, Dnyaneshwar, Eknath, Ramananda, Ramanuja and Tukaram rejected all caste-based discrimination and accepted disciples from all the castes. Many Hindu reformers such as Swami Vivekananda and Sathya Sai Baba believe that there is no place for the caste system in Hinduism.

The caste system has also been criticized by many Indian social reformers. Some reformers, such as Mahatma Jyotirao Phule and Iyothee Thass argued that the lower caste people were the original inhabitants of India, and were conquered in the ancient past by Brahman invaders.

Mahatma Gandhi coined the term "Harijan", a euphemistic word for untouchable, literally meaning Sons of God. B. R. Ambedkar, born in Hindu Dalit community, was a heavy critic of the caste system. He pioneered the Dalit Buddhist movement in India, and asked his followers to leave Hinduism, and convert to Buddhism. Periyar Ramasami, a Tamil rationalist fought against the caste practice of Brahmins and was a prominent Anti-Hindu.

The caste system has been often used to criticize Hinduism and India, in general. Kancha Ilaiah, a professor at Osmania University is known for his polemical attacks on Hindus and the caste system. Many Hindus, however point out that the caste system is related to the Indian society, and not Hinduism (as is evident by presence of caste among Indian Christians and

Muslims). Hindu Nationalist organizations such as the Rashtriya Swayamsevak Sangh have actively criticized the caste system.

Some activists consider that the caste system is a form of racial discrimination. The participants of the United Nations Conference Against Racism in Durban, South Africa in March 2001, condemned the discrimination due to the caste system, and stated that caste as a basis for the segregation and oppression of peoples in terms of their descent and occupation is a form of apartheid.

The Indian government denies the claims of equivalency between Caste and Racial discrimination, pointing out that the caste issues as essentially intra-racial and intra-cultural. Indian Attorney General Soli Sorabjee insisted that "The only reason India wants caste discrimination kept off the agenda is that it will distract participants from the main topic: racism. Caste discrimination in India is undeniable but caste and race are entirely distinct. "..Many scholars dispute the claim that casteism is akin to racism. The view of the caste system as "static and unchanging" has been disputed.

Sociologists describe how the perception of the caste system as a static .and textual stratification has given way to the perception of the caste system as a more processual, empirical and contextual stratification. Others have applied theoretical models to explain mobility and flexibility in the caste system in India. . According to these scholars, groups of lower-caste individuals could seek to elevate the status of their caste by attempting to emulate the practices of higher castes.

Sociologist M. N. Srinivas has also debated the question of rigidity in Caste. For details see sanskritization. In India, some observers felt that the caste system must be viewed as a system of exploitation of poor low-ranking groups by more prosperous high-ranking groups. In many parts of India, land is largely held by dominant castes high-ranking owners of property that economically exploit low-ranking landless labourers and poor artisans, all the while degrading them with ritual emphases on their so-called god-given inferior status.

Matt Cherry, claims that karma underpins the caste system, and the caste system traditionally determines the position and role of every member of Hindu society. Caste determines an individual's place in society, the work he or she may carry out, and who he or she may marry and meet. According to him, Hindus believe that the karma of previous life will determine the caste an individual will be (re)born into.

VARNASHRAMA DHARMA

Varnashrama Dharma refers to the system of classes of social life and stages of individual life in Hinduism. Varna refers to the belief that most humans were created from different parts of the body of the divinity Purusha and according to which part they were created from it defines their social standing for issues such as who they can marry and what jobs they can do.

The classes of society given in the Hindu scriptures: Brahmana ("scholarly community"), Kshatriya ("warriors or politicians community"), Vaishya ("mercantile community") and Sudra ("service providing community"). Asrama refers to the four stages of individual life prescribed for all Hindus: Brahmacharya ("student life"), Grihastha ("householder life"), Vanaprastha ("anchorite life") and Sannyasa ("renunciate life"). The Hindu tradition holds this system as a Dharma ("sacred law") sanctioned by the scriptures. While the above is the general belief and interpretation by some, there is no mention except at one place in Purusha Sukta (Yajurveda), of various Varnas or castes or classes, either natural or created, in any of the Vedas.

There are views held by some that even the stanza which talks about the four Varnas originating from Face, Hands, Torso and feet of the Hindu deity Purusha appears different from other Slokas and could have been altered at some later stages. One of the foremost Rishi in Rig Veda is Vishwamitra, who was a King and Kshatriya by birth. Vyasa was of mixed birth between Parasara, a Brahmin and Sathyavathi (a Soodra, fisher woman). Maharishi Matanga was from the Matanga Bhil tribe but was raised as a Brahmana. Hence to attribute caste system to Hindu scriptures is without substance. Only Manu Smriti talks clearly about caste system and their duties.)

The Sanskrit term Varna is derived from the root Vrn meaning "to choose (from a group)." This is contrary to the assumption that 'varna' denotes colour and hence signifies qualities of someone, just as Saguna Brahman means "with qualities. "In the context of social hierarchies, it means "arrangement".

When humans first settled down into agrarian and trading societies, many changes occurred in social relationships with this greater specialisation of labour. People got organised into structures that could be stable and accommodating diverse individuals in diverse occupations. Societies are organic wholes self-sustained by diverse groups with differing occupations that optimise that society's well-being and growth. The varna system is a functional hierarchy system proposed by the Brahmin texts to describe their society. It is an ideal system that did not exist anywhere in reality, as the Indian society was organised according to Jatis, since time immemorial.

The oldest mention of the varna system is in the Purusha sukta of Rig Veda 10. 90 which claims "Brahmana is the mouth of the purusha, rajanya his arms, vaishya is his thighs and shudra arose from his feet"-an obvious reference to the organic (purusha) nature of the society, sustained by the harmonious integration of functional groups (organs) working in unison. In such organic hierarchies, it is recognised that proper functioning of each part is necessary for the stability of the whole. This led to the importance given to kartavya or "duties" (deontology). Each one is obligated to perform their duties relevant to their position in the system. Proper functioning is of utmost necessity for the stability of the whole structure.

Etymology

Varna is a Sanskrit term (varna meaning type, order, colour or faith (faithless), preference, religious affiliation, conviction, or "to choose", or lustre.

- In the Zend Avesta and the Gathas, the word Varana or Varena (from the root Var ("put faith in, to believe in") is used in the sense of preference (or religious affiliation, conviction, faith, religious doctrine, choice of creed or belief). The language of the Gathas (the oldest part of the Avesta) is very similar to the language of the Rig Veda.
- It may also come from the root Var-"choose", as in "svayamvara", "(a girl's) own choice (of a husband)", or from the root vri (which means "one's occupation").
- In the Rig Veda, the word Varna occurs 22 times and means lustre. In 17 out of 22 times it refers to the "lustre" (*i.e.* "one's own typical light") of gods like Soma, Agni or Ushas. In RV 3. 34. 5 and RV 9. 71. 2 it refers to the lustrous colour of the sky at dawn.
- According to Hindu tradition, Varna refers to sounds of speech or language. Western Indologists have wrongly interpreted varna as "a letter of the alphabet". According to Welzer (1994 (229-230)), Varna can be grammatically derived from the term "class" (vide Panini), but it has acquired the incorrect meaning of "colour".

SOCIAL DEVELOPMENT

The caste system is used by Hindus, particularly in India, Bali and Nepal for reasons of determining lineage and is passed down through patrilineal descent. It is based on the older four-varna system varnas which later became attached to the members' families. Sometimes Mlechha (people excluded from caste) are referred to as fifth varna.

JATI

The terms Varna (class) and Jati (caste) are two distinct concepts. Varna ("class") (from Sanskrit, literally "arrangement") is a supposed unification of all the Hindu sub-castes or jatis into either four groups: Brahmin, Kshatriya, Vaishya, Sudra, or into one of several varna-sankaras. Jati (Caste) is an endogamous group. Generally a sub-caste is divided into exogamus groups based on same Gotras. Many of the Hindus could be classified into a specific varna. But not all. During the British rule, several cases went to court to settle the "varna" of a sub-caste. For example, the farmers are sometimes given Kshatriya status because many ruling Chieftains may have risen from them. On the other hand some classified them as Vainya, based on an older occupation of artisans. Orthodox Brahmins may classify them as Sudras, because they do not have a tradition of undergoing through the thread ceremony, that would make them Dvija.

THE TWICE BORN

The first three varnas are seen as 'twice born'. They are allowed to study Vedas. In India and Nepal the sub-castes within a Varna are called Jat or Jati (The varna is also used instead of Jat). Traditionally, each Jati members are allowed to marry only with their Jati members. People are born into their Jati and normally it cannot be changed, though there were some exceptions in Hindu Mythology. For example, sage Vishwamitra was born as a Kshatriya (ruling class) and by deep meditation (tapas) became a venerable Brahmin Rishi (saint). Once someone is born to certain sub-caste or Jati he or she cannot normally change their Jati, although some groups throughout history have risen or fallen according to their deeds. Caste is a permanent attribute among the Hindus.

The occupations of the Vaishya are those connected with trade, the cultivation of the land and the breeding of cattle; while those of a Kshatriya consist in ruling and defending the people, administering justice, and the duties, of the military profession generally and ruling and expounding all Dharma. Both share with the Brahmin the privilege of reading the Vedas. To the Brahmin belongs the right of teaching and expounding the sacred texts vedas. Sudras were the serfs, and performed agricultural labour. Muluki Ain has incorporated the entire ethnic group of Nepal into Caste hierarchy.

Instances in Hindu Texts and Tradition

The Rig Veda refers in the Purusha Sukta to the four principal varnas described in Manu's code, *viz.* Brahmins, Kshatriyas, Vaishyas, and Sudras. The term Varna is not associated with Brahmins or Kshatriyas in the Rig Veda, and the term Varna does not occur in the Purusha Sukta. It affirmed that Varnashram Dharma needs to be strictly followed as every soul has been given a specific duty by God. A soul is born into a varna as punishment/reward for its karmic influences-actions in past lives (Hindus believe in reincarnation).

The "Purusha Sukta' hymn (Rig Veda 10:90) mentions the varnas and compares them to the body of the "primordial man": "The Brahmana was his mouth, of both his arms was the Rajanya made. His thighs became the Vaishya, from his feet the Sudra was produced." (RV 10:90:12) In the Purusha Sukta hymn the word Varna is not used, and it is the only hymn of the Rig Veda where the words Vaishya and Sudra are used. The Purusha Sukta hymn is considered to be one of the youngest parts of the Rig Veda.

There is an Upanishadic story of a boy who went to a guru to study the various holy Hindu scriptures. His guru asked him what his varna was. Consulting his mother, who was actually a prostitute who didn't really know what her caste was, the boy returned to the guru and told him that he was all castes. He worshipped the Gods, thus fulfilling the duties that are ordinarily a Brahmin's, he earned his keep like a Vaishya, took care of cleaning the house, like a Sudra, and protected his family's interest like a Kshatriya. The guru was pleased and told the boy he was fit to be taught and initiated into the Brahmin's life. The Dharmashastras (a collection of collections of Hindu codes and laws) say that caste is not just determined by birth, but by action in life according to the Dharma of varna-ashram as well.

The Brahmins (priests), The Kshatriyas (warriors, nobility), the Vaishyas (the craftsmen and men of commerce), and the Sudras (agriculture workers; menial workers) were the four varnas. A person of each varna was said to possess certain set of characteristics: the Sudras, they believed, were of the tamasic nature; the Vaishyas were either tamasic or rajasic; the Kshatriyas were believed to be noble, learned and selfless, his or her duty being the administration of the people and fighting of battles against intruders, often very spiritually inclined; and that the Brahmins were religious, pure, Society's bank of knowledge and wisdom for their memory of holy scriptures, the performers of rituals. However, there is a dispute as to which varna holds the greatest spiritual purity. Brahmins are associated with the evil Daksha, an arrogant Brahmin that received the head of a goat, and according to scriptures caused all Brahmins to be cursed by Nandi to never attain the greatest spiritual heights in Hinduism as Daksha insulted Shiva.

Hindu tantrics are a part of Hinduism whose scriptural texts, the Agamic texts known collectively as the Tantras, assert their descent from the Vedas, especially the Atharva Veda. Claiming that the Vedic rituals no longer necessary in Kali Yuga, that the fourth and final epoch of humanity in Hinduism shall see morality ebb to complete dissolution until the end of the earth, the Tantrics see themselves as natural continuations of the Vedas through Hindu yogic practices—and not of any particular caste, yet not Untouchables.

Many Hindu yogis and sages have, over the centuries, constantly commented about caste. Shri Chaitanya Mahaprabhu (15th century), the powerful Bhakti of Krishna also denounced caste. He famously distributed the Hare Krishna Mantra to non-brahmins all around India, claiming this was the True path to Moksha.

Kanakadasa of the 15th century also denounced Casteism. He believed that Life in every human being is Divine, and that only the ignorant wrought injustice against their own brethren by practising the caste system.

RIG VEDA AND MANU SMRITI

In Sanskrit, Varna means colour, as in quality (just as the term "Shaguna Brahman") One of the hymns of the Rig Veda, one of the holiest Hindu scriptures, gives the following enumeration in the famous Purusha Sukta (RV 10. 90):

Its rough translation is: "What became of his (the Cosmic Spirit's) face or mouth? What became of his two arms? What became of His two thighs? What were (the products of) the two feet called? From His face (or the mouth) came the Brahmanas. From His two arms came the rajanya (the Kshatriyas). From His two thighs came the vaishyas. From His two feet came the shudras."

In the Purusha Sukta hymn the word Varna is not used, and it is the only hymn of the Rig Veda where the words Vaishya and Sudra are used. The Purusha Sukta hymn is considered to be one of the youngest parts of the Rig Veda.

Manu Smriti is often quoted in reference to the Varna-caste system. The Manu Smriti is a later work that does not form a part of Hindu Scriptures, so it is of questionable relevance. Use of the Manu Smriti by the British colonialists has been used by politicians and sociologists to denigrate those of the Hindu faith.

The Manu Smriti claims that by the time it was written, Hinduism included another class (untouchables) of people without a position in any of the four Varnas and therefore associated with the lowest of the jobs. The upper castes, who were supposed to maintain ritual and corporal purity, came to regard them as untouchables. The people of this "fifth varna" are now called Dalits (the oppressed) or Harijans; they were formerly known as "untouchables" or "pariahs".

It is very clear that in the early Vedic times, the Varna system (if at all it existed) meant classes with free mobility of jobs and intermarriage. One hymn of the Rig Veda states:

"I am a bard, my father is a physician, my mother's job is to grind the corn."

While intermarriage between Brahmana bridegrooms and Kshatriya princesses was extremely common (even sanctioned by the later Manu Smriti), in many instances, marriages between Kshatriya princes and Brahmana brides was also observed (severely condemned by Manu Smriti). One of such instances is marriage of Yayati, a Kshatriya King, with Devayani, a daughter of the sage Shukracharya. In later times, with the elaboration of ritualism, the caste system became absolutely hereditary (the historians disagree as to when) and the Sudras were not even allowed to hear the sacred word of the Vedas.

This text is not found in Manu Smriti: Request the author to remove this.

> *"If the shudra intentionally listens for committing to memory the Veda, then his ears should be filled with (molten) lead and lac; if he utters the Veda, then his tongue should be cut off; if he has mastered the Veda his body should be cut to pieces."*
> *(Manu Smriti XII. 4)*

A stark contrast to this is a mantra from the White Yajur Veda itself:

> *"I do hereby address this salutary (Vedic) speech for the benefit of humanity-for the Brahmanas, the Kshatriyas, the Sudras, the Vaishas, the kinsfolk and the men of lowest position in society. May I be dear to the learned in this world."*

OPPOSITION WITHIN HINDUISM

Critics point that the effect of the system was to bind certain castes to sources of influence, power and economy while locking out others and thus create more affluence for higher castes and severe poverty for lower castes and the outcast Dalit. In the last 150 years Indian movements arose to throw off the economic and political yoke of the caste system. And replace it with true Varnashrama Dharma, described in the Vedas.

In the religious scripture Mahabharata, Yudhisthira, is questioned by Yama in the form of a Yaksha, about what makes one a Brahmin. Yudhisthira, without hesitation, said that it is conduct alone that makes one a Brahmin.

Ramananda, an ascetic of the Sri Ramanuja's Sri Vaishnava sampradaya, accepted all varna as his disciples. Mirabai, the 15th century mystical poet and Queen of Chittor is known to have ignored varna distinctions and elected the cobbler, Sant Rohidas, as her guru. Annamacharya, a 15th century telugu poet's famous Bramhamokkada song, preaches equality of all in the eyes of God and condemns the caste system as un-Vedic. And proposed a return to traditional varnashrama Dharma. Which promoted equality and stressed the importance of all varnas. Ramakrishna Paramahamsa, the 19th century Hindu religious leader, also did not recognise varna distinctions and took his first alms as a twice-born Brahmin from a Sudra woman.

The late Swami Krishnananda, the successor to Swami Sivananda and former head of Divine Life Society, noted the following about caste in his autobiography:

> "*While the caste system was originally evolved for the necessary classification of human duty in order to preserve the organic stability of society, its original meaning and its philosophical foundation was forgotten through the passage of time, and bigotry and fanaticism took its place through the preponderance of egoism, greed and hatred, contrary to the practice of true religion as a social expression of inner spiritual aspiration for a gradual ascent, by stages, to God Almighty. Vidura,*

> *famous in the Mahabharata, was born of a Sudra woman. But he had the power to summon the son of Brahma, from Brahmaloka, by mere thought. Which orthodox Brahmin can achieve this astounding feat? It is, therefore, necessary for everyone to have consideration for the facts of world-unity and goodwill, Sarvabhuta-hita, as the great Lord mentions in the Bhagavad Gita. Justice is more than law. No one's body is by itself a Brahmin, because it is constituted of the five gross elements, -earth, water, fire, air and ether. Else, it would be a sin on the part of a son to consign to flames the lifeless body of a Brahmin father. It is, therefore, not proper to victimise a colleague by an action plan of any religious community wedded to fundamentalist doctrines."*

Paramahansa Yogananda also opposed what he called to the un-Vedic caste system as we know it today. He taught that the caste system originated in a higher age, but became degraded through ignorance and self-interest. Yogananda said:

> *"These were (originally) symbolic designations of the stages of spiritual refinement. They were not intended as social categories. And they were not intended to be hereditary. Things changed as the yugas (cycles of time) descended toward mental darkness. People in the higher castes wanted to make sure their children were accepted as members of their own caste. Thus, ego-identification caused them to freeze the ancient classifications into what is called the 'caste system. ' Such was not the original intention. In obvious fact, however, the offspring of a Brahmin may be a Sudra by nature. And a peasant, sometimes, is a real saint. "*
>
> *—from Conversations with Yogananda, Crystal Clarity Publishers, 2003.*

Ashrama

The traditional classification of the stages of a Hindu's life into Brahmacharya ("student life"), Grihastha ("householders life"), Vanaprastha ("anchorite life") and Sannyasa ("renunciate life") has been sanctioned in the Hindu scriptures. This classification is believed by the Hindus to lead to a fulfilment of the four aims of life, namely Dharma ("righteousness"), Artha ("wealth"), Kama ("sensual gratification") and Moksha ("salvation").

India's Caste System

Although many other nations are characterized by social inequality, perhaps nowhere else in the world has inequality been so elaborately constructed as in the Indian institution of caste. Caste has long existed in India, but in the modern period it has been severely criticized by both Indian and foreign observers. Although some educated Indians tell non-Indians that caste has been abolished or that "no one pays attention to caste anymore," such statements do not reflect reality. Caste has undergone significant change since independence, but it still involves hundreds of millions of people. In its preamble, India's constitution forbids negative public discrimination on the basis of caste. However, caste ranking and caste-based interaction have occurred for centuries and will continue to do so well into the foreseeable future, more in the countryside than in urban settings and more in the realms of kinship and marriage than in less personal interactions.

Castes are ranked, named, endogamous (in-marrying) groups, membership in which is achieved by birth. There are thousands of castes and sub-castes in India, and these large kinship-based groups are fundamental to South Asian social structure. Each caste is part of a locally based system of interdependence with other groups, involving occupational specialization, and is linked in complex ways with networks that stretch across regions and throughout the nation.

The word caste derives from the Portuguese casta, meaning breed, race, or kind. Among the Indian terms that are sometimes translated as caste are varna, jati, jat, biradari, and samaj. All of these terms refer to ranked groups of various sizes and breadth. Varna, or colour, actually refers to large divisions that include various castes; the other terms include castes and subdivisions of castes sometimes called sub-castes.

Many castes are traditionally associated with an occupation, such as high-ranking Brahmans; middle-ranking farmer and artisan groups, such as potters, barbers, and carpenters; and very low-ranking "Untouchable" leather workers, butchers, launderers, and latrine cleaners. There is some correlation between ritual rank on the caste hierarchy and economic prosperity. Members of higher-ranking castes tend, on the whole, to be more prosperous than members of lower-ranking castes. Many lower-caste people live in conditions of great poverty and social disadvantage.

According to the Rig Veda, sacred texts that date back to oral traditions of more than 3, 000 years ago, progenitors of the four ranked varna groups sprang from various parts of the body of the primordial man, which Brahma created from clay. Each group had a function in sustaining the life of society—the social body. Brahmans, or priests, were created from the mouth. They were to provide for the intellectual and spiritual needs of the community. Kshatriyas, warriors and rulers, were derived from the arms. Their role was to rule and to protect others. Vaishyas—landowners and merchants—sprang from the thighs, and were entrusted with the care of commerce and agriculture. Sudras—artisans and servants—came from the feet. Their task was to perform all manual labour.

Later conceptualized was a fifth category, "Untouchable" menials, relegated to carrying out very menial and polluting work related to bodily decay and dirt. Since 1935 "Untouchables" have been known as Scheduled Castes, referring to their listing on government rosters, or schedules. They are also often called by Mohandas Karamchand (Mahatma) Gandhi's term Harijans, or "Children of God." Although the term Untouchable appears in literature produced by these low-ranking castes, in the 1990s, many politically conscious members of these groups prefer to refer to themselves as Dalit, a Hindi word meaning oppressed or downtrodden. According to the 1991 census, there were 138 million Scheduled Caste members in India, approximately 16 percent of the total population. The first four varnas apparently existed in the ancient Aryan society of northern India. Some historians say that these categories were originally somewhat fluid functional groups, not castes. A greater degree of fixity gradually developed, resulting in the complex ranking systems of medieval India that essentially continue in the late twentieth century.

Although a varna is not a caste, when directly asked for their caste affiliation, particularly when the questioner is a Westerner, many Indians will reply with a varna name. Pressed further, they may respond with a much more specific name of a caste, or jati, which falls within that varna. For example, a Brahman may specify that he is a member of a named caste group, such as a Jijotiya Brahman, or a Smartha Brahman, and so on. Within such castes, people may further belong to smaller subcaste categories and to specific clans and lineages. These finer designations are particularly relevant when marriages are being arranged and often appear in newspaper matrimonial advertisements.

Members of a caste are typically spread out over a region, with representatives living in hundreds of settlements. In any small village, there may be representatives of a few or even a score or more castes. Numerous groups usually called tribes (often referred to as Scheduled Tribes) are also integrated into the caste system to varying degrees. Some tribes live separately from others—particularly in the far northeast and in the forested centre of the country, where tribes are more like ethnic groups than castes. Some tribes are themselves divided into groups similar to sub-castes. In regions where members of tribes live in peasant villages with non-tribal peoples, they are usually considered members of separate castes ranking low on the hierarchical scale.

Inequalities among castes are considered by the Hindu faithful to be part of the divinely ordained natural order and are expressed in terms of purity and pollution. Within a village, relative rank is most graphically expressed at a wedding or death feast, when all residents of the village are invited. At the home of a high-ranking caste member, food is prepared by a member of a caste from whom all can accept cooked food (usually by a Brahman). Diners are seated in lines; members of a single caste sit next to each other in a row, and members of other castes sit in perpendicular or parallel rows at some distance.

Members of Dalit castes, such as Leather workers and Sweepers, may be seated far from the other diners—even out in an alley. Farther away, at the edge of the feeding area, a Sweeper may wait with a large basket to receive discarded leavings tossed in by other diners. Eating food contaminated by contact with the saliva of others not of the same family is considered far too polluting to be practiced by members of any other castes. Generally, feasts and ceremonies given by Dalits are not attended by higher-ranking castes.

Among Muslims, although status differences prevail, brotherhood may be stressed. A Muslim feast usually includes a cloth laid either on clean ground or on a table, with all Muslims, rich and poor, dining from plates placed on the same cloth. Muslims who wish to provide hospitality to observant Hindus, however, must make separate arrangements for a high-caste Hindu cook and ritually pure foods and dining area.

Castes that fall within the top four ranked varnas are sometimes referred to as the "clean castes," with Dalits considered "unclean." Castes of the top three ranked varnas are often designated "twice-born," in reference to the ritual initiation undergone by male members, in which investiture with the Hindu sacred thread constitutes a kind of ritual rebirth. Non-Hindu caste-like groups generally fall outside these designations.

Each caste is believed by devout Hindus to have its own Dharma, or divinely ordained code of proper conduct. Accordingly, there is often a high degree of tolerance for divergent lifestyles among different castes. Brahmans are usually expected to be nonviolent and spiritual, according with their traditional roles as vegetarian teetotaller priests. Kshatriyas are supposed to be strong, as fighters and rulers should be, with a taste for aggression, eating meat, and drinking alcohol. Vaishyas are stereotyped as adept businessmen, in accord with their traditional activities in commerce. Sudras are often described by others as tolerably pleasant but expectably somewhat base in behaviour, whereas Dalits—especially Sweepers—are often regarded by others as followers of vulgar life-styles. Conversely, lower-caste people often view people of high rank as haughty and unfeeling.

The chastity of women is strongly related to caste status. Generally, the higher ranking the caste, the more sexual control its women are expected to exhibit. Brahman brides should be virginal, faithful to one husband, and celibate in widowhood. By contrast, a Sweeper bride may or may not be a virgin, extramarital affairs may be tolerated, and, if widowed or divorced, the woman is encouraged to remarry. For the higher castes, such control of female sexuality helps ensure purity of lineage—of crucial importance to maintenance of high status. Among Muslims, too, high status is strongly correlated with female chastity.

Within castes explicit standards are maintained. Transgressions may be dealt with by a caste council, meeting periodically to adjudicate issues relevant to the caste. Such councils are usually formed of groups of elders, almost always males. Punishments such as fines and outcasting, either temporary or permanent, can be enforced. In rare cases, a person is excommunicated from the caste for gross infractions of caste rules. An example of such an infraction might be marrying or openly cohabiting with a mate of a caste lower than one's own; such behaviour would usually result in the higher-caste person dropping to the status of the lower-caste person.

Activities such as farming or trading can be carried out by anyone, but usually only members of the appropriate castes act as priests, barbers, potters, weavers, and other skilled artisans, whose occupational skills are handed down in families from one generation to another. As with other key features of Indian social structure, occupational specialization is believed to be in accord with the divinely ordained order of the universe.

The existence of rigid ranking is supernaturally validated through the idea of rebirth according to a person's karma, the sum of an individual's deeds in this life and in past lives. After death, a person's life is judged by divine forces, and rebirth is assigned in a high or a low place, depending upon what is deserved. This supernatural sanction can never be neglected, because it brings a person to his or her position in the caste hierarchy, relevant to every transaction involving food or drink, speaking, or touching.

In past decades, Dalits in certain areas (especially in parts of the south) had to display extreme deference to high-status people, physically keeping their distance—lest their touch or even their shadow pollute others—wearing neither shoes nor any upper body covering (even for women) in the presence of the upper castes. The lowest-ranking had to jingle a little bell in warning of their polluting approach. In much of India, Dalits were prohibited from entering temples, using wells from which the "clean" castes drew their water, or even attending schools. In past centuries, dire punishments were prescribed for Dalits who read or even heard sacred texts.

Such degrading discrimination was made illegal under legislation passed during British rule and was protested against by preindependence reform movements led by Mahatma Gandhi and Bhimrao Ramji (B. R.) Ambedkar, a Dalit leader. Dalits agitated for the right to enter Hindu temples and to use village wells and effectively pressed for the enactment of stronger laws opposing disabilities imposed on them. After independence, Ambedkar almost single-handedly wrote India's constitution, including key provisions barring caste-based discrimination. Nonetheless, discriminatory treatment of Dalits remains a factor in daily life, especially in villages, as the end of the twentieth century approaches.

In modern times, as in the past, it is virtually impossible for an individual to raise his own status by falsely claiming to be a member of a higher-ranked caste. Such a ruse might work for a time in a place where the person is unknown, but no one would dine with or intermarry with such a person or his offspring until the claim was validated through kinship networks. Rising on the ritual hierarchy can only be achieved by a caste as a group, over a long period of time, principally by adopting behaviour patterns of higher-ranked groups. This process, known as Sanskritization, has been described by M.N. Srinivas and others. An example of such behaviour is that of some Leather worker castes adopting a policy of not eating beef, in the hope that abstaining from the defiling practice of consuming the flesh of sacred bovines would enhance their castes' status. Increased economic prosperity for much of a caste greatly aids in the process of improving rank. India has a hierarchical caste system in the society. Within Indian culture, whether in the north or the south, Hindu or Muslim, urban or village, virtually all things, people, and groups of people are ranked according to various essential qualities. If one is attuned to the theme of hierarchy in India, one can discern it everywhere. Although India is a political democracy, in daily life there is little advocacy of or adherence to notions of equality.

Castes systems in India and caste like groups—those quintessential groups with which almost all Indians are associated—are ranked. Within most villages or towns, everyone knows the relative rankings of each locally represented caste, and people's behaviour toward one another is constantly shaped by this knowledge. Between the extremes of the very high and very low castes, however, there is sometimes disagreement on the exact relative ranking of castes clustered in the middle. Castes system in India are primarily associated with Hinduism but also exist among other Indian religious groups.

Muslims sometimes expressly deny that they have castes—they state that all Muslims are brothers under God—but observation of Muslim life in various parts of India reveals the existence of caste-like groups and clear concern with social hierarchy. Among Indian Christians, too, differences in caste are acknowledged and maintained.

Throughout India, individuals are also ranked according to their wealth and power. For example, there are "big men" (bare Admi, in Hindi) and "little men" (chhote admi) everywhere. "Big men" sit confidently on chairs, while "little men" come before them to make requests, either standing or crouching down on their haunches, certainly not presuming to sit beside a man of high status as an equal. Even men of nearly equal status who might share a string cot to sit on take their places carefully—the higher-ranking man at the head of the cot, the lower-ranking man at the foot.

Within families and kinship groupings, there are many distinctions of hierarchy. Men outrank women of the same or similar age, and senior relatives outrank junior relatives. Several other kinship relations involve formal respect. For example, in northern India, a daughter-in-law of a household shows deference to a daughter of a household. Even among young siblings in a household, there is constant acknowledgment of age differences: younger siblings never address an older sibling by name, but rather by respectful terms for elder brother or elder sister. However, an older sibling may address the younger by name.

Even in a business or academic setting, where colleagues may not openly espouse traditional observance of caste or class ranking behaviour, they may set up effective kinship relations, addressing one another by kinship terms reflecting family or village-style hierarchy. For example, a younger colleague might respectfully address an older colleague as chachaji (respected father's younger brother), gracefully acknowledging the superior position of the older colleague.

Purity and Pollution

Many status differences in Indian society are expressed in terms of ritual purity and pollution. Notions of purity and pollution are extremely complex and vary greatly among different castes, religious groups, and regions. However, broadly speaking, high status is associated with purity and low status with pollution. Some kinds of purity are inherent, or inborn; for example, gold is purer than copper by its very nature, and, similarly, a member of a high-ranking Brahman, or priestly, caste is born with more inherent purity than a member of a low-ranking Sweeper (Mehtar, in Hindi) caste. Unless the Brahman defiles himself in some extraordinary way, throughout his life he will always be purer than a Sweeper. Other kinds of purity are more transitory—a Brahman who has just taken a bath is more ritually pure than a Brahman who has not bathed for a day. This situation could easily reverse itself temporarily, depending on bath schedules, participation in polluting activities, or contact with temporarily polluting substances.

Purity is associated with ritual cleanliness—daily bathing in flowing water, dressing in properly laundered clothes of approved materials, eating only the foods appropriate for one's caste, refraining from physical contact with people of lower rank, and avoiding involvement with ritually impure substances. The latter include body wastes and execrations, most especially those of another adult person. Contact with the products of death or violence are typically polluting and threatening to ritual purity.

During her menstrual period, a woman is considered polluted and refrains from cooking, worshipping, or touching anyone older than an infant. In much of the south, a woman spends this time "sitting outside," resting in an isolated room or shed. During her period, a Muslim woman does not touch the Quran. At the end of the period, purity is restored with a complete bath. Pollution also attaches to birth, both for the mother and the infant's close kin, and to death, for close relatives of the deceased (see The Ceremonies of Hinduism; Islam.

Members of the highest priestly castes, the Brahmans, are generally vegetarians (although some Bengali and

Maharashtrian Brahmans eat fish) and avoid eating meat, the product of violence and death. High-ranking Warrior castes (Kshatriyas), however, typically consume non-vegetarian diets, considered appropriate for their traditions of valour and physical strength. A Brahman born of proper Brahman parents retains his inherent purity if he bathes and dresses himself properly, adheres to a vegetarian diet, eats meals prepared only by persons of appropriate rank, and keeps his person away from the bodily exuviae of others (except for necessary contact with the secretions of family infants and small children).

If a Brahman happens to come into bodily contact with a polluting substance, he can remove this pollution by bathing and changing his clothing. However, if he were to eat meat or commit other transgressions of the rigid dietary codes of his particular caste, he would be considered more deeply polluted and would have to undergo various purifying rites and payment of fines imposed by his caste council in order to restore his inherent purity. In sharp contrast to the purity of a Brahman, a Sweeper born of Sweeper parents is considered to be born inherently polluted. The touch of his body is polluting to those higher on the caste hierarchy than he, and they will shrink from his touch, whether or not he has bathed recently. Sweepers are associated with the traditional occupation of cleaning human feces from latrines and sweeping public lanes of all kinds of dirt. Traditionally, Sweepers remove these polluting materials in baskets carried atop the head and dumped out in a garbage pile at the edge of the village or neighbourhood. The involvement of Sweepers with such filth accords with their low-status position at the bottom of the Hindu caste hierarchy, even as their services allow high-status people, such as Brahmans, to maintain their ritual purity.

Members of the Leather worker (Chamar) caste are ascribed a very low status consonant with their association with the caste occupation of skinning dead animals and tanning the leather. Butchers (Khatiks, in Hindi), who kill and cut up the bodies of animals, also rank low on the caste hierarchy because of their association with violence and death.

However, castes associated with ruling and warfare—and the killing and deaths of human beings—are typically accorded high rank on the caste hierarchy. In these instances, political power and wealth outrank association with violence as the key determinant of caste rank.

Maintenance of purity is associated with the intake of food and drink, not only in terms of the nature of the food itself, but also in terms of who has prepared it or touched it. This requirement is especially true for Hindus, but other religious groups hold to these principles to varying degrees. Generally, a person risks pollution—and lowering his own status—if he accepts beverages or cooked foods from the hands of people of lower caste status than his own. His status will remain intact if he accepts food or beverages from people of higher caste rank. Usually, for an observant Hindu of any but the very lowest castes to accept cooked food from a Muslim or Christian is regarded as highly polluting.

In a clear example of pollution associated with dining, a Brahman who consumed a drink of water and a meal of wheat bread with boiled vegetables from the hands of a Sweeper would immediately become polluted and could expect social rejection by his caste fellows. From that moment, fellow Brahmans following traditional pollution rules would refuse food touched by him and would abstain from the usual social interaction with him. He would not be welcome inside Brahman homes—most especially in the ritually pure kitchens—nor would he or his close relatives be considered eligible marriage partners for other Brahmans.

Generally, the acceptance of water and ordinary foods cooked in water from members of lower-ranking castes incurs the greatest pollution. In North India, such foods are known as kaccha khana, as contrasted with fine foods cooked in butter or oils, which are known as pakka khana. Fine foods can be accepted from members of a few castes slightly lower than one's own. Local hierarchies differ on the specific details of these rules.

Completely raw foods, such as uncooked grains, fresh unpeeled bananas, mangoes, and uncooked vegetables can be accepted by anyone from anyone else, regardless of relative status. Toasted or parched foods, such as roasted peanuts, can also be accepted from anyone without ritual or social repercussions. (Thus, a Brahman may accept gifts of grain from lower-caste patrons for eventual preparation by members of his own caste, or he may purchase and consume roasted peanuts or tangerines from street vendors of unknown caste without worry).

Water served from an earthen pot may be accepted only from the hands of someone of higher or equal caste ranking, but water served from a brass pot may be accepted even from someone slightly lower on the caste scale. Exceptions to this rule are members of the Waterbearer (Bhoi, in Hindi) caste, who are employed to carry water from wells to the homes of the prosperous and from whose hands members of all castes may drink water without becoming polluted, even though Waterbearers are not ranked high on the caste scale.

These and a great many other traditional rules pertaining to purity and pollution constantly impinge upon interaction between people of different castes and ranks in India. Although to the non-Indian these rules may seem irrational and bizarre, to most of the people of India they are a ubiquitous and accepted part of life. Thinking about and following purity and pollution rules make it necessary for people to be constantly aware of differences in status. With every drink of water, with every meal, and with every contact with another person, people must ratify the social hierarchy of which they are a part and within which their every act is carried out. The fact that expressions of social status are intricately bound up with events that happen to everyone every day—eating, drinking, bathing, touching, talking—and that transgressions of these rules, whether deliberate or accidental are seen as having immediately polluting effects on the person of the transgressor, means that every ordinary act of human life serves as a constant reminder of the importance of hierarchy in Indian society.

There are many Indians, particularly among the educated urban elite, who do not follow traditional purity and pollution practices. Dining in each others' homes and in restaurants is common among well-educated people of diverse backgrounds, particularly when they belong to the same economic class. For these people, guarding the family's earthen water pot from inadvertent touch by a low-ranking servant is not the concern it is for a more traditional villager. However, even among those people whose words and actions denigrate traditional purity rules, there is often a reluctance to completely abolish consciousness of purity and pollution from their thinking. It is surely rare for a Sweeper, however well-educated, to invite a Brahman to dinner in his home and have his invitation unselfconsciously accepted. It is less rare, however, for educated urban colleagues of vastly different caste and religious heritage to enjoy a cup of tea together. Some high-caste liberals pride themselves on being free of "casteism" and seek to accept food from the hands of very low-caste people, or even deliberately set out to marry someone from a significantly lower caste or a different religion. Thus, even as they deny it, these progressives affirm the continuing significance of traditional rules of purity, pollution, and hierarchy in Indian caste system.

CASTE DIVISIONS

It is difficult to define how castes are divided. However, there are two main sources:

1. Early British Census Records
2. Interpretations of the Manu Smriti

British Census Officers determined caste hierarchy based on the principle, *e.g.* someone who accepts food and water from another person but the other person does not reciprocate the same way, then the other person is superior to the former. It was contested at many places (a notable example is that the Koris of up who said they won't accept water from Brahmins, and so should be placed higher than them). Because it was met with rampant controversies, arbitration was very common during those days. The most notable arbitration stories are:

1. Caste status of Bhumihar
2. Caste status of Kayastha
3. Caste status of Kurmi
4. Caste status of Yadav

It raised more questions than it answered and subsequent census records varied radically, making it free for all, after some time. Manu Smriti is considered as the most ancient and authentic source regarding origin and hierarchy of castes. Though it answers most of the questions, it is ambiguous at most places. Other accounts which throw light on social structure in past are:

- Arthasastra by Kautilya
- Indica by Megasthenese
- Travel account by Fa-Xien
- Travel account by Alberuni
- Travel account by Ibn Battuta.

Caste division among Muslims was determined according to ancestry. One with ancestry matching with invaders were considered superior to converts. Some castes are based on occupation. For example, goldsmiths, carpenters, and barbers each form separate sub-castes. Often, a sub-caste with a significant number of members will be divided into further sub-castes. This further division may be due to:

- Geographical separation: For example, there are purabia (eastern) and pachchaia (western) sections of some castes.
- Variation in standards of conduct: For example, disagreements over the permissibility of widow marriages have caused some castes to subdivide.

VARNAS (CLASSES) AND JATIS (CASTES)

Although Varna Jati and caste sounds synonymous, they have different connotations. Varna is mentioned as caste equivalent in scriptures. Puranas use it in the context of skin colour too. Puranic deities are often described as belonging to

Shwet or "Gaur" meaning white and Shyam meaning black varnas. Scriptures describe Varnas as classification based o profession too. Manu Smriti identified four varnas in Indian society. These are Brahmin, Kshatriya, Vaishya, and Sudra according to origin. However, Lord Krishna in Bhagwadgita says Varna are according to Karma (work) nothing to do with origin.

Theoretically, according to the Manu Smriti, every caste belongs to one of the four varnas (Brahmin, Kshtriya, Vaishya, and Sudra). However, the division of Indian society into four castes was a generalization rarely held in practice. Consequently, there have been many disputes about the varna of many castes, such as castes being considered Kshatriya by some scholars, while described as Sudra by others. While texts such as the Manu Smriti attempted to rationalize ambiguous castes by placing them in varna-sankaras (*i.e.* mixed varna), the fact remains that Indian society was, and is, composed of numerous geographically diversified but endogamous groups.

With many occupational groups practising endogamy within a particular region, as well as numerous sub-divisions within the four main castes, a more complex system of sub-castes and jatis is evident. The jatis have broken up into clans like Agarwal, Iyer, etc. Unlike the varna system of Brahmins, which requires spiritual purity in order to ascend, a jati is able to move up or down the social hierarchy based on the aspirations of its members. Marriages are usually arranged within one's own sub-caste; however, they may occur between two affiliated sub-castes, or two sub-castes that are in the same region, and are as such termed inter-caste marriages. Over time, this grew more and more rigid, until every aspect was determined by birth, with various "justifications" as described below.

To simplify the perspective, often people use the classification based on Four varnas, given in Manu Smriti and other Dharmashastras: The Brahmins (Teachers, Scholars and Priests), The Khshatriyas (Kings and warriors), the Vaishyas (Traders, Landowners and some Artisan groups), and Sudras

(Agriculturists, Service providers, and some Artisan groups). There was another group, which was excluded from the main society, for various reasons, which was called Parjanya or Antyaja; these were the people called untouchables. The varnas (rather than Jatis), was used after the 1902 Census by the British, for consolidation of demographic data into manageable proportions. However no commonly agreed approach for classifying the castes into the four varnas exists, sometimes a caste may claim to be a Brahmin, but others may regard it to be a Vaishya.

In the past, members of different castes would not partake in various activities, such as dining and religious gatherings, together. In addition, the performance of religious rites and rituals were restricted to Brahmins, who were the designated priesthood. In recent years, more egalitarian reforms have enabled lower castes and even non-castes such as the Dalits to become religious clerics. The "Pandaram" priests are an example of an order of Dalit priests, based in Nepal and South India. The Pandaram maintain the same tradition as the Brahmin priests, including the use of the Sanskrit language (traditionally reserved for the Brahmins) for the rituals. While they are not generally as well trained as the Brahmin priests, they are highly respected within their community and are addressed with reverence.

MOBILITY AMONG THE CASTES

Although group mobility was not completely uncommon, individual mobility among castes was generally rare. While mobility among caste groups was not common, it was not unheard of. Groups of lower-caste individuals could seek to elevate the status of their caste by attempting to emulate the practices of higher castes.

The view of the caste system as "static and unchanging" has been disputed by many scholars. Sociolgists such as Bernard Buber and Marriott McKim describe, for instance, how the perception of the caste system as a static and textual stratification has given way to the perception of the caste system as a more processual, empirical and contextual stratification. Other sociologists such as Y. B. Damle have applied theoretical models to explain mobility and flexibility in the caste system in India.

Sociologist M. N. Srinivas has also debated the question of rigidity in Caste. In an ethnographic study of the Coorgs of Karnataka, he observed considerable flexibility and mobility in their caste hierarchies. He asserts that the caste system is far from a rigid system in which the position of each component caste is fixed for all time. Movement has always been possible, and especially in the middle regions of the hierarchy. It was always possible for groups born into a lower caste to "rise to a higher position by adopting vegetarianism and teetotalism" *i.e.* adopt the customs of the higher castes. While theoretically "forbidden", the process was not uncommon in practice. The concept of sanskritization, or the adoption of upper-caste norms by the lower castes, addressed the actual complexity and fluidity of caste relations.

When it comes to stance of a hereditary caste system, the Manu Smriti takes the position:

> *The above verse is believed to sanction support for vocational non-hereditary caste system, suggesting some flexibility in the propagation of the Castes. According to some economists, mobility across broad caste lines may have been "minimal", though sub-castes (jatis) may change their social status over the generations by fission, relocation, and adoption of new rituals.*

Historical examples of mobility in the Indian Caste System among Hindus have been researched. The "Noniya" Caste of salt makers have claimed to the higher status of the "Chauhan Rajput". They have risen well above the untouchable line and their leaders have, in the past, mobilized upwards along the caste hierarchy. There is also precedent of certain Sudra families within the temples of the Shrivaishava sect in South India elevating their caste.

A well-known precedent for mobility in the caste system is that of Shivaji, the founder and monarch of the Maratha Confederacy, who was born into a lower caste but was elevated to a higher caste to facilitate his coronation.

THEORIES ABOUT THE ORIGINS OF THE SYSTEM

The histories of many of the castes are available in form of an oral tradition. Many of these were recorded in the past few centuries. With the archaeological findings in the last one and half centuries, it is now possible to trace the emergence on several of the specific castes to 11-12th century or even a few centuries earlier. For example, Babb has attempted to trace the history of several castes in Rajasthan in his "Archemies of Violence", based largely on narratives recorded in the past few centuries. Prior to the availability of archaeological evidence, the histories of individual castes are often speculative.

One theory is, in its initial period caste system was flexible and it was merit and job based. One could migrate from one caste to other caste by changing one's profession. Evidence in support of it says that Rama's guru Rishi Vashishtha was a shudra and he became Rishi later. Also Rishi Valmiki was a dacoit before becoming a sage. Later, the caste system is said to have become rigid, and caste began to be inherited rather than acquired by merit.

According to 19th century theories, the caste system began with the arrival of the Aryans in India. Indo-Aryan culture arrived in India around 1500 BC, around the time of the collapse of the Indus Valley Civilization. The Indo-Aryans arrived in India from Central Asia. European scholars first supposed that they came as invaders, and were contemptuous of their newly-conquered subjects. This was often romanticized as a struggle between the native dark skinned culture and the invading light skinned one. Before the arrival of the Indo-Aryans, the dominant cultural and linguistic group would have been the Dravidians. The Dravidians were the largest community in India, and are by some scholars identified as the bearers of the Indus Valley Civilization. It was fully developed by 800 BC. It was at first assumed that the Indus Valley Civilization collapsed due to the apparent invasion of the Aryans, but it now seems more likely that the migration of Indo-Aryan culture came about as a result of the diminished power of the Indus Valley Civilization as it was collapsing due to internal pressures, much like the migrations period in Europe was brought on by the weakening of the Roman Empire.

The early Aryans organized among themselves in three groups, much like other Indo-European peoples. The different Jats (sub-castes) who professed different occupations were integrated in different Varnas according to their occupation. According to the invasion theory of caste origin, most of the c mmunities that were in India before the arrival of the Aryans w re integrated in the Sudra Varna or were made outcast dependin on the professions of these communities. Communities who pro essed non-polluting jobs were integrated in Sudras Varna. And communities who professed polluting professions were made outcasts or untouchables. Untouchables were not only disallowed to touch the high caste people but they also had to stand at a certain distance from the high castes.

This Aryan Invasion theory is today often claimed to have been formulated to undermine the historical significance of India and its cultural and religious heritage by the British, and subsequently the west. The British historians were writing under a Biblical time-frame where the world began only around 4000 BC. The theory was also exploited by the British to show that they had the right to invade India, as the Indians supposedly themselves were invaders. It indirectly also implied that the "indigenous" people were incapable of creating their religion or culture and that it was brought by outsiders. Recent genetic studies have supported the idea that the invasion did not occur, showing that most north Indians today are primarily of Indian, not Central Asian, descent suggesting that the influx of Indo-Aryan culture was one primarily of language, not genes.

MODERN STATUS OF THE CASTE SYSTEM

The caste system was first exposed to the modern Western world during the Portuguese occupation and rule of sections of India. Indeed, the word 'caste' in this context is derived from the Portuguese, casta. Later, other European empires, including the British, occupied parts of the subcontinent. The anthropologist Herbert Risley's The Tribes and Castes of Bengal, published in 1892, was one of the first works on the caste system in India written by a Western scholar.

SCHEDULED CASTES, SCHEDULED TRIBES AND OTHER BACKWARD CLASSES

Independent India officially documented castes and sub-castes, primarily to determine those deserving reservation (positive discrimination in education) through the census. The Indian reservation system relies entirely on quotas. The Government lists consist of scheduled castes, scheduled tribes and other backward classes.

Scheduled Castes (SC): Scheduled castes generally consist of former "untouchables" (the term "Dalit" is now preferred). Present population is 16% of total population of India *i.e.* around 160 million. For example, the Delhi state has 49 castes listed as SC.

Scheduled Tribes (ST): Scheduled tribes generally consist of tribal people. Present population is 7% of total population of India *i.e.* around 70 million.

Other Backward Classes (OBC): Other backward classes generally consist of cultivators, pastoralists, artisans, etc. The Mandal Commission has covered more than 3000 castes under OBC Category. According to the Mandal Commission, the present population of OBC's is approximately 52% of the population. The Mandal Commission has since been criticized for fabricating data. The National Sample Survey puts the figure at 32%. For example, Delhi places 53 castes in this group. There is substantial debate over the exact number of OBC's in India, with census data compromised by partisan politics. It is generally estimated to be sizable, but lower than the figures quoted by either the Mandal Commission or and national Sample Survey. Some Indian states are dominated by caste-based politics. Sometimes converts to other religions, such as Christianity or Islam, retain their caste identity, often due to the economic benefits it carries, and also to retain their ties with the community for social reasons. This practice, however, is often frowned upon by members of the same sub-caste.

CONTEMPORARY CRITICISM OF THE CASTE SYSTEM

There has been strong criticism of the caste system existing in India. Some activists consider that the caste system is a form of racial discrimination. The participants of the United Nations Conference Against Racism in Durban, South Africa in March 2001, condemned the discrimination due to the caste system, and stated that caste as a basis for the segregation and oppression of peoples in terms of their descent and occupation is a form of apartheid.

The Indian government denies the claims of equivalency between Caste and Racial discrimination, pointing out that the caste issues as essentially intra-racial and intra-cultural. Indian Attorney General Soli Sorabjee insisted that "The only reason India wants caste discrimination kept off the agenda is that it will distract participants from the main topic: racism. Caste discrimination in India is undeniable but caste and race are entirely distinct." In India, some observers felt that the caste system must be viewed as a system of exploitation of poor low-ranking groups by more prosperous high-ranking groups. In many parts of India, land is largely held by dominant castes high-ranking owners of property that economically exploit low-ranking landless labourers and poor artisans, all the while degrading them with ritual emphases on their so-called god-given inferior status.

Matt Cherry, claims that karma underpins the caste system, and the caste system traditionally determines the position and role of every member of Hindu society. Caste determines an individual's place in society, the work he or she may carry out, and who he or she may marry and meet. According to him, Hindus believe that the karma of previous life will determine the caste an individual will be (re)born into.

THE STATUS OF UNTOUCHABLES

The untouchable (or Dalit) in Hindu Society was a person who worked in what were seen as unhealthy, polluting work dealing with the dead bodies and animal carcasses, the collection and disposal of bodily waste, and other jobs that brought him/her into constant contact with what society considered disgusting and even dangerous. These occupations, although they were helpful to the society and improved sanitation, were considered unclean and polluted the individual, and such polluted individuals were considered unfit for physical or social contact with the non-polluted, "purer" sections of society. Untouchables used to live separately within a subcultural context of their own, outside the inhabited limits of villages and townships, made pariahs in every sense of the word. No other castes could, or would, interfere with their social life since untouchables were lower in social ranking than even those of the shudra varna. In the past, extreme poverty drove many untouchables to wear clothing off the bodies of the dead that they handled.

In their home they ate from broken dishes discarded by others. Untouchables suffered from many social restrictions. They were not allowed temple worship with others, nor water from the same sources. Person of higher castes would not interact with them. Untouchables were not allowed to use the same wells as the other castes as that would "pollute" the water and indirectly the other castes who drank it. If somehow a member of a higher caste came into physical or social contact with an untouchable, the member of the higher caste was defiled, and had to bathe thoroughly to purge her/himself of the impurity.

Such contact even included the shadow of an untouchable falling on the member of the higher caste. At the same time, the untouchables developed their own rich folk traditions with a lifestyle that was unhampered by the variety of restrictions on the rest of the society. The inclusion of lower castes into the mainstream was argued for by Mahatma Gandhi who called them "Harijans" (people of God). The term Dalit (downtrodden) is used now as the term Harijan is largely felt patronising. Gandhi's contribution toward the emancipation of the untouchables is controversial. This is usually highlighted by the commentary of his contemporary Dr. B. R. Ambedkar, an untouchable himself. Ambedkar was deeply suspicious of Gandhi's motivations and frequently saw his activities as detrimental to the cause of upliftment of his people.

For instance, Gandhi, a Vaishya, was not against the caste system, but tried hard to bring untouchables into the mainstream of society and get the other castes to discard the practice of untouchability. Ambedkar, influenced by liberal thinkers like Voltaire, was interested in the elimination of the caste system and untouchability altogether.

To him, Gandhi's efforts solved no problems of the untouchables as they would remain at the bottom of the hierarchy. Ambedkar suggested that the evils of the caste system would be eliminated if the upper castes (especially the Brahmins) would change their behaviour and eventually get rid of the caste system altogether.

4

HISTORICAL BACKGROUND OF RESERVATION

Realising the inequatious distribution of posts in the administration between different castes and communities, the rulers of some of the then Princely States, who were genuinely interested in the upliftment of disadvantageous sections of the society, took initiatives and introduced reservations in the administrative posts in favour of the backward castes and communities in their States as early as in the first quarter of the 20th century. Mysore and Kolahpur were amongst the first to do so. Because of the movement for social justice and equity started by the Justice Party, the then Presidency of Madras initiated the reservation in Government employment in 1921.

It was followed by Bombay Presidency comprised of the major portion of present States of Maharashtra, Karnataka and Gujarat. Thus, the first quarter of the 20th century saw reservations in Government employment in almost whole of Southern India. These reservations were not only in favour of the depressed classes which were rechristined as Scheduled Castes in the Government of India Act, 1935, but also in favour of other backward castes and classes including what were then known as intermediate castes. To identify the backward classes in the State of Mysore, Justice L. C. Miller Committee was appointed in 1918-20. Similarly in the Princely State of Travancore and Cochin, Justice C. D. Nokes Committee was appointed in 1935.

Poona Pact 1932

Before the Poona Pact 1932 the representation of depressed classes in public service was negligible except for a few pockets of old presidency of Madras and princely State of Mysore. In the Poona Pact under Clause 6 a provision was made under which Government should make every endeavour to secure fair representation of the depressed classes in elections to local bodies and appointments to public services.

RESERVATION PRIOR TO 1947-BRITISH INDIA

For the first time instructions were issued in 1934, without providing a formal reservation that candidates belonging to depressed classes and possessing the requisite qualifications should not be deprived of fair opportunities of appointment merely because they could not succeed in open competition. The term Scheduled Castes was used for the first time in the Government of India Act, 1935. In August, 1943, Government of India provided reservation at the rate of 8. 1/3 per cent for the Scheduled Castes in the vacancies filled up by direct recruitment through open competition. The relaxation in the upper-age limit and concessions in examination fee prescribed for appointment to a service or post were announced in favour of the Scheduled Castes candidates.

RESERVATION AFTER INDEPENDENCE

Soon after independence, orders were issued by Government on 21. 9. 1947 providing for reservations in services for Scheduled Castes at the rate of 12. 5% of vacancies in respect of direct recruitment through open competition. In the case of recruitment otherwise than by open competition separate reservation at the rate of 16 2/3% was provided in favour of Scheduled Castes. The question of providing reservations for the Tribal Communities in the Central Services also came up before the Government and instructions were issued in December, 1947, that the appointing authorities should consider as far as possible desirability of recruiting suitably qualified candidates from amongst the tribal communities. However, a decision to reserve a definite percentage of vacancies at the rate of 5% for candidates of Scheduled Tribes was taken only after the promulgation of the Constitution in 1950.

Constitutional Provisions for Reservation

The framers of the Constitution felt that unless special provisions were made for the protection of the right of Scheduled Castes and Scheduled Tribes to secure fair representation in public employment in proportion to their population, it would never be possible to catch up and compete successfully for securing public employment. Therefore, to secure fair representation of Scheduled Castes and Scheduled Tribes in services and posts under the State, special provisions of reservation under Article 16(4), Article 46 and Article 335 of the Constitution were made. Article 16(4) empowers the State for making any provision for the reservation of appointment or posts in favour of any backward class of citizens which in the opinion of State, is not adequately represented in the services under the State.

Article 16(4A) enacted by a Constitutional Amendment removes any misunderstanding of the meaning and scope of reservations.

The Article 16(4A) reads as under.

Nothing in this Article shall prevent the State from making any provision for reservation in matters of promotion to any class or classes of posts in the services under the State in favour of the Scheduled Castes and Scheduled Tribes which, in the opinion of the State are not adequately represented in the services under the State".

> *"Articles 46 says that the State shall promote with special care the educational and economic interests of the weaker sections of the people and in particular of the Scheduled Castes and Scheduled Tribes and shall protect them from social injustice and all forms of exploitation".*

Article 335 imposes upon the State a responsibility that the claims of the members of the Scheduled Castes / Scheduled Tribes shall be taken into consideration consistent with the maintenance of efficiency of administration, in making of appointments to the services and posts in connection with the affairs of the Union or of a State.

Under these constitutional backgrounds the Central Government provided reservation only for members of the Scheduled Castes and Scheduled Tribes. After the Constitution was promulgated, Ministry of Home Affairs in its Resolution of 13. 9. 1950 provided 5% reservation for Scheduled Tribes apart from the percentage fixed for Scheduled Castes already in force. The Census of 1951 showed that the percentage of Scheduled Castes in the total population was 15. 05 per cent and that of Scheduled Tribes 6. 31 per cent. The 1961 Census revealed that the Scheduled Castes and Scheduled Tribes population in proportion to the India's population stood at 14. 64 per cent and 6. 80 per cent respectively. Accordingly, the percentage of reservation for Scheduled Castes and Scheduled Tribes was increased from 12-1/2 per cent and 5 per cent to 15 per cent and 7-1/2 per cent respectively on 25. 3. 1970. The 1971 Census did not warrant any such review. As the census of 1981 could not be carried out in the State of Assam the actual impact of 1981 Census figures on all India percentages could not be known.

Since special provisions of reservations in services were required to overcome the socioeconomic and educational deprivation and discrimination suffered by the Scheduled Castes and Scheduled Tribes in the past the founding fathers of the Constitution made provisions of reservation for SCs/STs in the Constitution for giving opportunities to them to have a share in the governance and administration of the country. Accordingly, various orders providing for reservation and necessary relaxations in direct recruitment and in promotions were issued by the Government from time to time.

It has been observed that even after 50 years of independence and with the facilities of aforesaid provisions, the representation of Scheduled Castes and Scheduled Tribes in various Departments and PSUs of Government of India has not reached the prescribed level of reservation *i.e.,* 15 per cent for Scheduled Castes and 7. 5 per cent for Scheduled Tribes. A substantial shortfall of Scheduled Castes in Group A and B category and Scheduled Tribes in almost all categories of posts is noticed; the post basis analysis has indicated that percentage of representation of these communities in higher posts is far below the requirement.

The implementation of the constitutional safeguards to Scheduled Castes and Scheduled Tribes in services is done through executive orders issued by the competent Ministry presently by Ministry of Personnel, Public Grievances & Pensions Department of Personnel & Training) from time to time. While these Executive Orders on reservations were to show their result in due representation of Scheduled Castes and Scheduled Tribes in services, the spate of five Office Memoranda issued by DOPT in 1997 have completely turned aside the reservation policy and withdrawn a number of facilities that were available to these communities. These five memoranda have withdrawn the facilities enjoyed by the Scheduled Castes and Scheduled Tribes employees for the last 50 years.

The Committee note that keeping in view the social, economic and educational backwardness of SCs and STs the framers of the Constitution had felt that unless special provisions were made for the protection of their rights to secure representation in public employment in proportion to their population, it would never be possible for these communities to catch up and compete successfully for securing public employment. Therefore special provisions for reservation in services and posts under the State in favour of SCs and STs were made under Article 16(4), Article 46 and Article 335 of the Constitution.

The Committee also note that the term Scheduled Castes was used for the first time in the Government of India Act, 1935 and in August, 1943, the Government of India provided reservation at the rate of 8. 1/3 per cent for SCs in the vacancies filled up by direct recruitment. After Independence, orders were issued on 21.9.47 providing for reservation in services for SCs @ 12. 5 per cent in respect of direct recruitment through open competition. In the case of recruitment otherwise than by open competition this percentage was fixed at 16. 2/3 per cent.

The Committee further note that after the Constitution was promulgated Ministry of Home Affairs in its resolution of 13.9.1950 provided 5 per cent reservation for Scheduled Tribes apart from the percentage fixed for SCs already in force. As the census of 1961 revealed that the SC and ST population stood at 14. 64 per cent and 6. 80 per cent respectively, and accordingly the percentage of reservation for SCs and STs was increased from 12.1/2 per cent and 5 per cent to 15 per cent and 7. 1/2 cent respectively.

The Committee are constrained to note that even after 50 years of independence, the representation of Scheduled Castes and Scheduled Tribes in various Departments and Public Sector Undertakings of the Government of India has not reached the prescribed level of reservation, *i.e.,* 15 per cent for SCs and 7. 5 per cent for STs. The Committee observe that there is substantial shortfall of SCs in Group A and B category and STs in almost all categories of posts in various Departments and Public Sector Undertakings of the Government. In higher posts the percentage of representation of these communities is far below the required level.

The Committee note that the implementation of the Constitutional safeguards provided to SCs and STs in services is done through the executive orders issued by the competent Ministry (Presently by Ministry of Personnel, Public Grievances & Pensions Department of Personnel and Training (DOPT) from time to time. The Committee are perturbed to note that while the reservation policy in force has yet to show results in achieving adequate representation of Scheduled Castes and Scheduled Tribes in services, the spate of five office memoranda issued by DOPT in 1997 on the basis of certain Supreme Court judgements have withdrawn a number of facilities that were available to Scheduled Castes and Scheduled Tribes and completely turned aside the reservation policy.

In the opinion of the Committee these Office Memoranda are anti-reservation and, therefore, unconstitutional in toto. The Committee strongly recommend that Government should immediately withdraw these anti-reservation O.M.S.

The Committee also recommend that in order to avoid recurrence of such incidents, the Government should bring out a Comprehensive Legislation-Reservation Act to fulfil the prescribed percentage of reservation for SCs and STs in all grades and cadres. The Reservation Act should be included in the 9th Scheduled of the Constitution so that the judiciary has no access to it. Seniority of SC/ST officers promoted earlier vis-a-vis general candidate promoted later.

5

SPIRITUAL ASPECT OF CONVERSION

Uptil now, we have discussed why conversion is necessary for material gains. Now, I propose to put forth my thoughts as to why conversion is as much necessary for spiritual wellbeing. What is Religion? Why is it necessary?... 'That which govern people is religion'. That is the true definition of Religion. There is no place for an individual in Hindu society. The Hindu religion is constituted on a class-concept. Hindu religion does not teach how an individual should behave with another individual. A religion, which does not recognize the individual, is not personally acceptable to me. Three factors are required for the uplift of an individual. They are: Sympathy, Equality and Liberty. Can you say by experience that any of these factors exist for you in Hinduism?

No Equality in Hinduism

Such a living example of inequality is not to be found anywhere in the world. Not at anytime in the history of mankind can we find such inequality, which is more intense than untouchability... I think, you have been thrust into this condition because you have continued to be Hindus. Those of you who have become Muslims, are treated by the Hindus neither as Untouchables nor as unequals. The same can be said of those who have become Christians. That God is all pervading is a principle of science and not of religion, because religion has a direct relation with the behaviour of man. Hindus can be ranked among those cruel people whose utterances and acts are two poles apart. They have this Ram on their tongues and a knife under their armpits. They speak like saints but act like butchers.

Thus we are not low in the eyes of the Hindus alone, but we are the lowest in the whole of India, because of the treatment given to us by the Hindus. If you have to get rid of this same shameful condition, if you have to cleanse this filth and make use of this precious life; there is only one way and that is to throw off the shackles of Hindu religion and the Hindu society in which you are bound.

The taste of a thing can be changed. But the poison cannot be made amrit. To talk of annihilating castes is like talking of changing the poison into amrit. In short, so long as we remain in a religion, which teaches a man to treat another man like a leper, the sense of discrimination on account of caste, which is deeply rooted in our minds, can not go. For annihilating caste and untouchables, change of religion is the only antidote.

Untouchables are not Hindus

What is there in conversion, which can be called novel? Really speaking what sort of social relations have you with the caste Hindus at present? You are as separate from the Hindus as Muslims and Christians are. So is their relation with you. Your society and that of the Hindus are two distinct groups. By conversion, nobody can say or feel that one society has been split up. You will remain as separate from the Hindus as you are today. Nothing new will happen on account of this conversion. If this is true, then why should people be afraid of conversion? At least, I do not find any reason for such a fear.

Revolution-Not Reform

Changing a religion is like changing a name. Change of religion followed by the change of name will be more beneficial to you. To call oneself a Muslim, a Christian, a Buddhist or a Sikh is not merely a change of religion but also a change of name. . Since the beginning of this movement of conversion, various people have raised various objections to it. Let us now examine the truth, if any, in such objections.

A congenital idiot alone will say that one has to adhere to one's religion because it is that of our ancestors. No sane man will accept such a proposition. Those who advocate such an argument, seem not to have read the history at all. The ancient Aryan religion was called Vedic religion. It has three distinct characteristic (features). Beef-eating, drinking and merrymaking was part of the religion of the day. Thousands of people followed it in India and even now some people dream of going back to it. If the ancient religion alone is to be adhered to why did the people of India leave Hinduism and accept Buddhism? Why did they divorce themselves from the Vedic religion?... Thus this Hindu religion is not the religion of our ancestors, but it was a slavery forced upon them.

To reform the Hindu society is neither our aim nor our field of action. Our aim is to gain freedom. We have nothing to do with anything else.

If we can gain freedom by conversion, why should we shoulder the responsibility of reforming the Hindu religion? And why should we sacrifice our strength and property for that? None should misunderstand the object of our movement as being Hindu social reform. The object of our movement is to achieve social freedom for the untouchables. It is equally true that this freedom cannot be secured without conversion.

Caste can't be Destroyed

I do accept that the untouchables need equality as well. And to secure equality is also one of our objectives. But nobody can say that this equality can be achieved only by remaining as Hindu and not otherwise. There are two ways of achieving equality. One, by remaining in the Hindu fold and another by leaving it by conversion. If equality is to be achieved by remaining in the Hindu fold, mere removal of the sense of being a touchable or an untouchable will not serve the purpose. Equality can be achieved only when inter-caste dinners and marriages take place. This means that the Chaturvarnya must be abolished and the Brahminic religion must be uprooted. Is it possible? And if not, will it be wise to expect equality of treatment by remaining in the Hindu religion? And can you be successful in your efforts to bring equality?

Of course not. The path of conversion is far simpler than this. The Hindu society does not give equality of treatment, but the same is easily achieved by conversion. If this is true, then why should you not adopt this simple path of conversion?

Conversion is a Simplest Path

According to me, this conversion of religion will bring happiness to both the Untouchables as well as the Hindus. So long as you remain Hindus, you will have to struggle for social intercourse, for food and water, and for inter-caste marriages. And so long as this quarrel continues, relations between you and the Hindus will be of perpetual enemies. By conversi n, the roots of all the quarrels will vanish... thus by conversion, if equality of treatment can be achieved and the affinity between the Hindus and the Untouchables can be brought about then why should the Untouchables not adopt the simple and happy path of securing equality? Looking at this problem through this angle, it will be seen that this path of conversion is the only right path of freedom, which ultimately leads to equality. It is neither cowardice nor escapism.

Sanctified Racism

Although the castes exist in Muslims and the Christians alike, it will be meanness to liken it to that of the Hindus. There is a great distinction between the caste-system of the Hindus and that of the Muslims and Christians. Firstly, it must be noted that though the castes exist amongst the Christians and the Muslims, it is not the chief characteristic of their body social.

There is one more difference between the caste system of the Hindus and that of the Muslims and Christians. The caste system in the Hindus has the foundation of religion. The castes in other religions have no sanction in their religion... Hindus cannot destroy their castes without destroying their religion. Muslims and Christians need not destroy their religions for eradication of their castes. Rather their religion will support such movements to a great extent.

Conversion alone Liberates Us

I am simply surprised by the question, which some Hindus ask us as to what can be achieved by conversion alone? Most of the present day Sikhs, Muslims and Christians were formerly Hindus, majority of them being from the Sudras and Untouchables. Do these critics mean to say that those, who left the Hindu fold and embraced Sikhism or Christianity, have made no progress at all? And if this is not true, and if it is admitted that the conversion has brought a distinct improvement in their condition, then to say that the untouchables will not be benefited by conversion, carries no meaning.

After giving deep thought to the problem, everybody will have to admit that conversion is necessary to the Untouchables as self-government is to India. The ultimate object of both is the same. There is not the slightest difference in their ultimate goal. This ultimate aim is to attain freedom. And if the freedom is necessary for the life of mankind, conversion of Untouchables which brings them complete freedom cannot be called worthless by any stretch of imagination.

Economic Progress or Social Changes?

I think it necessary here to discuss the question as to what should be initiated first, whether economic progress or conversion? I do not agree with the view that economic progress should precede. Untouchability is a permanent handicap on your path of progress. And unless you remove it, your path cannot be safe. Without conversion, this hurdle cannot be removed. So, if you sincerely desire that your qualifications should be valued, your education should be of some use to you, you must throw away the shackles of untouchability, which means that you must change your religion. However, for those who need this Mahar Watan, I can assure them that their Mahar Watan will not be jeopardized by their conversion. In this regard, the Act of 1850 can be referred. Under the provisions of this Act, no rights of person or his successors with respect to his property are affected by virtue of his conversion.

Poona Pact

A second doubt is about political rights. Some people express fear as to what will happen to our political safeguards if we convert. But I feel, it is not proper to depend solely on political rights. These political safeguards are not granted on the condition that they shall be ever lasting. They are bound to cease sometime. According to the communal Award of the British Government, our political safeguards were limited for 20 years. Although no such limitation has been fixed by the Poona Pact, nobody can say that they are everlasting.

Those, who depend upon the political safeguards, must think as to what will happen after these safeguards are withdrawn on the day on which our rights cease to exist. We will have to depend on our social strength. I have already told you that this social strength is wanting in us. So also I have proved in the beginning that this strength cannot be achieved without conversion.

Political Rights

Under these circumstances, one must think of what is permanently beneficial. In my opinion, conversion is the only way to eternal bliss. Nobody should hesitate even if the political rights are required to be sacrificed for this purpose. Conversion brings no harm to the political safeguards. I do not understand why the political safeguards should at all be jeopardized by conversion. Wherever you may go, your political rights and safeguards will accompany you. I have no doubt about it.

If you become Muslims, you will get the political rights as Muslims. If you become Christians, you will get the political rights as Christians, if you become Sikhs, you will have your political rights as Sikhs. In short, our political rights will accompany us.

So nobody should be afraid of it. On the other hand, if we remain Hindus and do not convert, will our rights be safe? You must think carefully on this. Suppose the Hindus pass a law whereby the untouchability is prohibited and its practice is made punishable, then they may ask you, 'We have abolished untouchability by law and you are no longer untouchables.

Looking through this perspective, conversion becomes a path for strengthening the political safeguards rather than becoming a hindrance. If you remain Hindus, you are sure to lose your political safeguards. If you want to save them, leave this religion. The political safeguards will be permanent only by conversion.

The Hindu religion does not appeal to my conscience. It does not appeal to my self-respect. However, your conversion will be for material as well as for spiritual gains. Some persons mock and laugh at the idea of conversion for material gains. I do not feel hesitant in calling such persons as stupid.

Conversion brings Happiness

I tell you all very specifically, religion is for man and not man for religion. To get human treatment, convert yourselves.

CONVERT-For getting organized.

CONVERT-For becoming strong.

CONVERT-For securing equality.

CONVERT-For getting liberty.

CONVERT-For that your domestic life may be happy.

I consider him as leader who without fear or favour tells the people what is good and what is bad for them. It is my duty to tell you, what is good for you, even if you don't like it, I must do my duty. And now I have done it.

It is now for you to decide and discharge your responsibility.

THE CASTE NOTION AND THE NATION

Ambedkar counterpoised the concept of nation as against the concept of caste, which was the pre-eminent mode of social organisation in India. For him, the idea of a nation was not just political sovereignty. A nation was a people who were socially bound as one. India however was divided by caste groups and people were unable to think in any other terms except as caste groups or caste sub-groups.

"The Hindus often complain of the isolation and exclusiveness of a gang or a clique and blame them for antisocial spirit. But they conveniently forget that this antisocial spirit is the worst feature of their own Caste System. One caste enjoys singing a hymn of hate against another caste as much as the Germans did in singing their hymn of hate against the English during the last war. The literature of the Hindus is full of caste genealogies in which an attempt is made to give a noble origin to one caste and an ignoble origin to other castes. The Sahyadrikhand is a notorious instance of this class of literature. This antisocial spirit is not confined to caste alone.

It has gone deeper and has poisoned the mutual relations of the sub-castes as well. In my province the Golak Brahmins, Deorukha Brahmins, Karada Brahmins, Palshe Brahmins and Chitpavan Brahmins, all claim to be subdivisions of the Brahmin Caste. But the antisocial spirit that prevails between them is quite as marked and quite as virulent as the antisocial spirit that prevails between them and other non-Brahmin castes. There is nothing strange in this.

An antisocial spirit is found wherever one group has 'interests of its own' who shut it out from full interaction with other groups, so that its prevailing purpose is protection of what it has got. This antisocial spirit, this spirit of protecting its own interests is as much a marked feature of the different castes in their isolation from one another as it is of nations in their isolation.

The Brahmin's primary concern is to protect 'his interest' against those of the non-Brahmins and the non-Brahmin's primary concern is to protect their interests against those of the Brahmins. The Hindus, therefore, are not merely an assortment of castes but they are so many warring groups each living for itself and for its selfish ideal. There is another feature of caste, which is deplorable. The ancestors of the present-day English fought on one side or the other in the war of the Roses and the Cromwellian War. But the descendants of those who fought on the one side do not bear any animosity—-any grudge against the descendants of those who fought on the other side.

The feud is forgotten. But the present-day non-Brahmins cannot forgive the present-day Brahmins for the insult their ancestors gave to Shivaji. The present-day Kayasthas will not forgive the present-day Brahmins for the infamy cast upon their forefathers by the forefathers of the latter. To what is this difference due? Obviously to the Caste System. The existence of Caste and Caste Consciousness has served to keep the memory of past feuds between castes green and has prevented solidarity."

Ambedkar devoted much effort to illustrate this in great detail. This is no surprise. Ambedkar was the chairman of the Drafting Committee of Constituent Assembly that drafted the Indian Constitution, which has lasted up to date with several amendments. He, like other leaders of the independence movement, was aware of the deep division within the Indian society. Nehru, the first Prime Minister of India was very much saddened by this historic reality. In the famous book-The Discovery of India-which he wrote from prison, where he was confined to by the British Raj, there are several references to this tragic historic reality. Mahatma Gandhi was deeply aware of the problem and knew that future of India would very much depend on this issue.

In fact all the great thinkers, poets and writers of India have said something or other strongly on the issue. However, it fell on Ambedkar, the beloved leader of the Untouchables, who also belonged to this group, to analyse this problem in its full details and suggest a path to its solution. Ambedkar's writings have now been brought out in fourteen thick volumes. All his writings directly or indirectly refer to the issue of caste and the nation.

Ambedkar demonstrated how the absence of solidarity led to the weakening of a people, making them indifferent and fear-ridden; as a result cooperation becomes impossible.

> "*Indifferentism is the worst kind of disease that can infect a people. Why is the Hindu so indifferent? In my opinion this indifferentism is the result of Caste System which has made Sanghatan and cooperation even for a good cause impossible*"

The notional foundation of Sanghatan and cooperation is at the heart of Ambedkar's views on the concept of the nation. He, as an eminent jurist, realised that this foundation cannot merely be a juridical one. The juridical conception of the nation are based on the theory of sovereignty which based on the classical legal theory of contract. However, Sanghatan and cooperation are social realities, not merely legal or poli ical ones. Their existence or not is a ground reality. Thus the n tions of Sanghatan and cooperation have to be derived from the ground reality of a given society at a given time. India as a lega entity, a colony under British Raj for most his lifetime and later an independent sovereignty with a constitutional framework, in the formulation of which he participated, was one thing.

The ground reality of India as a society was quite another. A democratic constitution however liberal, could not create this ground reality. The ground reality was primarily a social issue and not a political or a juridical issue. Here, the notions must be derived from the ground reality and if different sets of notions were to be introduced it had to be done by a change in the ground reality, which would involves everyone in society. What then was at issue was not the contract, but consensus. The consensus is not an abstraction; it is a social reality.

In fact Ambedkar's thought can be divided into two parts. Why he thought there was a fundamental impediment-caste-which prevented Indian people from reaching a consensus regarding any important aspect of their social life, and the solutions he proposed to get rid of this great impediment.

The Concept of Power Involved in this Discourse

The concept of power that Ambedkar had to discuss in dealing with the above mentioned two issues were not juridical notions of sovereignty and of the sovereign individual who passed his power to the state, but the issue of social power as actually found in the existing Indian society. He clearly saw the illusion of political power, when divorced from the social bases of power, when such great leaders such as Gandhi and Nehru were unable to achieve any of the fundamental ambitions they had set out to achieve, on the use of Indian independence for altering the nature of Indian society.

Ambedkar engaged in many debates with both the Socialists and people who held right wing views, as well as those who held the view that economic development was the solution to the social division of castes.

> "*One may contend that economic motive is not the only motive by which man is actuated. That economic power is the only kind of power no student of human society can accept. That the social status of an individual by itself often becomes a source of power and authority is made clear by the sway, which the Mahatmas have held over the common man. Why do a millionaire in India obey penniless Sadhus and Fakirs? Why do millions of paupers in India sell their trifling thickets, which constitute their only wealth and go to Benares and Mecca? That, religion is the source of power is illustrated*

by the history of India where the priest holds a sway over the common man often greater than the magistrate and where everything, even such things as strikes and elections, so easily take a religious turn and can so easily be given a religious twist. Take the case of the Plebeian of Rome as a further illustration of the power of religion over man. It throws great light on this point. The Plebs had fought for a share in the supreme executive under the Roman Republic and had secured the appointment of a Plebeian Consul elected by a separate electorate constituted by the Commitia Centuriata, which was an assembly of Plebeian. They wanted a Consul of their own because they felt that the Patrician Consuls used to discriminate against the Plebeian in carrying on the administration.

They had apparently obtained a great gain because under the Republican Constitution of Rome one Consul had the power of vetoing an act of the other Consul. But did they in fact gain anything? The answer to this question must be in the negative. The Plebeian never could get a Plebeian Consul who could be said to be a strong man and who could act independently of the Patrician Consul. In the ordinary course of things the Plebeian should have got a strong Plebeian Consul in view of the fact that his election was to be by a separate electorate of Plebeian. The question is why did they fail in getting a strong Plebeian to officiate as their Consul? The answer to this question reveals the dominion which religion exercises over the minds of men. It was an accepted creed of the whole Roman populous that no official could enter upon the duties of big office unless the Oracle of Delphi declared that he was acceptable to the Goddess. The priests who were in-charge of the temple of the Goddess of Delphi were all Patricians. Whenever therefore the Plebeian elected a Consul who was known to be a strong party man opposed to the Patricians or 'communal' to use the term that is current in India, the Oracle invariably declared that he was not acceptable to the Goddess. This is how the Plebeian were cheated out of their rights. But what is worthy of note is that the Plebeian permitted themselves to be thus cheated because they too like the Patricians, held firmly the belief that the approval of the Goddess was a condition precedent to the taking charge by an official of his duties and that election by the people was not enough. If the Plebeian had contended that election was enough and that the approval by the Goddess was not necessary they would have derived the fullest benefit from the political right which they had obtained. But they did not. They agreed to elect another, less suitable to themselves but more suitable to the Goddess which in fact meant more amenable to the Patricians. Rather than give up religion, the Plebeian give up material gain for which they had fought so hard. Does this not show that religion can be a source of power as great as money if not greater?" He goes on to say.

"Religion, social status and property are all sources of power and authority, which one man has, to control the liberty of another. One is predominant at one stage, the other is predominant at another stage. That is the only difference. If liberty is the ideal, if liberty means the destruction of the dominion which one man holds over another then obviously it cannot be insisted upon that economic reform must be the one kind of reform worthy of pursuit. If the source of power and dominion is at any given time or in any given society social and religious, then social reform and religious reform must be accepted as the necessary sort of reform.

One can thus attack the doctrine of Economic Interpretation of History adopted by the Socialists of India. But I recognise that economic interpretation of history is not necessary for the validity of the Socialist contention that equalisation of property is the only real

> *reform and that it must precede everything else. However, what I like to ask the Socialists is this: Can you have economic reform without first bringing about a reform of the social order?"*

In this aspect of economic interpretation of power, Ambedkar's views expressed in the text published in 1937 and many other texts, which are a very integral to his analysis of caste, bear similar perspectives as the views of Foucault expressed in his lectures in 1971, on Truth and Power.

> *"What is at stake in all these genealogies is the nature of this power which has surged into view in all its violence, aggression and absurdity in the course of the last forty years, contemporaneously, that is, with the collapse of Fascism and the decline of Stalinism. What, we must ask, is this power-or rather, since that is to give a formulation to the question that invites the kind of theoretical coronation of the whole which I am so keen to avoid-what are these various contrivances of power, whose operations extend to such differing levels and sectors of society and are possessed of such manifold ramifications? What are their mechanisms, their effects and their relations? The issue here can, I believe, be crystallized essentially in the following question: is the analysis of power or of powers to be deduced in one way or another from the economy? Let me make this question and my reasons for posing it somewhat clearer. It is not at all my intention to abstract from what are innumerable and enormous differences; yet despite, and even because of these differences, I consider there to be a certain point in common between the juridical, and let us call it, liberal, conception of political power (found in the philosopher of the eighteenth century) and the Marxist conception, or at any rate a certain conception currently held to be Marxist. I would call this common point economism in the theory of power. By that I mean that in the case of the classic, juridical theory, power*

is taken to be a right, which one is able to possess like a commodity, and which one can in consequence transfer or alienate, either wholly or partially, through a legal act or through some act that establishes a right, such as takes place through cession or contract. Power is that concrete power which every individual holds, and whose partial or total cession enables political power or sovereignty to be established. This theoretical construction is essentially based on the idea that the constitution of political power obeys the model of a legal transaction involving a contractual type of exchange (hence the clear analogy that runs through all these theories between power and commodities, power and wealth). In the other case-I am thinking here of the general Marxist conception of power-one finds none of all that. Nonetheless, there is something else inherent in this latter conception, something which one might term an economic functionality of power. This economic functionality is present to the extent that power is conceived primarily in terms of the role it plays in the maintenance simultaneously of the relations of production and of class domination which the development and specific forms of the forces of production have rendered possible. On this view, then, the historical raison d'etre of political power is to be found in the economy. Broadly speaking, in the first case we have a political power whose formal model is discoverable in the process of exchange, the economic circulation of commodities; in the second case, the historical raison d'etre of political power and the principle of its concrete forms and actual functioning, is located in the economy. Well then, the problem involved in the researches to which I refer can, I believe, be broken down in the following manner: in the first place, is power always in a subordinate position relative to the economy? Is it always in the service of, and ultimately answerable to, the economy? Is its essential end and purpose to serve

> *the economy? Is it destined to realize, consolidate, maintain and reproduce the relations appropriate to the economy and essential to its functioning? In the second place, is power modelled upon the commodity? Is it something that one possesses, acquires, cedes through force or contract, that one alienates or recovers, that circulates, that voids this or that region? Or, on the contrary, do we need to employ varying tools in its analysis-even, that is, when we allow that it effectively remains the case that the relations of power do indeed remain profoundly enmeshed in and with economic relations and participate with them in a common circuit? If that is the case, it is not the models of functional subordination or formal isomorphism that will characterize the interconnection between politics and the economy. Their indissolubility will be of a different order, one that it will be our task to determine."*

In fact the whole study of caste by Ambedkar, which takes many volumes to fully study, falls under what Foucault describes as genealogy. Forced by the need to explain the theory and practice of caste, which could not be explained in terms of the usual economic and social theories, Ambedkar was forced to explain them in other ways. The learned jurist who had obtained many degrees from several western universities, was not able to rely on any of the theories he learned to explain the Indian caste system. What he wrote might fall under what Foucault later called subjugated knowledge.

> *"On the other hand, I believe that by subjugated knowledge one should understand something else, something which in a sense is altogether different, namely, a whole set of knowledge that have been as inadequate to their task or insufficiently elaborated: naive knowledge, located low down on the hierarchy, beneath the required level of cognition or scientificity. I also believe that it is through the re-emergence of these*

low-ranking knowledge, these unqualified, even directly disqualified knowledge (such as that of the psychiatric patient, of the ill person, of the nurse, of the doctor-parallel and marginal as they are to the knowledge of medicine-that of the delinquent etc.), and which involve what I would call a popular knowledge (le saviour des gens) though it is far from being a general commonsense knowledge, but is on the contrary a particular, local, regional knowledge, a differential knowledge incapable of unanimity and which owes its force only to the harshness with which it is opposed by everything-surrounding it-that it is through the reappearance of this knowledge, of these local popular knowledge, these disqualified knowledge, that criticism performs its work."

He further goes on to say, "What emerges out of this is something one might call a genealogy, or rather a multiplicity of genealogical researches, a painstaking rediscovery of struggles together with the rude memory of their conflicts. And these genealogies, that are the combined product of an erudite knowledge and a popular knowledge, were not possible and could not even have been attempted except on one condition, namely that the tyranny of globalising discourses with their hierarchy and all their privileges of a theoretical avant-garde was eliminated.

Let us give the term genealogy to the union of erudite knowledge and local memories, which allows us to establish a historical knowledge of struggles and to make use of this knowledge tactically today. This then will be a provisional definition of the genealogies which I have attempted to compile with you over the last few years."

In fact, the work of both Ambedkar and Grundtvig, are works that of genealogies, though they did not think of their work in that way. It is important to note this aspect when considering the contributions made to education within the context of discourse on power. Grundtvig beautifully combines erudite knowledge with folk memories. Folk School was a meeting place where erudite knowledge and folk thinking were to mix and merge, where academic and popular forms of thinking were to be fused. That was the living dialogue, and the genuine enlightenment.

GANDHI: PATRON SAINT OF THE INDUSTRIALIST

During the years of the Indian independence movement, a leading Indian industrialist, G. D. Birla, was Mahatma Gandhi's most generous financial supporter. While Birla has been described as a devotee of Gandhi, the relationship between the two men was more one of collaboration than of one-sided devotion. Gandhi's campaigns were made possible by drawing from Birla's vast financial resources while Birla benefited not only from the social and religious prestige which his association with Gandhi brought him, but his economic role and position as a wealthy capitalist was strengthened and glorified. Gandhi gave his blessing to the abundant wealth of Birla with his teaching on trusteeship, a concept which asserted the right of the rich to accumulate and maintain wealth, as long as the wealth was used to benefit society. Gandhi apparently borrowed the concept of trusteeship from the writings of the American millionaire, Andrew Carnegie, who had used trusteeship to promote capitalism over socialism.

The close relationship between Gandhi and G. D. Birla did not escape scrutiny. B. R. Ambedkar, a leader of the untouchable castes, accused Gandhi of pretending to support the cause of the oppressed while actually supporting the forces of social conservatism. Lord Linlithgow, the Viceroy of India, questioned the Gandhi-Birla connection. Linlithgow, who had blamed Gandhi for the sabotage and violence of the Quit India Movement of 1942, had suspicions that Birla, as representing big business, was actually the hidden hand behind the violence. Investigations by the governments of both colonial and independent India into Birla's economic and political association with Gandhi and the Congress failed to bring criminal indictment. Nevertheless, the relationship between the two men had consequences for the future of India and deserves attention. Gandhi and Birla, both strong defenders of social conservatism, shared objectives that were not brought out openly. In the shadow of Gandhi's public persona and popular teachings, Gandhi and Birla were able to weave conservative policies into the social, political, and economic fabric of independent India.

Ghanshyam Das Birla (1894-1983) was from a Marwari merchant family of Pilani in Rajasthan. His grandfather, Seth Shivanarain Birla, set out for Bombay on a camel in 1862. In Bombay, Shivanarain began trading in seeds and bullion. His only son, Baldeodas, joined him in the business at age thirteen in 1875. The Birla's trading business thrived and the family established an export-import business in Calcutta. In Bombay the family moved into trading in cotton, wheat, rape-seed and silver. G. D. began his apprenticeship in the family business at age thirteen. G. D. was sixteen when he started his own brokerage. G. D. 's business took him into contact with the British. He was offended by their racial arrogance. Birla wrote, "I was not allowed to use the lift to go up to their offices nor their benches while waiting to see them. I smarted under these insults and this created in me a political interest."

When G. D. was in his early twenties he found himself a wealthy man. World War I had produced great profits in his trading business. He was also a wanted man. G. D., in his frustration with the British had become involved with the Bara Bazaar Youth League, a group that engaged in terrorist activities against the British. Birla denies participating in terrorism, but in 1916 he was accused of stealing a shipment of armaments. He went into hiding for several months until friends could have the charges dropped against him.

Birla, restored to his business, decided to steer clear of terrorism. He would meet the British on the playing fields of business. There were British businessmen though who did not want him to play. When the Birlas attempted to open a jute factory in Calcutta, a British competitor started buying up all the land adjacent to the plot on which the Birlas were to build their factory, forcing the Birlas to move elsewhere. The Birlas were not deterred. G. D. and his brothers prospered in the jute business, as well as in their other enterprises. At the beginning of World War II, the Birlas were worth $3. 3 million. By the end of the war, they had holdings of $20 million. Before independence in 1947 the Birlas had 20 companies. Today they own 175 businesses and are prominent in textiles, sugar, jute, automobiles, bicycles, boilers, calcium carbides, industrial alcohol, linoleum, woollens, flax, ghee, margarine, and also starch, confectionery, banking, and insurance. The Birlas owned several newspapers including the Hindustan Times and a large interest in radio. In the summer of 1993, the Birla fortune was $1. 5 billion. G. D. Birla's political activities were a factor in the success of the Birla empire.

G. D. Birla's association with Mahatma Gandhi began in 1915. Gandhi had just returned to India from South Africa as a hero for championing the rights of Indian workers. In Calcutta, where Gandhi was to make a speech, Birla arranged a grand reception for him. Birla related his first impressions of Gandhi:

> At this first meeting he appeared rather queer.... I was rather puzzled about him when I first saw him, and then gradually I came to know him.... He gave us a new conception of politics. We felt him a saint as well as a politician.... That meeting was thirty-two years ago, and since then I have been associated with him and have been giving him such service as I can.

The service that Birla provided amounted to supplying practically every financial need Gandhi brought to him. Gandhi had other sources of income, including the assistance of the industrialist Jamnalal Bajaj, as well as the accumulated donations from multitudes of poor supporters, but Birla was the major financier. Birla's brothers also contributed to Gandhi, but sometimes G. D.'s gifting was seen by them as an extravagance. Birla rarely refused any financial request on Gandhi's part and Gandhi's requests were numerous. The following request from Gandhi was not atypical:

My thirst for money is simply unquenchable. I need at least Rs. 2, 00, 000—for khadi, untouchability and education. The dairy work makes another Rs. 50, 000. Then there is the Ashram expenditure. No work remains unfinished for want of funds, but God gives after severe trials. This also satisfies me. You can give as you like for whatever work you have faith in.

With Birla's beneficence Gandhi was able carry on his massive political campaigns, as well as to maintain a semblance of poverty and simplicity in lifestyle, while enjoying almost limitless financial resources.

While Gandhi appeared to share the living standards of the typical Indian villager in his Ashram, the annual expenditure of his Ashram was 100, 000 rupees, a considerable sum in pre-Independence rupees. In a similar vein, Gandhi was known for his humility in insisting on travelling by third-class trains. To get a seat in a crowded third-class car was difficult, so when Gandhi and his entourage travelled, the entire third-class car, cars, and sometimes even the whole train was paid for to ensure Gandhi's comfort. When Gandhi attempted to make a symbolic action by temporarily moving into an untouchable colony in Delhi, half the residents were moved out before his visit and the shacks of the residents torn down and neat little huts constructed in their place

The entrances and windows of the huts were screened with matting, and during the length of Gandhi's visit, were kept sprinkled with water to provide a cooling effect. The local temple was white-washed and new brick paths were laid. In an interview with Margaret Bourke-White, a photo-journalist for Life magazine, one of the men in charge of Gandhi's visit, Dinanath Tiang of the Birla Company, explained the improvements in the untouchable colony, "We have cared for Gandhiji's comfort for the last twenty years."

Gandhi put forward the illusory image of poverty and simplicity while he was actually living very comfortably. We can only speculate whether this image-making was political posturing on Gandhi's part or whether the amenities were forced on him by the practicalities of operating a massive movement. When Gandhi was questioned by the journalist Louis Fischer about the percentage of his budget which was funded by the rich, Gandhi told him practically all of it was, adding, "In this Ashram, for instance, we could live much more poorly than we do and spend less money. But we do not and the money comes from our rich friends." Gandhi was not oblivious to the expense laid out for him.

We can also only speculate on whether certain statements Gandhi made were representative of his opinions or whether they, too, could have been political tactics. Gandhi was well known for espousing seemingly contradictory positions. As a result it is a difficult task to decide what Gandhi's true positions were. For example, Birla criticized Gandhi for his public support of the Swaraj party. Birla did not care for the party due to its violent propensities. Gandhi responded:

I shall talk to you about the Swaraj party when we meet. I do not want you to change your view because by justifying your views I seek to justify my position as well.

Apparently Gandhi had reasons for publicly seeming to support a party which he admitted in private he was against. Similarly, Gandhi voiced radical views against capitalism and industrialism in his public speeches and writing:

Industrialism is, I am afraid, going to be a curse for mankind.... Industrialism depends entirely on your capacity to exploit.

To change to industrialism is to court disaster... The one great change to make is to discard foreign cloth, and reinstate the ancient cottage industry of hand spinning. We must thus restore our ancient and healthgiving industry if we would resist industrialism. I do not fight shy of capitalism. I fight capitalism... I do picture a time when the rich will spurn to enrich themselves at the expense of the poor.

These radical positions do not seem to correspond to other elements in Gandhi's life and thought, especially his close relationship with the industrialists. Margaret Bourke-White, having read Gandhi's seemingly revolutionary writings, was very puzzled to learn that for a quarter of a century Gandhi had spent much of his time living in G. D. Birla's palatial mansion in Delhi, where he was later assassinated.

Margaret Bourke-White's investigations into working conditions at one of Birla's mills in Delhi revealed a equally puzzling attitude on Gandhi's part to Birla's labour practices. Bourke-White was present when Gandhi was fasting in December 1947. During his fast, all the trade-unions sent delegations with peace pledges and pleas for Gandhi to end the fast. One trade-union, the largest union in India, did not send delegates. The textile workers union, whose chief employer was Birla, was noticeably absent. On December 8, shortly before Gandhi was to begin his fast, workers at Birla's textile mill in Delhi went to the manager asking for a cost of living bonus to meet rising prices.

When their requests were answered with gunfire and rifle butts, the workers sent a delegation of five workers to see Gandhi at the Birla House. According to Bourke-White, Gandhi refused to see them. On an earlier occasion, the workers at Birla's Delhi mill wrote to Gandhi directly to complain of bad working conditions. Instead of answering the letter or questioning Birla about the matter, Gandhi forwarded the letter to Birla. Birla responded by telling Gandhi that the workers were lying. Margaret Bourke-White visited Birla's mills and found conditions to be appalling. The squalid living quarters Birla provided for his workers were no better than those at mills belonging to owners who were not devotees to Gandhi. She wondered why Gandhi never visited the mills, as it would have been easy for him to do so. In none of the voluminous correspondence between Birla and Gandhi is Gandhi critical of the working conditions in Birla's mills.

Birla once defensively wrote Gandhi, not in response to rebuke from Gandhi, but to reports that conditions were bad in his mills. Birla tells Gandhi that he is improving conditions in one factory and hopes to do so in others. He blames any atrocities at his mills on the mill managers, claiming he cannot control them. While it would seem natural for the Mahatma to take an interest in Birla's workers, Gandhi refrained from criticizing or questioning Birla personally.

In other cases, Gandhi did not shy away from public criticism of companions who did not abide by his views. He frequently complained about his longtime friend Pandit Madan Mohan Malaviya. Gandhi had called for a boycott of all British education. Malaviya, the founder of Banaras Hindu University, refused to comply. In one of many attacks against Malaviya's position, Gandhi accused him of the greatest Adharma (unrighteousness).

I do not want to go into why this Empire in Satanic. But an Empire which has been guilty of the atrocities in the Punjab, which killed children six or seven years old... to study in the schools of such an Empire is, to my mind, the greatest adharma of all. To Panditji, an elder brother to me, this seems to be Dharma.

Though Gandhi continued to say he respected Malaviya, in reality there was a break in their friendship. In Gandhi's thirty-two year friendship with Birla, he never publicly criticized Birla's actions. Gandhi at times would make suggestions to Birla, but if Birla failed to follow them, Gandhi did not complain. Gandhi did not have the upper hand in the relationship. He considered Birla one of his mentors and would act on his advice. In Gandhi's letters to Birla he does not lecture him, except with regard to dietary matters.

Their correspondence is remarkably free from spiritual concerns, quite unlike the writing which Gandhi puts forward to the public. In Birla's collection of his correspondence with Gandhi, one letter by Gandhi stands out in addressing spiritual matters. Birla writes that he cannot remember the context or for whom the letter was meant. Though the letters between Gandhi and Birla are very amicable, the subject matter concerns mostly mundane affairs of finances and strategy.

When Gandhi disagreed with Birla, he found a way of avoiding argument. In one instance, Gandhi publicly complained that people were buying mill-produced khadi under the mistaken impression that it was homespun. Birla understood this as an indirect criticism of his textile industry, which was producing milled khadi, and gave quick retort to Gandhi's complaint:

Do you not think that you are unnecessarily exaggerating the results of the khadi propaganda?... You could find this out yourself if you send hawkers with mill-made as well as shuddha khadi who may ask some villagers to select their choice after explaining the latter properly about the quality as well as the price of the cloth, I have not the least doubt that if you made the experiment you will find that 90% of the consumers will pick up the cheaper and more lasting of the two stuffs. Mill khadi is popular because people find it cheap, durable besides it being Swadeshi make.

Gandhi answered a week later: "I got both your letters. But even today there is not time for reply." Gandhi never allowed the khadi issue to become an object of contention between himself and Birla. Instead he found a place for mills in the khadi movement. Later Gandhi wrote to Birla:

I am convinced that the boycott will be successful only through khadi. This does not mean that the mills have no place in the scheme at all. The mills can have their deserved place by recognizing the worth of khadi. The conception of God envelopes all Gods. Gandhi was clearly making concessions to Birla in incorporating textile mills into his homespun khadi movement. Gandhi was as much interested in pleasing his patron as Birla was in pleasing his saint.

A useful model for examining the give and take of the Gandhi-Birla relationship is that of the patron and publicist as presented by the historian C. A. Bayly. Bayly examines the relationship between wealthy patrons and leaders of reform movements such as the Hindi movement and the cow-protection movement in the late 1880s. Bayly uses for example the patronage of Madan Mohan Malaviya, a leader of the Hindu revivalist movement, the Hindu Mahasabha, by the wealthy magnate Ram Charan Das. Bayly holds that the goal of the patron-publicist relationship was not exclusively concerned with protection of the patron's financial interests:

Two forms of relationship can be seen between patron and publicist, as also between various levels of political activity. One was the relationship between patron and publicist designed to protect material interests, or to promote them within new political arenas—the vakil relationship. The other concerned the protection or enhancement of particular conceptions of status conceived within the bounds of revived Hinduism—the Dharmik relationship. It is difficult to separate them.

Desire for enhanced religious standing in the community, which affected all avenues of social interactions, from marriage arrangements to business deals, was an important element of the patron-publicist relationship. Religious patronage was a means to enhance social and economic status in the community. Avenues of religious patronage went beyond the traditional practices of temple construction and maintenance, feeding of Brahmans, sponsoring of festivals, etc. With the advent of religious reform movements in the 1800's, sponsoring such causes as the Hindi movement or the cow-protection movement became a religious and status-enhancing act. Elements of some of the earlier religious reform movements, such as the use of the vernacular and revived cultural identity, as well as the political undertones and organizational capabilities of the movements, later played a role in the growth of nationalism. These causes were sponsored by the wealthy, whose economic and social standing profited therefrom. Later, the relationships of patrons and publicists became an important element of Congress.

Aspects of the Birla-Gandhi relationship can be described by Bayly's model. Birla's fame and social standing did not rest on his raw wealth alone. Birla did not neglect to develop his reputation for generous religious patronage. He is well known for his religious gifting, particularly in the construction of magnificent temples. Birla admitted that he did not construct the temples from personal piety, "Frankly speaking, we build temples but we don't believe in temples. We build temples to spread a kind of religious mentality." Birla's financial support of the publicist Gandhi, as a form of religious patronage, would serve him well.

The mere association with Gandhi conferred on Birla a measure of Gandhi's religious stature. It is easy to see that Birla's generous patronage of Gandhi could have been perceived as a sign of devotion and Gandhi's acceptance of that patronage as a sign of approval of Birla. Gandhi's role in the independence movement was as much religious as it was political. He was the Mahatma, the Great Soul. Gandhi captured the hearts and imaginations of his fellow Indians by drawing upon a wealth of traditional Hindu symbolism. The political entity that Gandhi called for would be a Ramarajya, a kingdom likened unto that of the righteous Lord Rama. The British, Gandhi often said, were the equivalent of the evil demon Ravana, who Lord Rama and his entourage defeated. Gandhi, not only discarded his Western garb and lifestyle to appear to identify with the Indian masses, but also to take upon himself the attitude of the Brahmacari, the holy renunciant. He renounced material possessions, sexual relations, and held to a strict vegetarian diet as part of his regime of holiness. At the same time he was the guiding inspiration to a massive political movement. According to Bayly's model, Gandhi would be the exemplar publicist.

As Birla's publicist, Gandhi was able to deftly weave Birla's interests into a seemingly spiritual context. A blatant example of this is found in Gandhi's support for Birla's position against government regulation of prices. On several occasions Gandhi brought up the need for decontrol in his sermons during his evening prayer meetings. Gandhi also allowed the issue of decontrol to be promoted in his newspaper Harijan, a publication that was supposedly devoted to the needs of the oppressed. As part of the campaign for decontrol, Gandhi's son, Devadas, as managing editor of the Hindustan Times, Birla's chief New Delhi newspaper, also published an editorial calling for decontrols. When Margaret Bourke-White questioned Birla about decontrols, he responded: "I never was in favour of controls. I am not built that way.

The greatest virtue of capitalism is free competition." He went on to add that since the recent decontrol of sugar prices, the price of sugar had gone down. Gandhi followed this line of argument in his prayer meetings. Bourke-White's investigation of decontrol found that it was true that the price of su ar went down for the for the wealthy, who could buy on the black market. As for the man on the street, the price of sugar had doubled. Though in theory prices could go down for poor consumers with decontrol, in this case, it was the wealthy consumers and industrial producers who prospered.

Gandhi did not have anything against wealth. He was not inclined towards socialism and taught that there should be no forced redistribution of wealth in India. Gandhi called for social justice and alleviation of suffering, but believed that change brought about by government intervention would be ineffective. Change must first come in the individual heart. The wealthy should not be coerced into sharing their wealth; they should do it voluntarily. Gandhi taught that the wealthy should be trustees of their wealth, using only what was necessary for their own use and distributing their surplus for the benefit of society. Gandhi's idea is very much like the ideas of trusteeship that were being expounded in England and America in the late 1800s and early 1900s. Andrew Carnegie, a self-made American millionaire, had published a series of articles between 1886 and 1899 that sought to justify private wealth in the industrial society increasingly burdened with social concern and unrest.

Although some conservative Christian spokesmen had condemned corporate oppression, financial dishonesty, and growing poverty, many American and British religious leaders supporting the capitalistic economic system saw these social realities as prices that must be paid for progress. Carnegie in his essays set "in authoritative form the ideas that many Christian authors and most of the church press had been preaching for at least a generation." In England the articles were reprinted and commented upon in the Fortnightly Review, Nineteenth Century, Saturday Review, and Pall Mall Gazette. The articles received much attention, including a review and praise by the British Prime Minister, William E. Gladstone. Carnegie believed that the articles were better-received in England, because England was "more clearly face to face with socialist questions." Carnegie's articles offered an alternative to socialism. He stressed individual effort and responsibility instead of government control. He urged the wealthy to adopt the principle of trusteeship:

> This then, is held to be the duty of the man of wealth: To set an example of modest, unostentatious living, shunning display or extravagance; to provide moderately for the legitimate wants of those dependent upon him; and, after doing so, to consider all surplus revenues which come to him simply as trust funds, which he is called upon to administer... the man of wealth thus becoming the mere trustee and agent for his poorer brethren, bringing to their service his superior wisdom, experience, and ability to administer, doing for them better than what they would or could do for themselves.

Gandhi was a student in England from 1888 to 1891, at the time some of Carnegie's articles were published. As the articles were a subject of some controversy at the time they wer published and afterwards, it is possible that Gandhi was exposed to these ideas that served to promote capitalism over socialism. Gandhi's teachings are remarkably similar to Carnegie's:

> The rich man will be left in possession of his wealth, of which he will use what he reasonably requires for his personal needs and will act as a trustee for the remainder to be used for society.

Carnegie made a list of worthy causes on which surplus wealth should be spent which included educational institutions, hospitals, churches, etc. To provide for the required surplus wealth, Carnegie called for unbridled capitalism: He who manages the ships, the mines, the factories, cannot withdraw his capital, for this is the tool with which he works wonder ; nor can he restrict his operations, for the cessation of growth and improvement in any industrial undertaking marks the beginning of decay.

Birla's lifestyle and actions could almost be used to illustrate Carnegie's ideas. Birla was known for his unostentatious living and philanthropy. Rajendra Prasad, the first President of India, in the foreword to G. D. Birla's book In the Shadow of the Mahatma, puts forward Gandhi's version of trusteeship and points to G. D. Birla as being a worthy trustee. The beneficiaries of Birla's patronage curiously match Carnegie's list of the institutions deserving of surplus wealth:

It has been one of Gandhiji's teachings that those who are blessed with wealth should regard themselves as Trustees and treat their wealth as trust property for the benefit of others. The large number of institutions which are to be seen in so many parts of the country in the shape of educational institutions or religious temples and Dharmshalas or Hospitals with their apex at Pilani and Delhi are testimony to the fact that Birlas have imbibed this part of Gandhiji's teachings in no small manner. They have earned abundantly and likewise spent also generously and abundantly on every good cause.

All this, whatsoever moves on the earth, is to be hidden in the Lord (the Self). When thouhast surrended all this, then thou mayest enjoy. Do not covet the wealth of others.

Perhaps by making such a claim Gandhi hoped to give credence to the concept of trusteeship in the eyes of the Indians. Attributing the basis of contemporary ideas or practices to ancient texts, even while the connection is spurious, is not an uncommon means of legitimization. This is not to say that it was impossible for Gandhi's idea of trusteeship to be original or inspired by Hindu tradition. The Manu smirti, for instance, contains a verse in a section on the duties of castes, which encourages the vainya caste to accumulate wealth for the benefit of others:

He (a vaishya) should expend the greatest effort in justly increasing his goods, and he should also take pains to bestow at least food on all creatures.

Theoretically, the verse could be developed into the idea of trusteeship. But Gandhi did not bring forward such an explicit text on which to claim trusteeship was founded. Judging from the popularity of Carnegie's writings and the simultaneity of Gandhi's stay in England with the publication of Carnegie's "Gospel of Wealth," it is highly probable that Gandhi borrowed from Carnegie's ideas on trusteeship.

Gandhi's first application of trusteeship was with regard to Britain's trusteeship of the colonies well before Gandhi called for independence. While Gandhi changed his mind about the ability of the British to be beneficent trustees, he did not change his mind about the trusteeship of capitalists in India.

Gandhi's support for capitalists is expressed in his writing concerning industrial workers. On one hand, Gandhi suggested in Young India that mill owners should provide the following improvements for their workers:

1. The hours of labour must leave the workmen some hours of leisure.
2. They must get facilities for their own education.
3. Provision should be made for an adequate supply of milk, clothing and necessary education for their children.
4. There should be sanitary dwelling for the workmen.
5. They should be in a position to save enough to sustain themselves during their old age.

In the same article Gandhi makes a strong statement of the intellectual superiority of the capitalist over the workers:

When labour comes fully to realise its strength, I know it can become more tyrannical than capital. The millowners will have to work dictated by labour if the latter could command the intelligence of the former. It is clear, however, that labour will never attain to that intelligence. If it does, labour will cease to be labour and become itself the master. The capitalists do not fight in the strength of money alone. They do possess intelligence and tact.

In another article Gandhi worries that increased wages and reduced work loads will be squandered by the workers:

It is now time to examine the use we should make of increasing wages and hours saved. It would be like going into the frying pan out of the fire to use the increase in wages in the grog-shop and the hours saved in gambling dens. The money received, it is clear should be devoted to education of our children, and the time saved to our education. In both these matters the millowners can render much assistance.

Gandhi implies that the workers are incompetent to spend their wages properly and that the mill-owners are better able to use the increase in wages to provide milk, reading rooms and harmless amusements and games for the workers. Gandhi counsels the workers that it would be a sin to request higher wages and less hours if they were unable to controls their passions. Higher wages and reduced hours, according to Gandhi, required clean minds and hearts. Gandhi does not grace the capitalists with a lecture to the effect that increased profits require a clean heart. According to Gandhi's version of trusteeship, the capitalists had a right to their profits owing to their superior abilities. They were to make decisions that would benefit their less able workers.

Birla, while prospering from his textile mills and making use of Gandhi to promote his own industrial interests, daily wore khadi and occasionally worked at the spinning wheel. At Gandhi's suggestion he had been active in the Harijan upliftment movement. Though Gandhi and Birla are supposed to be strong supporters of the untouchables there is a noticeable lack of emotion or enthusiasm about the issue in their letters. The Harijans are spoken of as a cause, perhaps one that they would not want pushed too far. Gandhi did not want to abolish the caste system that had assigned the Harijans to their degraded position. B. R. Ambedkar, an untouchable leader, was strongly critical of Gandhi's motives and policies regarding untouchable castes, including the euphemistic designation of untouchables as Harijans. Ambedkar was also critical of Gandhi's connection with businessmen:

> *If the Bania is financing the Congress it is because he realized and Mr. Gandhi has taught him—that money invested in politics gives large dividends.*

Gandhi's call for Harijan upliftment, like Gandhi's ideas on abolition of capitalism and industry would be revolutionary if put into actual practice. But Gandhi's lofty teachings were otherworldly and seemingly unattainable, perhaps purposely so. That most people would not follow them literally was understood, even by Gandhi. Birla once wrote of the exaggerated expectations Gandhi had aroused in the untouchable castes:

> *Especially among the educated Harijans, hopes have been encouraged which could under no circumstances be fulfilled. Many educated Harijans seem to be under the impression that the society of ours is going to create a millennium.*

Ambedkar accused Gandhi of exploiting social problems, such as the plight of the untouchables, for political gain, while actually preventing social change. Ambedkar pointed out for example that Gandhi had publicly supported a bill for temple-entry for Harijans, but when election time came, he, along with Congress withdrew support for the bill.

Birla realized that behind all the revolutionary rhetoric, Gandhi was socially conservative. Gandhi might make public statements against industrialism, but he was no threat to Birla's industrial interests; he was a boon. Birla, as Gandhi's patron, basked in the aura of Gandhi's popularity, while Gandhi went about securing Birla's interests. Among Birla's chief concerns was Indian independence.

There had been times that Birla had profited from his relations with the British, and for some time had served as a go-between for Gandhi and British officials. But developments in British economic policies in India in 1937 had not been favourable to Birla and other industrialists:

> *The (British) refusal to change the rupee ratio, the willingness to sacrifice large-scale Indian interests in Burma, new encroachments of foreign capital in some profitable fields, austerity budgets and... open hostility to India's industrialization and to planning combined to produce a marked shift in the traditionally cautious line pursued by big business towards the government.*

Resentment on the part of industry grew against the government and led to closer ties with Congress. B. R. Tomlinson, a historian, credits a group of industrialists, which included G. D. Birla, Sir Purshottamdas Thakurdas, and J. R. D. Tata, with presenting in 1944 the most complete survey of India's postwar economic requirements, as well as detailed planning to achieve them.

Tomlinson writes that the industrialists began to regard Congress, rather than the British, "as the body best able and most willing to secure for them a place in the domestic economy and polity they desired." From 1944 onwards, business interests openly supported Congress. It was clear that big business, including Birla, would stand to profit by independence.

There was a major obstacle remaining in Birla's path. Jawaharlal Nehru, as president of the Congress in 1936, put forward two proposals. The first was to establish a joint anti-imperialist front. He was willing to yoke himself to any sympathetic party for this cause, including Madan Mohan Malaviya, whom Nehru had criticized for the communal politics of his Nationalist Party. Nehru's other proposal was the affiliation of trade and peasant unions to the Congress. Nehru in his presidential speech at the Lucknow Congress presented his plea for radical changes in the status quo of India:

> *I see no way of ending the poverty, the vast unemployment, the degradation and the subjection of the Indian people except through socialism. That involves vast and revolutionary changes in our political and social structure, the ending of vested interests in land and industry, as well as the feudal and autocratic Indian States system. That means the ending of private property, except in a restricted sense, and the replacement of the present profit system by a higher ideal of cooperative service.*

The outcome of the Lucknow Congress was that Nehru's idea of yoking the Congress to the unions was gently pushed aside to a committee who was to consider the matter. Satyamurti, a Congressman from Madras, announced that it was the triumph of Gandhi over socialism.

Birla had earlier tried to bring Nehru into his camp. When Nehru was having severe financial difficulties, Birla had offered him a handsome monthly allowance, such as the Birla family was providing Gandhi and other Congress leaders. Nehru was angry with the offer and refused it. Now Birla expressed his pleasure with Gandhi's victory over Nehru:

> *Mahatmaji kept his promise and without his uttering a word, he saw that no new commitments were made. Jawaharlalji's speech in a way was thrown into the waste paper basket because all the resolutions that were passed were against the spirit of his speech.*

A disappointed, but undeterred Nehru went on tour to promote his proposals. In Bombay, he was met with hostility by businessmen. On 20 May 1936, The Times of India published a response to Nehru's speech signed by twenty-one Bombay businessmen:

> *We are convinced that there is a grave risk of the masses of the country being misled by such doctrines into*

> *believing that all that is required for the improvement of their well-being is a total destruction of the existing social and economic structure. The inculcation of any such ideas into the mind of unthinking millions of this country would lead to a situation in which not only the institution of private property but the peaceful observance of religion, and even personal safety, are likely to be jeopardized. The business communities and the propertied classes of this country played not a small part in the furtherance of the national movement for the achievement of political freedom and have supported all practical measures for the amelioration of the lot of the toiling masses of this country.*

Birla himself avoided a public confrontation with Nehru. In a letter to one of the signers of the Bombay businessmen's manifesto, he criticized the open display of hostility towards Nehru's policies:

> *You have rendered no service to your caste men. It is curious how we businessmen are so short-sighted.... It looks very crude for a man with property to say that he is opposed to expropriation in the wider interest of the country.*

Birla's preferred method was to quietly strengthen the opposition to Nehru by bolstering the non-revolutionary, right-wing elements in the anti-British camp. He left it to Vallabhbhai Patel, Rajendra Prasad, Rajagopalachari, and Gandhi to criticize Nehru for taking it on himself to try to push forward his minority viewpoint against propertied interests to the forefront of Congress policies.

Gandhi's friendship with Birla endured until Gandhi's assassination at the Birla mansion in Delhi in January 1948. Gandhi has come to be remembered as a saint and leader of the Indian nationalist movement. He is not remembered as a supporter of capitalism and social conservatism. History's memory of Birla is somewhat fainter. After all, an industrialist is an industrialist. It is noted to his credit that he was also a devotee of Gandhi. This recollection distorts what transpired between Gandhi and Birla, as well as neglects their mutual influences. The relationship between the two men was too complex to be reduced to simple manipulation on the part of either. Theirs was a friendship involving an interplay of nationalism, social conservatism, the exigencies of business, politics, and patronage, as well as shared membership in mercantile castes, religion, and genuine affection.

The relationship between Gandhi and Birla reveals that Gandhi in many ways supported capitalism and policies that were favourable to the industrialists, particularly in respect to his teachings on trusteeship. It cannot be denied that Gandhi and Birla had a hand in the fact that after independence there was no social revolution and the socialist aspirations of Nehru were discouraged. When one reads a letter from Birla written as early as 1942 calling for the formation of Pakistan, and further mentioning that Gandhi told Birla at that time that he was willing to be converted to the idea, ones wonders if the full extent of Birla's influence is yet to be told.

6

DR. AMBEDKAR FOR MOVEMENT OF DALITS

Various icons that the post-Ambedkar movement of dalits appear to have built up, characterise Ambedkar as the maker of the Indian Constitution, provider of the present order, a Bodhisatva, a constitutionalist, a messiah, a saviour, an SC leader, a liberal democrat, a staunch anti-Communist, a social engineer who believed in the reform process and disliked revolutions. It is heavily sculpted by the petty-bourgeoisie outlook that has completely hegemonised the Dalit movement. It rarely reflects the dreamer in him who was perpetually in search of ways and means to see the human society sans exploitation, injustice and humbug.

Many students of the Dalit movement are influenced by these post-Ambedkar reflections in characterising Ambedkar as the bourgeoisie liberal democrat. Does it really project what Ambedkar stood for? Does it capture the full essence of his movement? More importantly, is that the Ambedkar whom we are going to use as the weapon in the emancipatory struggle of dalits?

Dalits as a social group, are still the poorest of poor. A negligible minority has managed to escape poverty limits and to locate itself on to a continuum ranging up to a reasonable level of prosperity with the help of certain State policies like reservation and political patronage. In social terms however, all dalits, irrespective of their economic standing, still suffer oppression. This social oppression varies from the crudest variety of untouchability, still being practised in rural areas, to the sophisticated forms of discrimination encountered even in the modern sectors of urban life. Although, the statistics indicate that dalits have made significant progress on almost all parameters during the last five decades, the relative distance between them and non-dalits seems to have remained the same or has increased. More than 75 per cent of the Dalit workers are still connected with land; 25 per cent being the marginal and small farmers and the balance 50 per cent being landless labourers.

The proportion of dalits landless labourers to the total labourers has shown a steady rising trend. In urban areas, they work mainly in the unorganised sector where the exploitation compares well with that of a feudal rural setting. Out of the total Dalit population of 138 million, the number of dalits in services falling in the domain of reservations does not exceed 1. 3 million including sweepers; less than even a percent. And this too would be grossly misleading, as out of this 1. 3 million the relatively well-off group A and B officers (in which most of the clerical staff of the PSUs also come), count only 72, 212 as against 131, 841, sweepers.

With the new politico-economic order emerging in the world, the grammar of the Dalit liberation struggle is going to be totally different from that familiar to dalits. The onslaught of the adversarial forces is being felt world over by all the oppressed people and it would be folly for dalits not to feel a part of the latter. Their objective situation as a social block is not represented by the minuscule minority that managed to find themselves in the organised sectors of economy, but by the vast majority who are left behind in the villages or the numbers who toil in the unorganised sectors in towns and cities. They need the weaponry for battling out their salvation. This battle is to be waged simultaneously on two fronts, marked by the caste and class.

These terms under segmented and sectarian usage came to bear an erroneous exclusivity. Since, Ambedkar still provides a better framework for their problems than any other, and since he commands an unchangeable place in their hearts, the weapons in his armoury needs dusting and sharpening. They will need a review for their effective application in the changing context and possibly, substantial supplementation and replenishment. Ambedkar, quite similar to Buddha in his own hands, needs redefinition. The folklore 'Ambedkar' needs to be replaced by the radical 'Ambedkar', who would inspire people to claim the whole world as theirs and not to beg for petty favours from the robbers.

It is the responsibility of all those who are capable of seeing the reality, to contribute to this task. For, without such a redefinition, Ambedkar could be fossilised as god but would fail in the emancipation project; he might be raised to the highest pedestal by the vested interests but then he would be unable to reach out to where he is most needed; he would lose out to the parody of history.

REDEFINING AMBEDKAR

Ambedkar's thoughts are variously presented by scholars. Some tend to put them in familiar academic slots, *viz.* : social, political, economic, religious etc. The other method may be bracketed as biographical. The problem with the former is that it tends to discretise his thoughts within the artificial compartments of academic disciplines. The latter tends to be narrational, eulogical and scarcely analytical. Both of them are likely to miss out the underscoring vision and more so the futuristic dimension, which are essentially the attributes of the holistic conception.

VISIONS AND ICONS OF GREAT PERSON

Every great person has a vision that impels all her/his works. Its discernibility may vary from case to case, generally being the function of the degree of turbulence around her/him, her/his relative position within the power structure in the given environment, her/his own equipment and conception of self-role.

Marx, for instance, offers an articulate vision in clearest terms as he assumed the primary role of a philosopher to bring about revolutionary change, whereas Ambedkar had donned the mantle of mass-leadership in his primary role to spearhead the change; the degree of turbulence in the work domain of Marx had been minimal as he basically struggled in the realm of thought spanning complete human history whereas Ambedkar situated himself in the political turbulence that obtained in

India as his strategy; Ambedkar's position in the power structure that bounded his work domain was certainly weak relative to Marx's. This is neither to undermine the role of Marx as the activist constantly trying out his philosophy in the realm of practice nor to belittle the problems he suffered in life. With regard to personal equipment, both Ambedkar as well as Marx, could be taken to be equally equipped to undertake their respective tasks that they had undertaken.

Marx had started off with philosophy and adopted the class-consciousness of the proletariat quite unlike Ambedkar, in whose case it was his own consciousness-the consciousness of an untouchable built up through concrete experience that had propelled his philosophical search. Marx was well aware of his role in the revolutionary project, that he had to provide requisite tools and tackles for the working class for bringing about a change in the overall interest of humanity.

But, Ambedkar was always loaded with anxiety as he had to strategize his way through the political maze around him, winning for dalits the maximum he could in a short span of time. In process, his role also underwent transformation with the expanse of the battleground. Inevitably, his thoughts and action always remained context-laden, polemical and pragmatically purposeful. It is therefore a relatively difficult task to discern a coherent vision underscoring the life work of Babsaheb Ambedkar.

It is a moot point as to what extent a great person, who is essentially anchored in her/his space and time, could transcend these barriers and be equally effective in a different situation. A great person basically is the product of prevailing social relations. It is a particular moment in history that reflects an acute demand for such a person. Depending upon her/his location in the social setting, she imparts her/his individual feature to the historical moments and movements in terms of working out specific means for resolving contradictions that engender them and releasing the forces of history in a specific direction.

The masses whose cause she/he espouses throng around her/him in this process, depending upon the level of their collective consciousness. The longevity of the ideas a great person propounds in a historical setting depends upon the nature of contradictions, the size and expanse of problems and the time domain in which they are situated. Generally, the classes that share the vision and ideology of such persons tend to iconise them with specific attributes of their class choice, in an attempt to institutionalise the latter.

In this process, they would de-contextise some of the ideas and proffer them as universal theorems, if they perceive a pay-off for themselves in the sphere hegemonised by them. This phenomenon becomes clear only over a long time horizon. For instance, the religious principles that were sprouted in the soil of certain specific social relations have basically blossomed in an alien soil with the help of the nutrients of class interests. Very broadly speaking, the trend of iconisation of great persons and the attempt of institutionalising their ideas is a gauge to assess the forces of status quo in the society.

AMBEDKAR: COMMITMENT AND CONSTRAINT

In the case of Babasaheb Ambedkar, iconisation was inevitable. The combination of factors like his high stature, his devotion to the cause of his people; the historical setting in which he lived, the low level of literacy and political consciousness in masses; and the vested interests of internal as well as external people have been its cause. The problem is not with iconisation as it is with its multiplicity. A question may be pertinently asked can Ambedkar be uniquely represented by a single icon? As Prof. Upendra Bakshi had outlined in one of his articles during the centenary year of his birth anniversary that there were many Ambedkars and had questioned as to which Ambedkar do we commemorate? When he said so, Prof. Bakshi was referring to different facets of Ambedkar's personality that could be virtually segregated.

One can even periodise some of them. For example, the pre-1942 Ambedkar as a young, untouchable man endowed with highest scholastic distinctions, struggling within and without for the emancipation of his people is a grossly different personality than the Ambedkar as a member of the viceroy's Executive Council or the Ambedkar as the law minister in the Nehru cabinet in the post-independence India or the Ambedkar as the chairman of the drafting committee for the Indian Constitution or even the Ambedkar of still later years who had completely identified himself with Buddhism and in a way completely spiritualised himself.

What comes clearly however, from this review is that the changes in his outlook and role were essentially driven by his unstilted commitment to the cause of emancipation of oppressed humanity in general and dalits in particular. He might not have had appropriate methodological tools to deal with the problem at hand. With the equipment that basically belonged to a school of social engineers, he tried to dissect history. Paradoxically, he attempted to demolish the establishment with the very tools that were forged to serve the ruling classes. By training he did not have the facility to look at history as the continuum of human struggle with a certain inherent logic. He did use history as a repertoire of human episodes and attributed even logic to it but its source was externalised.

Non-Dialectical Solution: State and Religion

It appears that Babasaheb Ambedkar had really internalised the doctrine of momentariness (Anityatawad and later Kshanikwad) of Buddha and therefore even refused to care for consistency in his views and opinions. This doctrine states that every thing changes every moment, that things are constantly becoming. It follows that in this situation of flux not even mental processes could be static, they had essentially to match the dynamicity of the material world. He thus never hesitated in changing his thoughts or strategy as per the unfolding situation. Viewed another way, these changes can be understood in relation to foci of control.

The degree of consistency in thought and action is generally inversely proportional to the distance of the subject from the foci of control of its surrounding. Ambedkar had nil or little control over his situation. He had to consistently create space for himself and strategize to influence the situation to his advantage. (The dynamics of the situation was propelled by the forces that were variously placed in the adversary camps.) The framework within which he conceived his struggle had exposed him to his lot to respond to this dynamics. The hallmark of Ambedkar's thoughts is the dynamic rationale, which he has consistently employed to comprehend situations and to strategize his response thereto. 'Ambedkar' therefore cannot be captured in static terms. His icon will have to represent the dynamism that he lived. Since, this is an infeasible proposition; we will have to discern the underscoring vision behind his works, the intransient essence of his entire mission to create a suitable icon. This icon, even if it does not resemble the familiar Ambedkar, alone could be the beacon of the Dalit movement.

The concept of Anityawad in Buddhism essentially belongs to dialectics that has made Buddha an early dialectician philosopher. The dichotomy that creeps in can only be resolved by dialectical method. It may be questioned whether Ambedkar's method was dialectical. It appears that while he accepts constant becoming of things as the principle underscoring the universe, he faces a dilemma with respect to the conception of order in this State. It could be resolved dialectically in terms of systemic attribute of self-regulation-a characteristic of internal control. But the conventional conception of order, essentially a non-dialectical conception, leads to externalisation of control.

Ambedkar, having experienced the brutal aspects of history and unbridled exploitation of man by man, appears in need of a control mechanism operating at two levels, *viz.*, internal and external, so as to maintain the societal order in the desired State. His internal control mechanism is the moral code provided by the religion and the one for external control is the State. If this moral code is internalised by all individuals and in turn by society as the summation of the latter (as the liberal tradition held), society is expected to have an internal order.

If however the baser instincts of some people or group of people defy this order, either as a result of conflicting codes they follow or for any other reason, then in such case the State will step in and restore the order. The will of the collective is supposed to be embodied in the State by the Constitution. It is therefore that Ambedkar has reservation in agreeing with Marx that 'religion was the opium of masses' or the 'State shall eventually wither away'. Ambedkar certainly did not know that the order could be the attribute of the system itself. It is only in the sixties that Cybernetics principles came to lime light that the complex probabilistic systems, which the social systems certainly are, do have the inherent capability of self-regulating and self-organising control.

LIBERALISM AND REFORMISM

By upbringing and training Ambedkar was influenced by western liberalism. The openness and liberal values of the western society had struck him with pleasant surprise by his own admission. There is a reason to believe that he had studied Marxism. His first essay on caste reflects some amount of analytical orientation of Marxism. One of the subjects in his curriculum also happened to be related to Marxian socialism and his guide Prof. Seligman was well versed with the economic interpretation of history. However, as his later work reveals, Ambedkar reflected more closeness with the liberal tradition than Marxism. However, consciously he never identified himself with the Liberalism. Being aware of its pitfalls, he needed to declare that he was not a liberal reformist, although while having reservations with the postulations of Marxism he could never hide his attraction towards it.

The pitfall of his thinking emanates from his conception of the moral force of religion divorced from the material reality. He therefore hopes that without any bloodshed, the society based on liberty, equality and fraternity could be created. Of course as hypothesized above, he conceptualizes the constitutional State based on these principles. With this wishful thinking, he tends to ignore the fact that regardless of the pretensions of ruling classes, the impact of liberal governance in the multicentric iniquitous society is bound to result in sustaining multicentricity and inequality.

This liberalism rather promotes politics of casteism and communalism, schism among dalits, their use in political power games, subversion of their real problems and protects the interests of the few rich. It was a kind of contradiction in terms to assume that liberal democracy, which is actually the manifestation of the political power of the bourgeois, will do justice to the paupers. It might appear to extend certain concessions to the weaker sections, but its real motive is to maintain the existing rule of the ruling classes. Liberal democracy might appear better than the decadent Hindu caste system but it is incapable of bringing any real change in favour of dalits. It muffles the tension of the exploitative system and kills the revolutionary motivation of its victims.

Redefinition Project

Many of the constructs employed by Babasaheb Ambedkar in his working have a qualified meaning. Firstly, they are not absolute as they appear. They are the derivatives of his thought process, the source of which could be traced to his basic objective of annihilation of castes and creating a society based on equality, liberty and fraternity. Even these three principles that he held so dear to his heart, bear very different meaning from the familiar ones associated with the French Revolution. He said he had them from Buddha.

What Buddha said also is to be understood from his interpretation, which could be as different from the accepted version as to be disproved by the Buddhist church. His Buddha and His Dhamma, for instance, had faced this kind of disapproval initially from many Buddhists. Understanding Ambedkar thus essentially demands extra consideration and care about the specific meanings of the constructs and concepts he uses. The lack of it has already caused much misunderstanding among many people. It is one thing to have a clear understanding of what he said or meant but quite another to extrapolate it to something congruent to his basic objective or vision that may be useable in shaping the future movement. Quite like Marx had said of philosophy, it could be said that the issue is not to understand Ambedkar as he is but to possibly think of him as a weapon in the struggle to which he devoted his life.

The redefinition referred to here will have to essentially address both these issues. From the viewpoint of one seeking a revolutionary change, there are indeed many dimensions on which Ambedkar calls for critical interpretation. Many of the concepts that seem to act as the props for his formulations are rooted in the reactionary camp. Paradoxically, he brings them to work for his emancipatory project, which potentially is no less than a revolution. Predominant among these concepts are identified as State, religion, liberal democracy, constitutionalism, revolution, socialism, violence and Marxism, that some way or the other have been the cause of misunderstandings about him.

It is important to appreciate that Ambedkar employed the search process that is essentially rational and the underlying objective undoubtedly radical. There could be flaws in the specific design or the application of the search process, depending upon the State of his knowledge and complexity of the situation to which it is applied. Besides this, the end result depends upon the repertoire of alternatives used for the search. What it means is that the specific method, thought or action of Ambedkar may constitute the historical facts but they cannot be taken in their face value if one wants to comprehend the ideological aspects of Ambedkar.

In his usage of the above concepts for instance he does not always exercise the academic rigour. Besides the reason that much of his usage was addressed to the un-academic lot, most of the times he tended to impart his own meanings to the terms he used. With the changed contexts or with the change in information, he readily changed his opinions. For, hypothetically speaking, if Ambedkar had lived longer he would have certainly changed his views, looking at more information available or experiencing the undesired aftermath of some of his own beliefs and opinions.

Had he not disowned the Constitution, which he had so laboriously written and so forcefully defended, saying that he was used as the hack to write it? Whatever he had done had several limitations. He never hesitated to change his opinion or stand if he was convinced that it was right. The redefinition project proposed here, in a way, is something, which he has done himself, all his life and would have continued doing if he had been alive. It is essentially something in the nature of continuing his unfinished task.

The methodological aspects of this exercise consists in the process of conceptualisation of the core vision and ideological proclivities of Ambedkar through the analytical study of his life within its contextual parameters, oriented towards capturing its intransient content. It should reflect the basic purpose, that is, to see whether and how he could catalyse the emancipatory movement of dalits and in turn democratise the Indian society. This process may not be free from bias. The bias could be in favour of the change craved for by the have-nots, not of the ruling classes that has necessarily been colouring the history so far. It cannot escape the viewpoint of the latter. The viewpoint is rather embodied in the basic intention to forge Ambedkar as the weapon for the future struggles of dalits.

The process of conceptualisation may be formalised by drawing out multiple ideological patterns based upon the constituent parameters of the hypothesised vision and testing them with the facts in their macro and micro settings. The test results could be used to refine the definition of the parameters and repeating the exercise until they can no more be improved. The iterative process will eliminate the tactic-based episodes and increasingly highlight the intransient dimensions. The radicalisation consists in derivation of the programme from these dimensions with any scientific methodology.

It is not possible to demonstrate adoption of this methodology within the space of this paper. The following discussion therefore directly deals with the salient dimensions of Ambedkar's life in order to capture its intransient essence.

'AMBEDKAR' FOR THE MOVEMENT OF DALITS

'Ambedkar' for the Dalit movement, first of all, should be shorn of all the sectarian outlook that unfortunately came to be associated with him. He was an iconoclast and therefore should inspire us to break such icons that are imbued with this outlook. Dalits have to demolish all the handiwork of the reactionaries and vested interests. The project of redefinition of Ambedkar should liberate him from the dens of the ruling class and bring him back to the huts in slums and villages where he rightly belongs.

The greatest thing about Ambedkar is his consistent anti-dogmatic stance. He never accepted any thing in name of authority. He hated humbug of every kind. He always approached problems with a student's sincerity and researcher's intellectual honesty. He gave a vision that even the ideologies are bound by the tenet of impermanence and no body should claim them validity beyond their times. His followers therefore can assume absolute liberty to think through things as per their own experience in changing times. Here, we can discuss certain issues, clarity on which may contribute to this task.

'AMBEDKAR' AGAINST EXPLOITATION

The underscoring vision in Ambedkar's thought and action is to be found in his yearning for the end of all kinds of exploitation. Whenever and wherever he smelt exploitation, he raised his voice against it. The caste system that subjugated more than one fifth of the population to levels worse than animals' for more than two millennia and which represented institutionalisation of the most heinous inequality by the Hindu religion as ordained by its gods, became the prime target of his life. He attacked it from the standpoint of its victims-the untouchables.

He waged many battles; initially targeting the citadels of Brahmanism-the custodian of the Hindu religious code, and later politicised the battle, realising the ineffectiveness of the former. He did not let this objective out of sight even for a moment and worked incessantly for its achievement. This Herculean task almost completely overshadows the fact that his struggles extend well beyond the caste struggles and rather encompass all other forms of exploitation.

Even the credit for struggling against untouchability was reluctantly granted to him by the establishment which had belittled him initially as merely a leader of his own caste-Mahar. This prejudicial treatment of Ambedkar could itself be taken as a measure of the severity of the problematic of caste. The facts are clear today that not only was his struggle directed towards the emancipation of all the untouchables but also towards annihilation of the entire caste system. It was basically against the systemic exploitation that ran unabated for centuries. The protest against this inhuman system could be articulated only in a concrete situation, not in a vacuum. He did not theorise the struggle on a hypothetical plane. He built it on the basis of real problems in a concrete situation.

Unlike many cases, the motive force for his life mission was provided by his experience itself. Although he pitched his tents against Brahmanism, he never bore any enmity against the Brahmins or identified any one for his friend or foe by caste. The Bahishkrit Hitkarini Sabha that was the launch vehicle of his movement had majority from the forward caste people in its executive body. Even later, this intention of having a non-caste base for the organisation could be consistently seen in his movement, be it the Mahad struggle or the Indian Labour Party. He was perceptive enough to say that the Brahmanism could exist in all the castes including the untouchables, for that was the essence of the casteism. It is tragic to find his legacy being monopolised today by only the scheduled castes.

Although, he considered the magnitude of the problem of emancipation of dalits is such as to warrant his sole attention, he did take cudgels for other oppressed entities like workers, peasants and women. At one occasion in response to the accusation that he did not care for the tribals, he had to squarely admit the fact that he considered the problem at hand big enough to outlast his life and provokedly put that he never claimed to fight for whole humanity. Such instances though disturbing enough could be understood within their specific context. While dealing with the socioeconomic depravation of dalits, he comprehensively exposed certain systemic dimensions that help perpetuate exploitation. For instance, he was well aware of the capitalist and imperialist oppression besides the decadent feudalism within which domain his problem lay.

Capitalism

During the colonial British regime, capitalism started taking root in India with the collaboration of Indian mercantile capital and British capital. Unlike Europe, it did not have to battle against feudalism; rather it was implanted on the trunk of the latter in India. As a result, even in the capitalist institutions in the cities, caste discrimination simultaneously existed. Ambedkar was quite aware of the exploitative potential of capital and hence he had declared capitalism and Brahmanism as the twin enemy of his movement. Capitalism was in an infantile stage then but Brahmanism encompassed the phases of slavery, feudalism and extended its tentacles as we see to the phase of imperialism.

Moreover, he noted the reactionary compradore character of rising capitalism in the contemporary sectors of the economy and the inhuman exploitation of workers that it unleashed. His, Indian Labour Party (ILP) was an attempt to take up the question of capitalist exploitation, as well as to combine the struggle on both caste and class basis. Various workers' problems were taken up by the ILP, the leadership of combined strike of the mill workers, parliamentary fight for the workers' interest in relation to the Industrial Disputes Act, and various legal reforms that were brought about while he was in the Executive Council of the Viceroy, can be the examples of his concern for workers' exploitation. It cannot be denied that his approach to these contemporary problems was closer to that of the Fabian socialists with whom he was more familiar.

But, it was a model adopted out of familiarity and pragmatism, a matter of strategy, never thought out on an ideological plane to be a theoretical plank. Although, there cannot be any doubt that he stood against capitalism, he could not articulate a sound theoretical basis for doing so. Resultantly, his efforts remained constricted with a short view of workers' welfare but could not provide them a vision of their liberation.

Imperialism

Ambedkar's attitude towards imperialism has been projected in a distorted manner right from the beginning, mainly because he refused to take part in the freedom struggle or opposed Gandhi who for certain category of ignoramuses was the anti-imperialism personified. He strategically sought to maintain neutrality vis-a-vis the colonial State. As per him, it would not be possible for the resourceless dalits to fight its mighty foes all together. He did not want to dissipate and squander his extremely limited resources on several fronts. He however knew the basic exploitative character of the colonial regime. At several occasions, he burst out saying that British imperialism and Indian feudalism were the two leaches that clung to Indian people. (BB, 58 (8)). However, there was a fundamental difference between his and others' viewpoint. For instance, he did not approve equating opposition to imperialism with opposing the British. He noted that the opposition to imperialism couldn't be effective until its supporters within the country are left untouched.

The then leader of the Communist Party of India-Manabendranath Roy once met him at his residence and during discussions insisted that destruction of imperialism had to be the first and foremost objective of Indian politics. Ambedkar's response to him summarised his outlook towards this problem. He replied to Roy in explicit terms that without struggling against the landlords, mill owners, moneylenders-the friends of imperialism within the country, it was not possible to wage an effective fight against imperialism. It may be a matter of research but a priori his anti-imperialist attitude pervades even his writings as a student.

The validation of his stand comes from an entirely unrelated corner and nearly half a century later. Suniti Kumar Ghosh, (1985 and 1995) in his books has shown in great detail how the Congress representing landlords and capitalists had played a compradore role to serve the interest of imperialism during the so-called freedom struggle and how even after the transfer of power in 1947 the grip of imperialism instead of weakening became stronger. Does it not indicate that he was more correct than any of his contemporary politicians?

The ones who biasedly wish to pronounce their half baked verdict that Ambedkar was a stooge of British merely on the basis of his acceptance of membership of Viceroy's Executive Council or talking to the Simon Commission, not only display their ignorance of history but also their casteist fangs. They ought to rethink the comparison between Ambedkar who, even being apparently a part of the imperialist apparatus was perhaps striking at its roots by empowering the people and many others, so called nationalists, who after wearing the mask of anti-imperialism were indirectly strengthening its pillars.

In relation to British rule, Ambedkar basically makes two points. The first is that he questions the so-called freedom struggle launched under the leadership of Congress as an anti-imperialist struggle. He contended that the Congress basically represented the class of feudal lords and the urban capitalists-the twosome exploiters of Indian masses. Although, it succeeded through the charismatic leadership of Gandhi in galvanising masses in its support, it essentially relied on bargaining with the colonial rulers for securing itself more share of power. It always throttled the mass spontaneity as in the case of 1942-uprisings and actively opposed the genuine anti-imperialist struggles of the revolutionaries like Bhagat Singh. Ambedkar reflects the understanding of true character of the Congress in his own way, when he says that if Congress was fighting a real anti-imperialist war, he would whole heartedly support it. The rhetoric of such statement apart, for he never appears to even take a note of other truly anti-imperialist struggles like the one referred to above, it is enough to reveal his attitude towards imperialism and understanding of the class character of the Congress. He knew that the class character of the Congress would not permit it to don this role in reality.

Ambedkar could see through the anti-imperialist masks the real fangs of an exploiter of masses. He thus not only saw no point in siding with this more real exploiter of people than perhaps the colonial rulers, but also did not hesitate to openly oppose it when it came in the way of Dalit liberation. He smelt rot in all such struggles that refused to notice existence of inhuman exploitation of some of their own people within their precincts and tended to over-externalise their woes. Here lay his second point when he raised a question of Hindu imperialism perpetrated through its caste system that was certainly seen as more vicious by its victims than the British rule. It may be pertinent to ask of those who raise the issue of Ambedkar's attitude and conduct towards imperialism, to answer as to why the problem of untouchability or caste system that reduced its one-fifth of the population to subhuman levels did not find a mere mention in the lofty discussions of freedom struggle that pre-dated Ambedkar's raising it.

The anti-imperialist aspiration also could be seen in the context of the class/caste division in the society. The battle for the lost kingdom waged by the vanquished lords also could be camouflaged as an anti-imperialist struggle and at the same time the genuine peoples' anti-imperialist aspiration manifested in the form of say anti-feudal struggle could be condemned as the pro-imperialism, merely because it directed its gun towards the props of the imperialism. The real anti-imperialist aspirations belong to the masses of people the manifestation of which is possible only through the peoples' war. Whatever anti-imperialist struggle people waged were soon hijacked by the phoney war whose real intent was to extract political power to native ruling classes. While the scenes of anti-British struggles were being enacted for the 'mother' India of exploiters, Ambedkar busied himself to liberate the other India-the India of the exploited and oppressed.

Oppression of Women

Besides these mainstream forms of exploitation even the subaltern forms like women's exploitation, could not escape his agenda. He viewed them as the most oppressed of all. His approach to the problems was typically that of a liberal democrat constitutionalist. This certainly constrained his articulation of this problem as in many others. This issue will have to be seriously rethought by dalits under the redefinition project. But suffice here to say that at any opportunity, he raised his voice against women's discriminatory situation in the society. His basic law of social engineering was that the social revolutions must always begin from the standpoint of the most oppressed or the ones on the lowest rung of the society.

Right from the days of Mook Nayak and Bahiskrit Bharat, he appears to take cudgels for women. He always involved women in his struggles and tended to give them vanguard positions. For example, about 500 women had marched at the head of the historical procession at Mahad to assert the untouchables' right to drink water from the public tank. He was immensely pained to see the permanent denial of education and religious rights to women ordained in the Shastras of the Hinduism (*e.g.* Manu Smriti). His democratic consciousness never reconciled with any thing lesser than the equality of men and women though its expression was acutely constrained perhaps by his anxieties about the possibilities, so much so that it might even be mistaken as the male centric tactic.

While he asked women to be good mothers so as to shape up their son or to be good wives to their husbands or be a carrier of community's cultural baggage, he did struggle for their equal rights as in the case of Hindu Code Bill. He described sacramental marriages (Mathew, 1991) as polygamy for men and perpetual slavery for women because under no circumstances within that system the latter would get liberty from their husbands, however bad or undesirable they may be. He insisted that women should have the freedom to break this contract.

7

AMBEDKAR—COMMITMENT AND CONSTRAINT

CONSTITUTION: AN EXERCISE IN LIBERAL DEMOCRACY

Although, Ambedkar was conscious of the limitations of liberal democracy in the emancipatory project he had undertaken and at times had even declared that he was not a liberal democrat, for many reasons he could not escape its clutches completely. He could not be unaware that liberal democracy basically was born as the ruling class ideology in 19th century Europe. It takes individuals and their groups as basically selfish units as its premise. It holds that individuals and social groups progress only through competition. It had however to take cognizance of weaker sections in the society, paradoxically in a large number, who cannot enter this competition openly and hence could be potentially be spoilers of the game.

The French Revolution had demonstrated this potential in ample measure. As the Whigs in the English Liberal party had thought "the best way to ward off revolution was to adopt a liberal generous attitude toward the lower classes. The upper classes should make concessions gracefully and in good time, and not wait until the lower classes are roused to exact them. If a revolution happens, it doesn't show that the people are bad and should have been repressed more thoroughly... repression is self-defeating. What it shows is that the upper classes were not wise enough and self-confident enough to make reasonable concessions in good time." It accommodates the relatively weaker sections by extending them some concessions or aids for some time, basically to equip them for this universal competition. The State performs the role of a referee in this competition. This State is supposed to be run by the representatives of all the social groups. Notwithstanding his awareness of the above facts, Ambedkar's schema does reflect the expectation that the State would perform the role of independent referee.

The influence of liberalism on Ambedkar is more pronounced after he accepted the role of the chairman of the drafting committee for the Indian Constitution in collaboration with the Congress. In the light of his own proposals of State socialism submitted to the Constituent Assembly on behalf of the Scheduled Caste Federation, this ideological somersault could only be understood as the situational compulsions acting upon him. Just before entering the Constituent Assembly he had experienced the bitter phase of political oblivion and had seen from closer angles the prospect of his life's mission ending without any result. He had a dire need to enter the Constituent Assembly and include certain provisions for his people in the future Constitution.

When Congress offered him this role, he had to perform it within bounds in exchange for his life's ambition to provide for his people. The compulsions are too obvious to be ignored. His States and Minorities envisages most of the productive assets to be the State property. This was against the principle of liberal democracy. The liberal theory of property right from the days of John Locke and Thomas Hobbes in the 17th century stressed on private property and on the duty of the government to protect it. It was the Congress liberalism that he had to submit to and had to plead for property rights that were considered pivotal within the Constitution.

The same holds true for the centralization of power and certain basic rights, which were congenial to the capitalist class. He had to accept all such provisions that considered the existing power structure from status quo viewpoint instead of transformation. He was compelled to accommodate the principles of social democracy, which he has been regarding as the basic soul into the ineffective chapter of the directive principles of the constitution. He himself had to accept the same parliamentary executive that he had always misgivings about as being dangerous to the life and freedom of ex-untouchables.

He could not be unaware of the fact that from the viewpoint of the oppressed and dalits, except for the reservations, the Constitution was not making any material difference. On the contrary, it had made all the arrangements for letting all the benefits of power stay with the wealthy and traditional elite classes while dangling the carrot of Constitutional safeguards and reservations for dalits and the oppressed people. The existing socioeconomic structure was kept in tact in the Constitution underneath the western democracy which proclaimed the principle of 'one vote, one value' in political arena.

Ambedkar could not hide his discomfort at this dichotomy and had to burst out in his famous warning that if equality in the socioeconomic sphere is not achieved within a reasonable time, the disadvantaged people would blast off the structure of the political democracy. He was aware of the fallacy in the assumption that political democracy would catalyze the social revolution through universal franchise and periodic elections. He had himself tested the bitter fruits of this process through the electoral defeats. Politics run on the principles of free market economy can never entail equality.

The slogans like socialism, social justice, equality etc. were merely masks to fool the people. The grammar of the game of electoral politics foreordained the politicians serving the interests of big landlords, capitalists and compradore bourgeoisie. They could not survive free political competition without the latter's blessings. Ambedkar should have been aware that liberal values and liberal institutions are incapable of arresting the monopolistic hold of the moneyed classes on political power.

On Revolution

Revolution, on the face of it, appears to be an anathema to Ambedkar who seems to dread it and instead advocates reforms. But it would be disaster to take it at face value. For, like many other terms, his usage of the term 'revolution' does not bear the same meaning as is in vogue, particularly in Marxist circles. What Ambedkar seems to detest in revolution is the violence. At many places he tends to equate rebellion, revolution and revolt with violence. He also seems to disagree with the method of insurrection. He thought that without mass consciousness being ripe enough for revolutionary change, insurrectionary methods would not succeed.

Moreover, he appears to be sceptical of the justness of revolutions as they invariably represent the triumph of the collective over the individual. It may be attributed to the influence of liberal democracy in which he got his indoctrination in his formative days. Liberal democracy always put an individual on a high pedestal and considered it precious. His concern for the individual is not again doctrinaire but emanates from the value that any and every human being is precious and the belief that alone can act as the best guarantee against the collective tyranny and totalitarian excesses any time.

In the context of the collapse of erstwhile Soviet block, where the totalitarian states that came into being in the name of dictatorship of proletariat and played havoc with people, this human-centric value assumes importance. One needs to be however reminded that even the values do need to have some material bases. They do not fall from sky. The contradiction between collective and individual has thus to be resolved in the concrete situation. As for Ambedkar, apart from this scepticism, he does not seem to have any dispute with the general aim and object of revolution.

Revolution, inasmuch as it seeks to bring about a fundamental change in the social relations in the society, will always be opposed by the forces of status quo, whose material interests are directly threatened by this change. In corollary, it becomes imperative for the forces of revolution to overcome this resistance whatever be the means. Whereas, the antagonist camp will always project codes of ethics and morality for their tactical defence in face of the onslaught of revolution, the revolutionaries discard them as decadent; for them revolution itself represents the highest value. Being the upsurge of the suppressed ones, revolutions do have a tendency to be bloody, but it is always in response to the resistance of its opponents.

Therefore it is a representation only by the vested interest to associate violence or moral turpitude with revolutions. On the contrary, it would be more logical to say about the revolutionaries that being propelled by an external motivation to deliver mankind from the existing traps at the risk of their own lives; they cannot be bloodthirsty people. The revolutionary violence is almost an inevitability that arises at the instance of the oppressors. In that sense Marx called "violence as the midwife of history", emphasising its inevitability. It is the inevitability that marks the compulsion of the vast majority of people to resist the anti-revolutionary violence of the minority. The pre-requisite here is that the revolution truly represents the majority consciousness. If it does not, then the violence of the few exercised with howsoever a lofty objective could transform into its anti-thesis, fortifying itself against the majority will. In this sense and insofar as the recent history showed the scepticism that revolutions trample upon individual's rights therefore cannot be dismissed as baseless.

Historically, revolution is the process of identifying and destroying the obstacles in the existing order to take productive forces to the qualitatively next higher level, for the overall progress of human race. The progress achieved by mankind so far is basically due to the qualitative transformation from quantitative continuum that characterises revolutions. The qualitative transformations always need concentrated inputs, akin to latent heat in the case of phase transformation of water. In social transformation it takes the form of revolutionary energy that in turn may manifest into violence. Ambedkar does not neglect the necessity of violence. As he himself said that if dalits wanted to be effective they would need the canons.

It is erroneous to construe that his opposition to violence was idealistic or doctrinaire. Violence was not a taboo for him; it could be practised when it was absolutely necessary. Even his mentor Buddha, who is respected as the greatest apostle of nonviolence had the same pragmatic approach towards violence. Ambedkar was not obsessed either with the idea of nonviolence or the value of individualism professed by the classical school of liberal democracy. His reservations were against the possibility of the cunning of a few overriding the will of majority as had happened in the case of caste institution. He would hate to see any thing like caste getting institutionalised again. In his scheme of things he therefore was not ready to compromise the value of democracy, the will of majority of people, whatever may be the end.

Ambedkar did not juxtapose reform against revolution, as many people tend to do. He does not reflect comprehension of technicality of dialectical materialism in his usage of these terms. Often his revolution is the violent overthrow of the existing rule and establishment of the new rule. Likewise, he does not seem to mean that reforms will not entail a qualitative transformation. What he certainly means by revolution is the change brought about in a 'big bang' manner. Notwithstanding what Ambedkar said about his own work, revolution does not always entail a 'big bang'; it is not a point concept as mistakenly regarded in common parlance, but a line concept. Mao's Great Proletarian Cultural Revolution may be a good example of this. There could be many bits of work, which contributes to taking society to a qualitatively higher rung in the ladder of progress that qualify to be the revolutionary work. The qualitative change itself occurs over a discrete time horizon and not a moment. The moment that marks out transformation of power and looks like a 'big bang', alone is not the revolution. The particular phase of history puts constraints on the kind of changes that can be conceived in its womb. Some one dreaming of a socialist revolution in the slave society would only at best be a daydreamer; a romanticist but he cannot be a revolutionary. Likewise, certain phase of history demands a lot of quantitative preparation before a revolutionary change can be planned for. Ambedkar largely reflects these kinds of concerns while dealing with the issue of revolution. He did not see Indian situation ripe enough for any revolutionary change. Any change without resolution of the caste question, according to him, would not only be detrimental to dalits but also be an extremely short-lived.

The importance of Ambedkar's work can be gauged in relation to contemporary social situation and its transitional social context. Indian society was ridden with a peculiar brand of feudalism, the most prominent feature of which was caste. Caste had incapacitated over 15 per cent of its population and maintained them at the subhuman level. The large part of the balance population also suffered the degradation in a varying degree. This decadent institution had far outlived its minimal utility and as a result for centuries kept Indian society in a fossilised form.

It served the material needs of a handful of people but all perceived varying stakes in the system on account of its hierarchical structure and faithfully practised it because they internalised it as their Dharma ordained by none other than God. The possible exception in generic terms were dalits who were placed at the lowest rung of the caste ladder and had hardly anything to their share. However, in particular terms only a few castes from the Dalit castes, who did not have any specific caste profession and hence little stake in the system and consequently who as the general workmen of villages had better exposure to the changing urban life than any one else came out of the hegemony of Brahmins to articulate the challenge to the system.

The hierarchy among dalits however prevented them to come together and consequently this challenge had to be articulated caste by caste. Capitalism that took root in India in big cities also had struck compromise with the caste institution like its harbingers, the British imperialism. It was an arduous task, as it still is, to conceive a model for this struggle and still more difficult to build. During the colonial times for various reasons these struggles had germinated largely in Maharashtra and Southern states where the social structure reflected sharper polarisation between dalits and balance society. Ambedkar's advent in the Indian sociopolitical scene marked their zenith.

It articulated its attack on Brahmanism and capitalism that accepted its alliance, focused its organisation on dalits and gave a clarion call for annihilation of castes for achieving the ultimate aim of society based on Liberty, Equality and Fraternity to provide wider umbrella for all progressive forces to work. It reflects the distinct historical need to democratise Indian society without which it was bound to suffer constriction of its productive forces. This work had to have large content in the sociocultural realm; it is a credit to Ambedkar's acumen that he gave it a political dimension. It had to be approached as reform. Ambedkar clearly found the talks of communist revolution as out of phase with the history although he never fully accepted the tenets of historical materialism as he thought it negatived human ingenuity and carried it through a predetermined channel. He insisted that India did not provide congenial soil for germination of class-consciousness because of castes. Their annihilation therefore constituted the first task in the revolutionary agenda.

It is unfortunate that many communist revolutionaries still parrot the same characterisation of his work as in years back their predecessors proclaimed using the spoon fed theories from the West. One day it is hoped that the contributions of all the caste struggles to democratisation of Indian society would be restored as a native revolutionary heritage by these well meaning people. Till then it will always sound puerile to pigeonhole the historical work as reform or revolution merely on the basis of syntax and not the content. However, it is much more unfortunate for Ambedkarite dalits to deny themselves the credit for this historical contributions by dissociating from the revolutionary agenda, mistakenly thinking that it something alien to them. Effectively, not only they are denying themselves a historical opportunity to contribute to revolution but also delaying their own emancipation.

Dalits have to rethink their position vis a vis revolution. Ambedkar's dream of a society based on liberty, equality and fraternity cannot be realised except through revolution. They will have to understand Ambedkar's life and mission only from this perspective. His contribution to Indian revolution lies in the fact that he tried to comprehend Indian reality independently and tried to contribute to the resolution of its contradictions in his own way. Indian history held out the gauntlet of fossilised Indian feudalism for so long to the Indian revolutionaries but every one conveniently wished it away, initially as a superstructural matter that would disappear automatically when the material base is revolutionised and now after seven decades as a problem belonging to both structure and superstructure, that could be solved through revolutionary practice.

It still lacks the clarity and courage to hold the bull by horn. Ambedkar did not confuse issues, he saw clearly that the annihilation of caste will have to be consciously worked for before taking up any revolutionary project. He went beyond and found out the institutional base of castes in the Indian village whose economic support lay in the land-relations and caste division of labour.

But, unlike many communists who still use the stereotype of land reform-a slogan of land to the tiller as the only revolutionary programme, he did not hamper on it because he knew that firstly it was economically impossible to satisfy the land hunger of the landless in the country, secondly the likely transformation of landless to a marginal farmer through land reforms was unlikely to solve the problems of dalits and thirdly, as the later empirical data showed, contrary to expectations the land reforms could aggravate the problem of caste. Instead, he proposed nationalisation of land and co-operativisation of farming. He realised the necessity of detaching substantial village population from land and absorbing it into the industrial sector that was to be mainly under State sector. Even in retrospect, these points could have constituted a viable agenda for democratic revolution. As one naxalite scholar-(Ashok Kumar, 1995) perceptively puts it, for having independently seen the question of annihilation of castes linked with the question of land one could unhesitatingly call Ambedkar as the torchbearer of the people's democratic revolution.

'AMBEDKAR' AS THE RADICAL THINKER

Dalits are never tired of projecting Ambedkar as the greatest of all the leaders. That unfortunately smacks of sectarian attitude and of their blind devotion to him. They need to understand that the measure of greatness of any person could only be her / his contribution to better the human situation, in terms of correct understanding of its ailment and contribution to cure it. What Ambedkar did could be seen in relation to the broad five currents in Indian politics of his times:

- The Reformists current that wanted to bring about development on the western pattern, possibly with the support of British imperialism,
- Congress, that represented Indian capital and which demanded self-rule under the domination of British imperialism,
- The Terrorist Nationalists who had taken up arms in their fight for freedom against British imperialism,
- The Communists who were trying to implant Bolshevik revolution in India, and
- The Muslim League which opened up a separatist front of Muslims.

All of them scarcely reflected an understanding of the Indian situation. For instance, none showed even a cursory concern about the problems of one fourth of their countrymen who were forced to live worse than animals as ordained by their decadent religion. It was indeed surprising that although all craved for self-rule from the British, none concerned with the caste-system which basically was responsible in pushing the country repeatedly into slavery. None seemed to attempt an objective analysis of either the history or the present of this country.

It could circumstantially be said that their motivations came from their narrow class-caste interests. These movements were motivated by the desire of an abstract freedom for country and a refusal to see the concrete slavery of their own people. Granted that the problems before the country were really intricate, still no one would dare say that the need for democratisation was in anyway subordinate. The real people's movement in the country was required to wage simultaneous war against imperialism, internal compradore bourgeoisie, landlords and Brahmanism.

It was only Ambedkar who clearly indicated this requirement. In this light, he was certainly ahead of all others. His own bitter experiences with untouchability had stood him in good stead in seeing this more clearly than any other. He strove to build his movement along this understanding but unfortunately it was neither in his power to deal comprehensively with all the issues, nor was there an ideological and programmatic clarity required therefore. He inevitably had to focus his attention on dalits who were the worst victims of this multifaceted oppression. It was the misfortune of Indian history that this struggle progressed in a constricted manner and eventually got dissolved into regressive statist politics. It reflected both the limitation of Ambedkar as well the situational compulsion on him.

The anti-caste movements before Ambedkar were mainly welfare oriented. Some wanted a higher rank for their own caste in the caste hierarchy and some taking the inferior culture of their caste to be the reason for their suffering, aimed at improving the same. Mahatma Phuley's movement was an exception to this trend insofar as it attempted to unite the Sudra and Ati-Shudra castes against the exploitation by the parasitic castes of Shetjis (capitalists) and Bhatjis (priests).

While Ambedkar accepted the lineage/inheritance of this movement and held Phuley in greatest esteem as his one of the three Gurus, he went beyond to declare annihilation of caste to be the object of his movement in the direction of the goal of 'liberty, equality and fraternity'.

In the historical context it certainly was a radical step. He rightly diagnosed that the caste system is basically sustained by the peculiar economic constitution of the Indian village of which the land relations were the main features. Towards breaking this link he toyed with an idea of separate settlement for dalits at one time and at another exhorted them to leave villages for cities. He had clearly understood that castes stood on multiple props, *viz.,* the religio-cultural relations, feudal relations in village setting of which land relations constituted the crux and the sociopolitical nexus with the State. Annihilation of castes thus needed destruction of all of them. He soon realised the necessity of political power for this multi-fronged attack. Even to bring about the residual change in the belief system either through the cultural or religious route, he stressed the necessity of political power. In this way, for the first time he brought the problem of untouchability and caste out of the confines of culture to the political agenda.

Unfortunately, this political agenda got lost into the maze of parliamentary politics that soon became be-all-end-all with Dalit leaders. Even during Ambedkar's times the economic aspects of the problem remained largely untouched giving the impression to his followers as though they did not count. In the overall context it can be seen that they could not be as easily dealt with as the religio-cultural and political aspects of the problem. Moreover, it meant direct confrontation with the State for which Ambedkar was certainly not prepared.

Alternately, the feudal relations in villages could be destroyed only if the private ownership of land is abolished and co-operativisation of farming is introduced. He thought, this structural change could be effected through the Constitution.

It was a folly that he would soon realise when even as the 'chief architect' of the Constitution he failed so much as to bring this point on the agenda of the Constituent Assembly.

Conception of an Ideal

Babasaheb Ambedkar envisioned his ideal in the famous three principles: liberty, equality and fraternity. They were the basis for the ideal society of his conception. (BAWS, 1/57). He denied that he had adopted them from the French Revolution. He said he had derived them from the teachings of Buddha. These principles were the clarion call of the French Revolution but later became the ideological props of the liberal bourgeoisie in Europe. Since Marx had ridiculed these principles as the fantasy of the bourgeois society, many people tended to stereotype Ambedkar as the petty-bourgeois liberal democrat.

As according to Ambedkar the source of these principles is different from the French Revolution, familiar to Marx, there is a prima facie scope to argue that Marx's ridicule does not apply to him. His conception of these principles is indeed substantially different from that associated with the liberal bourgeoisie. Actually, what Marx refers to are the slogans of liberty and equality of the bourgeois parliamentary democracy. There, 'liberty' is the liberty to contract and 'equality' refers to equality in market. Ambedkar insists that the conception of the ideal society ought to have them all the three together. Absence of any would not be acceptable to him.

The ideal society of his dream could only be seen within a kind of spiritual frame. It would be interesting to compare this society with the communist society of Marx's conception. Marx reached his inference following the dialectical track of historical materialism. In Ambedkar' case it was just his vision. Inevitably, he had to attribute the origin of them to some spiritual source. For Ambedkar they meant to denote the State of society sans exploitation and with an emotive ambience of fellow feeling. It was beyond him to describe this State further in concrete terms and much so to indicate the forms of struggle to reach it. Known for his obsession with pragmatism and belief that any definitive laws could not bind the flow of human history, he would avoid the speculative construction of this distant stage of human society.

Not even Marx could describe what his dream communist society would be like beyond that it would be freed of the familiar contradictions. It essentially reflected a contradiction between human desire and material reality. It would be disaster to derive the meaning of this ideal State of Ambedkar's conception from what he did. He left that to posterity to decide as per their circumstances. But, rationally there could be little doubt that the vision of Ambedkar can only be realised in the communist society of Marx's conception where most (not all) of the contradictions in human society would have been resolved.

Dalits ought to internalise this vision and strive for its realisation. Ambedkar had a radical enough interpretation of his principles of liberty, equality and fraternity so as to feel inadequacy even in Marxism. He said that Marxism supported only equality (BAWS, 3/462). He was in need of a body of thought that would give equal importance to all these three principles. He met it with a convenient conceptualisation of religion. It is paradoxical that a person who is rational enough not to bind the posterity with his vision volitionally binds himself with what is said more than 25 centuries before. It is natural to find ideals better articulated in spiritual spheres but it is equally true that these dream worlds are incapable to provide any clue for their realisation on the earth except for their pet prescription to ignore the material reality and imagine it happened in the mind.

They run away from the fact that the evil humans suffer from are the attributes of the divisions in human society, and their abolition essentially calls for struggles by the sufferers against those who perpetrate sufferings. Howsoever, inherently rational the religion may be or radical its interpretation may be it cannot fully escape these limitations. It can be seen in relation to Buddhism handed down by Babasaheb Ambedkar with his radical interpretation. Notwithstanding the familiar quibbling around the Dhamma and Dhamma among dalits, what remained of Buddhism with them is what would happen to any religion. It is a different question whether Marxism embodied Ambedkar's ideals or not but it is certain that they are neither realisable neither through any kind of constitutional acrobatics nor through any religious practice.

State

Ambedkar's conception of State reflects some amount of autonomy from the hegemony of the ruling classes. It is why he expected it to act as per the constitutional structure and endeavoured to incorporate the pro-Dalit bias into the Constitution. He must have realised the true nature of it, the boundaries of the autonomy and basic class bias of the State, when he actually reached not only the Constituent Assembly but also became the chairman of its Drafting Committee. In his anxiety to secure some provisions in favour of dalits, he accepted to be the 'hack' to write what was acceptable to the ruling caste-class representatives. He must have thought that within the given constraints he had done a good job of making the Constitution responsive to the needs of the downtrodden people.

Indeed, many of the provisions in the directive principles and elsewhere apparently bear clear imprint of his zeal and owe their existence to him. But, even they had to be within the strategic space provided by the rulers. His realisation of the folly was near complete when he had to burst out in utter dejection at its ineffectual implementation, that he would be the first man to burn the Constitution as it was of no good to any one. He was inaccurate, as the Constitution had proved good enough to the upper caste-class combine who had hegemonised complete political space in post-1947 India. He attributed it to the 'devils' in the Congressmen who had occupied the constitutional 'temple' he and others had built. Had he lived little longer, he would have realised that the ones that he considered his co-workers to build the temple were themselves the agents of the very devils.

He hoped to thwart the devil's march by people's power conceived in the form of a parliamentary party called Republican Party of India. It was within the very precincts of the temple inhabited by devils and therefore it soon proved to be the devil's feast. Ambedkar could not reach the point of understanding that the State is a mere instrument in the hands of the ruling classes to coerce the ruled ones into submission to their interests. Until the downtrodden themselves become the ruling class, they cannot expect the State to do good to them. Whatever good that appears to come to their share, in ultimate balance accrues to the other side in multiple measure.

The post-1947 State, which has never tired of propagandising its concern for dalits and poor, has in fact been singularly instrumental in aggravating the caste problem with its policies. Even the apparently progressive policies in the form of Land Ceiling Act, Green Revolution, Programme of Removal of Poverty, Reservations to Dalits in Services and Mandal Commission etc. have resulted against their professed objectives. The effect of the Land Ceiling Act, has been in creating a layer of the middle castes farmers which could be consolidated in caste terms to constitute a formidable constituency.

In its new incarnation, this group that has traditionally been the immediate upper caste layer to dalits, assumed virtual custody of Brahmanism in order to coerce Dalit landless labourers to serve their socioeconomic interests and suppress their assertive expression in the bud. The Green Revolution was the main instrument to introduce capitalisation in agrarian sector. It reinforced the innate hunger of the landlords and big farmers for land as this State sponsored revolution produced huge surplus for them. It resulted in creating geographical imbalance and promoting unequal terms of trade in favour of urban areas. Its resultant impact on dalits has been far more excruciating than that of the Land Ceiling Act.

The much publicised programme for Removal of Poverty has aggravated the gap between the heightened hopes and aspirations of dalits on one hand and the feelings of depravation among the poorer sections of non-dalits in the context of the special programmes especially launched for upliftment of dalits. The tension that ensued culminated in increasingly strengthening the caste-based demands and further aggravating the caste-divide. The reservations in services for dalits, notwithstanding its benefits, have caused incalculable damage in political terms. Reservations created hope, notional stake in the system and thus dampened the alienation; those who availed of its benefit got politically emasculated and in course consciously or unconsciously served as the props of the system.

The context of scarcity of jobs provided ample opportunity to reactionary forces to divide the youth along caste lines. Mandal Commission, that enthused many progressive parties and people to upheld its extension of reservation to the backward castes, has greatly contributed to strengthen the caste identities of people. Inasmuch as it empowers the backward castes, actually their richer sections, it is bound to worsen the relative standing of dalits in villages.

Thus, the State, its welfare mask notwithstanding, has viciously and consistently acted against dalits and poor people. It is a complete contra-evidence to hopes of Ambedkar who strove to maximise and make use of the autonomous space of the State for the benefits of the have-nots, particularly dalits. It is one thing to assume autonomous space but quite another to equate it with caste-class neutrality. Unfortunately, the Dalit political behaviour always reflected this erroneous notion of caste-class neutrality of the State. It has already caused great damage to the Dalit interests. The radical Ambedkar might have strategy to use State for Dalit cause but would never see it as caste-class neutral.

Socialism

Despite his ambivalence and reservations about the emphasis on the economic dimension in socialism, Ambedkar broadly remained a socialist. Some scholars do find little scope for suspecting his socialist credentials because of his disapproval of Russell's criticism of property, his non-acceptance of Marxian formulations and his placement of social issues higher than the economic and political issues. He called the complaint against love of money as 'philosophy of sour grapes' (BWAS 1/ 489) and ridiculed materialism as 'the ideology of pigs'. This impression is moreover strengthened by his reservations to accept the economic interpretation of history.

But, in all fairness it may be said that what he appears to mean is the integrative consideration of all the factors that are needed for any society to be based on liberty, equality and fraternity. Notwithstanding his variant conception, there should not be any doubt about his socialistic antecedents. His conception of socialism also underwent evolution. Once he had stated that there was hardly any difference between his socialism and communism. As such, his disagreement with the communists was about the means and not about the aim. He warns the communists that the classless society can emerge only after the emergence of a casteless society. It implies that his quarrel with the then communists was over the stages of revolution.

In the 1920s and 30s, these people had borrowed the communist dogma and parroted class struggle in utter disregard of the reality. Ambedkar, on the contrary, was firmly rooted in it. They believed that the soviet Russian model of revolution was importable for bringing about a socialist revolution into India whereas Ambedkar realistically postulated that unless the consciousness of the working class was congenial for revolution, there was no question of it materializing.

And, unless the caste system is destroyed, creation of the pro-revolution consciousness was out of question. His annoyance with the Bombay communists was largely because of their dogmatic behaviour. It is unfortunate that the ideal of classlessness that was latent in his agenda never really surfaced during his lifetime (Rao, 1979).

Ambedkar relies on the concept of 'State' for materialisation of his conception of socialism. His conception of State is largely idealist. He wanted the State to intervene in the economic structure and its monitoring. He wanted to constitutionalise this State intervention so that it would not be subject to change any time with the whims of simple majority vote in the legislation. Ambedkar who taught, "The lost rights cannot be regained by making appeals or requests to the robbers; it needs struggles"; did not say anything on how the oppressed people will get such strength as to create the constitutional provisions, that would put the class structure upside down. On behalf of his party-Scheduled Caste Federation, he had submitted a draft for the future constitution to the Constituent Assembly for the independent India.

It was published later as "States and Minorities". This book has really aided students in understanding some aspects of his conception of socialism. Nevertheless, one cannot afford to forget the constraints placed by the context in which it was written.

The context was that he had failed to get into the Constituent Assembly and was therefore anxious to strike a feasible and still radical note that could find the support of the vast majority of the have-nots which might then create some pressure either for its inclusion in the Constitution or for his entry into the Constituent Assembly. For some years, during the preceding turbulence of negotiations for transfer of power, he found himself totally marginalised. Notwithstanding the probable limitations of this draft, its provisions in operational terms were still very radical. The main provisions are:

- All important industries and services shall belong to the nation.
- Insurance industry shall be in public sector and insurance will be compulsory for every citizen.
- Private sector and entrepreneurs shall have a role in the economy but it shall not be dominating.
- Nationalisation of land and promotion of cooperative farming on a collective principle.

These provisions, if implemented, would have gone a lo‑ way towards supporting democratic revolution in the coun‑

It would have limited inequality and exploitation in the economic and political sphere. Politically, it would have had far-reaching impact.

Ambedkar till the end could not completely remove the Fabian influence (which he might have gathered while in England) on him. In his times, particularly before World War II, few people in India were well versed in Marxist philosophy. The knowledge of Marxism seldom exceeded some broad principles and 'Stalin's dictatorship' painted by imperialists or the 'revolt of the workers, the insurgency of the poor. Ambedkar also does not seem to have gone very far from this point. Without indulging into the debate of ifs and buts, there should not be any iota of doubt that the ideal society of his co ception could materialise only through socialism.

Democracy

Ambedkar had unshakeable faith in democracy. In his conception of an exploitation-less society, democracy has an extraordinary role. Democracy means 'one person, one vote'; and 'one vote, one value'. Democracy means empowerment of any person for participating in the process of decision-making relating to her/him, democracy means liberty, equality and fraternity-Ambedkar's definition of democracy had such a tone. Because he presided over making of the Constitution and is being projected as its chief architect, there is a misunderstanding that parliamentary democracy is what he wanted. But nothing could be farther from the truth than this. He himself spoke against parliamentary democracy. For instance, he defined parliamentary democracy as "voting by the people in favour of their owners and handing over the rights of ruling over themselves" (BAWS 10/36). This provides a glimpse of the expanse of his ideal, which certainly was much beyond the Indian Constitution or any common place understanding about him.

His conception of democracy appears to be purely people oriented. He showed that the bookish concepts of equality are detrimental to the disabled sections of society in the prevailing social setting and proposed a fundamental change in the concept of equality. It envisaged complete abolition of inequality. His principle of positive discrimination is based on this very concept of equality. But the operational aspects of this concept involved the need for some kind of autonomous institution, which was met by 'State' and 'religion'. It is necessary to stress that his greatness lies in the radicality of his conceptions, his vision of a human society sans any kind of exploitation; not in the remedies or apparatus he proposed in the circumstances prevailing in his time.

Buddhism

Religion was the institution envisaged to control the organisation at the level of an individual and society to curb their latent exploitative instincts. It was a philosophical device that would regulate their lives, including the interface between them at the most primary level. Ambedkar viewed it as a code of behaviour, a way of life that is upheld by the multitude. He insisted that this code should be based on and be compatible with the precepts of modern science. The religion as normally defined or that became a pill of opium for Marx, was not the religion of his concept either. When ultimately he embraced Buddhism he claimed to have used the criteria of modern science. Buddhism, as it was propounded by Gautama the Buddha hardly qualified to be called religion in so far as it did not have even a single of the three necessary features of religion-*viz.* : belief in God, permanent entity and a set of rituals. But it is a matter of opinion whether its institutionalised form that we are familiar with still retains its uniqueness. Shunning the futile debate, it could be definitely said and has been acknowledged that the Buddhism that he embraced was far more radical than its familiar version. His 'Buddha and His Dhamma' is replete with instances where he reconstructs and redefines Buddhism with a near-scientific approach.

Buddhism, in its purer form, puzzled many people with its radical outlook and rational approach. It did not have a place for God, ritual of any kind or for any permanent entity that characterise all other religions. Morality is said to be its basis and surprisingly a pure democratic criterion of 'happiness and welfare of many' (Bahujan Hitay, Bahujan Sukhay) as its motto. He exhorted Bhikkus (monks) and Bhikkunis (nuns) to wander all over the world carrying the Dhamma to people and not to rest at one place. Even by this, he did not mean spread of his creed; it was essentially an expression of the compassion and concern he had for suffering humanity. For, he had repeatedly advised people not to take his word for granted but test it on the touchstone of their experience and intellect before accepting or rejecting it. He never claimed any role in their emancipation asking them to be their own light-" Atta Deep Bhava". He treated the Sangha (the order of his Bhikkus and Bhikkunis) as a microcosm of the society. The Bhikkus and Bhikkunis were not allowed to have any private property except for the basic eight things for their personal use. In economic and political sphere, he put forth the ideal of service before the monks and nuns. The people who did not observe this ideal are said to be the parasites, consuming national wealth.

In the realm of philosophy, Buddha's contributions were far reaching. Several centuries before Hegel, he presented full-blown dialectics in his philosophy. Hegel had provided the basis for Marxism, in a sense that Marx had just to make the reality in Hegel upside down. Buddha's reality also had shades of Hegel, although he never explicitly accepted, unlike Hegel, the primacy to the consciousness, but he did not get his Marx to resurrect his dialectical non-materialism. The principle of impermanence is the fundamental tenet of Buddhism. For Buddha, any thing that is not permanent does not exist; its application is all pervading. Somewhat as a corollary of this principle, Buddha proposed the tenet of dependent origination (Pratit Samutpad). With regard to materialism, and consciousness, Buddhist philosophy goes quite close to materialism, in the sense that it does not regard independent existence of consciousness without the body. Significantly, Buddha's approach reflects his orientation to help people emancipate themselves and not pontificate on things irrelevant.

It is quite the same as Marx insisting on 'changing the world' as the object of philosophy. There are many 'un-knowables' on which he kept his famous silence. His 'middle path' appears to provide for the grey areas where a definite stand could be erroneous.

Ambedkar's attraction to Buddhism is basically on account of its moral base and absence of irrationality. On this account it has been the subject of admiration and awe of scores of intellectual people. A person like Einstein had opined that it was the only religion suitable for the scientific age. Ambedkar must have had multiple motives behind embracing Buddhism. Basically he was in search of a religion as an instrument of internal control on individuals' instincts and social behaviour. He had a social need of an appropriate cultural identity for his people after they had discarded the chains of Hinduism. He was moreover aware of the aberrations that had crept in Buddhism and had to redefine it to present its rational version. Basically, he included many a rational interpretation presented by scholars like Dharmanand Kosambi, and left a mirror to posterity to have a glimpse of his worldview. This worldview, does take cognisance of the material reality of living, subscribes to law of causation, relies on humane rational to interpret the world and finally embodies a craving for changing it. Although, there is no difficulty in understanding or empathising with his decision, the claim that Buddhism could be the substitute for Marxism or a liberating philosophy for the whole world is not only anachronistic but also grossly magnified idealistic hyperbole.

Another notable feature is his repeated reference to Marxism in relation to Buddhism. Many of his disciples misused it as his opposition and even extended it to enmity to Marxism. It is untrue and unfortunate. Like his claims to have checked the consistency of Buddhist tenets with those of modern science, he claimed that his Buddhism was Marxism plus some thing. It certainly shows that he did not hold Marxism in the same esteem as science, but there is no doubt that he considered Marxism as the near-best and willed that his chosen religion should contain all of it and be superior to it. It is interesting to study what aspects he considers important in Marxism and what methodology he employs to compare them with corresponding contents in Buddhism. What is important is to note that with the amount of information available on Marxism to him, he considered it great enough to serve as a benchmark to assess Buddhism.

On Marx and Communism

Babasaheb Ambedkar thought that the communists while attempting to bring about revolution do not bother about justice or injustice, truth or untruth; atrocities and taboos and if times demand, are prepared for bloodshed to establish the State with soviet methods. It was shocking to his moral philosophy and therefore he always expressed his reservation and even disapproval for these methods. He says "The object of communism is as economic and social as it is political. About social, the revolution in public opinion has not taken place. Moreover, majority of people does not have ability to understand the economic and political aims of communism" (BB, 337 (7)). Elsewhere, he cites the historical examples in the context of historical materialism of Marx and says that the political revolution has always taken place on the background of social revolutions.

Howsoever congenial the objective situation for revolution may be, it should be an axiom that till the revolutionary consciousness in people does not impel them to revolt, revolution cannot take place. He could not agree with the communists of his times who reared a mechanistic belief that revolutionary consciousness would automatically be born out of the material reality around. He wanted to stress the importance of the mediation of the conscientisation process in creating the revolutionary consciousness. He had little difficulty in visualising the communist prospects of a stateless and classless society as many people have. But there cannot be any doubt that he wished materialisation of some such 'utopia' where all kinds of exploitation would be deeply buried in the past and all the people would enjoy liberty, equality, and fraternity in their sublimest part in full measure.

One of the main problems with the prevailing icons of Ambedkar is that they project him uniformly as anti-Marx. It is the single saddest aspect for the moribund state of the Dalit movement. Ambedkar often referred to Marx in various ways but never discussed him at the philosophical plane where essentially Marx resides. It is notable that he has not much to disagree with Marx on the ideological level except for the derogatory comments on materialism. Any one knowing even the basics of Marxism would say that these comments do not have anything to do with Marxism. They relate with the mechanical materialism and not with the dialectical materialism of Marx. What prompted these comments perhaps was the practice of the then communists who vulgarised materialism in tending to ignore anything not material and have been spiteful of the movements of dalits. Beyond this nowhere he appears to discuss basics of Marxism *viz.*, dialectical materialism, historical materialism and scientific socialism. He did express doubt about the uni-linear flow of human history but unfortunately not in any depth to discern the areas of disagreement. Insofar as it implies that the history can develop divergent streams under certain conditions, the validity of the doubt cannot be dismissed.

Ambedkar and Marx share many common spaces. Both were driven by the same goal of reaching the society sans exploitation. Both had a firm commitment to the most oppressed people (technically not so for Marx, though), and saw them in the vanguard role for bringing about the revolutionary change for overall progress of the mankind. Marx arrived at his formulation by scientific study of history and found that in the era of capitalism the working class would be the vanguard of the socialist revolution. Ambedkar did not see working class in India and any probability of its emergence until the castes were annihilated. He therefore saw the necessity of launching the anti-caste movement with its worst victims-the untouchables in the vanguard role.

The language and syntax certainly differed because of different frameworks they came to follow. Marx laboured on rigorous philosophical formulation and came out with his own body of thought or a science of revolution. Ambedkar got drowned into the turbulence of present and used philosophy for his reassurance or as a support for practice. A large part of his thoughts have a polemical hue and therefore cannot be used shorn of its context without risk. Ambedkar quite like Marx felt that the object of philosophy was to change the world. His statement that he does not believe in any 'ism' can be considered anti-dogma. It is with the same sense he used to say He was a realist. What a coincidence between this and the statement of Karl Max, when he said, "I am not a Marxist "!

Besides these similarities, Marx was always referred to by Ambedkar as a kind of benchmark right up to his last days though unfortunately he never reflected the rigour that is expected in such discussions. It hovered around the superfluous and hearsay features of Marxism. Serious thinkers of Marx are surprised at his conception of Marxism till they are reminded of their location in times.

Notwithstanding Ambedkar's claim that he had read more number of books on Marxism than that read by all the communists in India, in those days the philosophical material on Marxism does not seem to be easily available. What was available was the stuff that talked about the Bolshevik revolution and what went in the Soviet Russia. Rarely does one find a purely philosophical discussion even in Marxist circles in those times. The point is that the impression spread by the vested interests that Ambedkar had rejected Marxism after careful consideration is firstly not true. Whatever his understanding of it, his interest in Marxism had never waned. He prophesied that if Buddhism failed to deliver the results, the whole world would go in for Marxism. Secondly, his feeling of inadequacy of Marxism was related to the superfluous picture of Marxism available to him.

Obviously, Marxism did not have what he was looking for, to readily offer. In the realm of practice, the natural possibility of an alliance between him and the communists seems to have been thwarted by the mechanical outlook of the Indian communists who refused even to take cognisance of the problem of castes. Their ostrich like behaviour towards the frozen reality of this land was more unmarxist than anything conceivable. Still, Ambedkar had joined hands with them during the ILP days to protest against the anti-labour bill and had led the historical strike of the workers in Bombay.

But this alliance was short-lived. Endowed with the most potent tools for analysing the social phenomena, it was the duty of the communists to understand Ambedkar and not vice versa. They not only failed in that but also went further to antagonistically oppose him. The Brahminical puritanism that they brought in Marxism was totally misfounded as the times proved. On the sheer consideration that dalits as the most oppressed people of this country did constitute their potential base, their strategy should have had a place for them if they were really committed to revolution. But, it is a fact that dalits just did not exist in their scheme of things. If any one were to be held responsible for betrayal of the revolution in India, it would be these mistaken comrades and not Ambedkar.

Unlike the frontline communist leaders in Bombay, Ambedkar did not need to declass himself to internalise the proletarian class-consciousness. Ambedkar belonged to the working class, he lived in the chawl-the mill workers quarters in Bombay. Even during his stay in USA and Europe, he lived the life of utter depravation, not even having enough food to eat. But for his western attire, which was supposed to reflect disgust for humbug prevalent in those days, he continued to identify himself with the masses and working classes in their trials and tribulations.

He did not have any necessity to demonstrate this identity by any extraneous means. The overpowering politician in him in the later days certainly eroded this consciousness and consequently led him increasingly after the short solutions shunning the direct struggles.

The communists basically had their base in the Trade Unions (TU) of the textile mill workers of Bombay. These TUs were tight-lipped on the discrimination faced by dalits in not getting the jobs in better remunerative departments like weaving in textile mills. The economic condition of dalits was much worse than their savarna counterparts. Ambedkar observed that the communists used these TUs for their political gains rather than for the welfare of the working class. Whenever they took precipitate action to strike the work, the workers tended to suffer differentially, owing to their castewise placements. Ambedkar's objection to this 'irresponsible' TU behaviour was on two counts: (i) they were driven by raw 'economism' to the detriment of prospects of enhancing the political consciousness of the working class, (ii) they were using them as cannon fodder in the promotion of their political interests. Ambedkar's writing on communism or Marxism is heavily imbued with his annoyance with the Bombay-communists. This legacy to identify Marxism with its self-appointed practitioners still appears to be followed by dalits. They cite examples of the parliamentary communist parties to show the lacuna or inapplicability of Marxism. It is necessary for them to understand that Marxism needs criticism but it presupposes its careful study.

One of the greatest barriers the communists pose to others is their unmarxist and puritanical attitude. In India that was naturally likened to Brahmanism with which all were familiar and because by default the communist leadership happened to come from Brahmin and other Dwija castes. Marxist essence presupposes scientific enquiry, a dynamic understanding of the situations and requisite tolerance for divergent views. But the institutionalised Marxism always appeared ready with the glued labels like renegade, reactionary, revisionist etc. to mark out those who did not toe the official line.

These fallen comrades then are treated as the worst class enemies nullifying in one shot their life time contribution to the revolution. This tradition has unconsciously induced a dogmatic behaviour in the Marxist circles. By virtue of the powerful analytical tools of Marxism their analyses still read superior to any one around but it could be generally said that they have not made full use of their potentialities. They are adept at stuffing new facts into the old inferences to demonstrate eternal validity of their dogma.

For instance, if they had seen the objective reality in Ambedkar's time as they did now about the problem of castes, the history of this country could have been a bit different! What worries the committed revolutionists is this attitude of the 'official' Marxists. For instance, there does not appear any significant appreciation of the changes in the mode of production under capitalism with the advances in communication and computational (information) technologies. The capitalist organisations have undergone sea change with adoption of them from the Fordist models that constituted the reference for the Marxist schema. These organisations have re-engineered themselves into delayered, downsized, flexible, decentralised units and are tending to destructure so as to reduce the cycle times with the fullest use of information technology.

In place of factories employing huge numbers of workers engaged in monotonous assembly line tasks, alienated from the product of their labour are coming the distributed production units with knowledge workers, fairly autonomous in their work sphere, located in apparently authority neutralised teams, with flexi-times and profit sharing avenues. The policy package of globalisation that is out to increasingly marginalise and crush the people in poorer countries is just the corollary of this paradigm change. Although, contrary to opinion of many, this so-called flexible capitalism does not any way affect the validity of the theory, one worries to note no influence of these changes in the strategy and tactics of the Marxists. The redefinition project will have to take into account this emergent shape of the world. One of the problems Ambedkar appears to face in accepting Marxism is its prescription of the 'dictatorship of proletariat' during the post-revolutionary transition period to communism.

For him any kind of dictatorship was an anathema. He equates it with monarchy. While it is true that he had not understood the basic rationale behind or rather derivation of this concept, his apprehensions cannot be said to be mis-founded as the later developments in the socialist countries revealed. To overcome this lacuna he devises a via media solution of State socialism without demolishing the parliamentary democracy. To cover up the inherent lacunae in the parliamentary democracy, he proposes to incorporate the structure of the economy in the Constitution and limit the sovereignty of the parliament. He visualised this solution as bringing in socialism without 'shedding a drop of blood' or resorting to dictatorship. It is unfortunate that instead of understanding the inherent defect of the framework of the political economy, he strove to propose such unrealistic solutions.

The separation of the Dalit and communist movements has caused the greatest loss to the revolution in India. The fact that Dalit and oppressed people, who constitute the backbone of this movement were kept away from it, restricted its growth. On the other side, on account of discarding the ideology of class struggle, the Dalit movement could never come to grips with the real problem of dalits and comprehend the means to solve them. As a result, the condition of this community went on deteriorating, their movement remained revolving around the trifling, temporary and emotional issues thrown in their front by the cunning of ruling classes and their leaders remained entangled with their self interests and politics of status quo. The project of redefinition of Ambedkar will consist in systematically examining Ambedkar's conceptions and relocating him in relation to Marxism.

Aspects of the Strategy and Tactics

In the context of strategy, some of Ambedkar's contributions are really noteworthy. He brought the struggle against

Brahmanism into the political battlefield. He inferred that without political power the social and religious structures will collapse and motivated his followers to capture political power. But his conception of political power being acutely constrained by the parliamentary framework where bargaining is the predominant medium of securing political power, inevitably it made way for all kinds of aberrations and perversities to creep in. The prevailing politics being the game of possibilities, he was soon sucked into its vortex. Politics came to dominate the other aspects of his personality. Slowly, the impact of politics started becoming visible everywhere. This phase significantly contributed to multiplication of his inconsistencies out of tactical imperatives. Dalits have taken this legacy of parliamentary politics very seriously, almost as the be all and end all of their political being. It may be, interesting to probe how much damage this kind of political orientation inflicted on the Dalit movement.

It is altogether a different question whether Ambedkar had any other alternative to parliamentary politics for political practice. It may be argued that in the context of his resources, adversarial environment and to some extent his personal limitations, he had none. Even if it is taken as correct, it should not be forgotten that it was a matter of strategy and tactic that presuppose contextual variables: it cannot be taken as the lasting value.

The fundamental source of most of Ambedkar's political thoughts and action is his conception of State and religion, that he had adopted as the extraneous instruments to reconcile the state of flux of things and the necessity of order in them. It is necessary to understand that both, the State as well as religion, are the products of the evolutionary process of the human society. There is nothing inevitable about them. Marx took State as the instrument of coercion in the hands of ruling classes and religion as the opium of the masses. Dalits have a long experience of nearly five decades with the so-called welfare State of Ambedkar's design. What does it say? Does the State side with them in their conflict with the landlords? Does it come to their rescue when every day three or four of their daughters are raped?

Does it come to save the shame of their women when they are paraded naked in the streets? Does it take their side when they come in conflict with landlords, moneylenders in villages or with management in the modern settings? Does it really ensure they get their dues as provided in the Constitution or punish the defaulting management for noncompliance? To all of such questions the answer could only be in the negative. It is not a matter of 'devils occupying the temples' as Ambedkar lamented seeing the people occupying the Constitutional positions. The State possesses the characteristics of its master class. In India the upper caste capitalists, landlords, top bureaucrats, etc. being the ruling class, the State can never have saints who would favour dalits. It is a fact that even the government by a Dalit party like the BSP could not transform it into a Dalit State.

Religion, in Ambedkar's conception is necessary to maintain the moral order of the society. It may be interesting to examine to what extent it conforms to this idealistic expectation. Buddhism, which undoubtedly is the most rational of all the religions, does not have any evidence of having created over its near millennium long tenure in India such an order of the society which could claim liberty, equality and fraternity of Ambedkar's conception. Ambedkar's argument that the Bhikku Sangha in Buddhism was the prototype of this kind of society becomes invalid once we call into question the role of Sangha in the production process.

Before that, the order that envisaged nostalgically to recreate the value of the vanishing Gana Rajya in microcosm against the evil of rising monarchies, cannot just sublimate to the era of capitalism without being an alley of exploiters unless it transforms itself in some way as a catalyst for the revolution. The moral tenets of Buddhism likewise cannot submerge the lure of surplus extraction, that is its dominating ethos. If at all, it may help it become more pronounced by weakening the resistance of the exploited masses. As we empirically see, the Buddhism of his conception could not produce even a trace of morality in its adherents. On the contrary, for the masses it presents the distorted, if not inverted, worldview; it orients them to look inwards for their misery and be blind to the reality that some one exploits him. He could certainly derive mental peace and pleasure but it is a state of an intoxicated mind. Keeping in mind the causal links in Ambedkar's adoption of these instruments, the redefinition project needs to address these issues afresh.

The strategy of the ruling class always stresses on diversion of peoples' attention from their real problems and their disarmament-both in physical and ideological terms. They invariably have a multilayered strategy in place for this purpose. The vanguard parties of the ruling classes open up sentimental fronts and attempt to divert the attention of people as their real problems get aggravated. Secondly, their time-tested methods of adulterating radical ideas with the masses are always in operation. Towards this end, we see all the ruling parties vying with each other in co-opting Ambedkar. 'Ambedkar' represents a potentially dangerous ideological weapon in the hands of the Indian proletariat and so the ruling class will be hell bent on blunting its edge. They will do everything to eulogise him not only for wooing dalits for their immediate electoral gains but also to neutralise him as the radical ideological force by propagandising a distorted version of the latter. Dalits will have to exercise vigil over their ideological assets even after redefining Ambedkar.

Conclusion

For at least over last four decades Dalits have devotedly followed Ambedkar as their ideal, as a virtual God and zealously practised, as they claim, his teachings. Their social being could be seen to be totally imbued with what they call Ambedkarism-the veritable science of their emancipation. If it is true, and no one would deny it is not, it should be pertinent to ask why despite this flawless following of Ambedkar they continue to be in a pathetic state in every sense. Barring a handful dalits in the government and public sector services and of course politicians, they continue to occupy the lowest rung in the social as well as economic hierarchy of Indian society. Their politics, notwithstanding the media hype, gauged by the measure of general empowerment, continues to be in shambles. Over these decades, their relative situation either shows stagnation or decline. The insinuation to relate this State with their faith in Ambedkar itself would be distasteful for many dalits. But, it is vital for ones that are committed to their liberation to squarely face the facts and dispassionately find out where the rot lay.

Generally, beyond the first burst of anger in reaction to this question, one would face the defensive arguments to discount this relationship. Typically, they tend to attribute their miserable situation to the lack of competent leadership after Babasaheb Ambedkar, to the educated dalits who they think have become Dalit Brahmins and have deserted the community; and sometimes to the people themselves for their extreme self-centredness. Sometimes, the finger is raised at the high caste hegemony that has neutralised the impact of the Constitution that Ambedkar created. Some, particularly the leadership, even would dismiss the basic premise itself that there is something wrong with the Dalit movement.

They might even go so far as to claim net achievements indicating the prosperity of themselves or some others of their ilk. More sober may argue that what is seen is the transition state. Conceding them all some amount of validity even would not erase the stark fact that the general situation of the vast majority of Dalit masses remains still alarmingly pathetic. Externalisation of the reasons for this state has not helped dalits any bit. The time has come for dalits to self-critically see whether anything was wrong with their ideology and / or with their practice thereof.

Reviewing the post-Ambedkar Dalit movement at some significant milestones, one finds a queer underscoring behaviour, believed to be in accordance with the teachings of Babasaheb Ambedkar, that is certainly incongruent with the essence of what he taught. This dichotomy between the essential Ambedkar and the 'Ambedkar' in the faith of Dalit masses-the icon of Ambedkar, comes out as the problematic in this review. In relation to almost every aspect of his teaching there emerged an icon that represented varying amount of distortion. Insofar as they constituted the ideology that gripped the masses, these icons can be seen to be at the root of the Dalit pathos. Among the myriad sources for these icons, Ambedkar himself might come out as the major source. Because, even a myth can not sustain for long without some material base.

The icons of Ambedkar thus could be linked to some such bases, howsoever tenuous, within his own life. The rationalist in Ambedkar never hesitated to change his opinions and behaviour if the facts so warranted. They appear to be inconsistencies to the ones who see it sans context. His distance from the focus of control in his sociopolitical environment, the vastly varying target audience (ranging from the Englishmen to the illiterate dalits) to whom he had to communicate, the exigency to respond to the dynamics of communities set in motion by the pre-independence politics, his anxiety to accomplish as many gains for dalits as he could in his life time, the exigencies for 'short' actions at the expense of 'long' vision inevitably led to mark patterns that could support array of behaviours. The first to take advantage of it were his own lieutenants for serving their personal ambitions that set the trends of distortion of Ambedkar in the minds of gullible Dalit masses.

The ruling classes that always look for the grounds to divide masses had severally reinforced this distortion and accelerated fragmentation of dalits in every field. They, along with willing collaboration of Dalit politicians and emerging elite, promoted and sustained the particular icons of Ambedkar that would prevent political coalescence of dalits and suck them into the vortex of parliamentary politics in order to bring the establishment much needed legitimacy. Dalits failed to note this cunning and let themselves flow in the currents of confusion the ruling classes deliberately created. Today, with increasing political crises the ruling classes seem vying with each other in co-opting Ambedkar, as though that may be their last chance of survival. If dalits stood their grounds well, that might have proved to be their last act. But, unfortunately dalits are giving them new leases of life by blinding themselves to the reality. Not only that they have not resisted these ruling class machinations but on the contrary they are curiously seen to swell the cadres of these castiest, communalist and anti-poor groups and parties. These parties who openly profess the ideology of Hindu revivalism and represent all that is decadent in Indian tradition show the temerity to project Ambedkar among their ideologues. Apart from the reasons of security that propel Dalit youth into their fold, the compradore behaviour of Dalit elite certainly has influenced the phenomenon. What is common in all the attempts by the ruling classes is to sap 'Ambedkar' of its rebellious content.

It is advantageous for them to show that he was the chief architect of the Indian Constitution, committed to parliamentary democracy and opposed to any ideology that propagates violence or revolution. He is projected to favour gradual change implying that dalits should patiently wait and strive persuasively to better their own lives. He is projected as the Bodhisatva that inspires nirvana-the State of total detachment from worldly matters. All these images have caused significant damage to the emancipatory struggles of dalits. Some of these images might be the purposeful and blatant disfiguring of Ambedkar but some of them represent genuine dilemma arising from Ambedkar's own stands on various issues. From the viewpoint of the comprehensive pro-people change in the present historical phase a democratic revolution is an imperative.

The motive force for this revolution ought to sprout from dalits. The history provides a strong testimony that any radical movement in the country could be sustained by dalits and tribals at its base. Ambedkar as a symbol for Dalit aspirations holds a key to the barrage that has so far bound the revolutionary upsurge in India below the alarming levels. If one concedes that Ambedkar's framework is going to haunt revolutionary commitment till the Indian Democratic Revolution actually happens and that Ambedkar represents the ideological weaponry in the hands of dalits who along with other oppressed people are going to be the axis of this revolution, then one would clearly see the need to redefine Ambedkar in radical terms commensurate with this purpose.

Many aspects of confusion with regard to the facts could be cleared with rational interpretation of his thoughts. But much might need the logical extrapolation of his basic thinking which for some reason appears to have settled in erroneous forms. As he himself showed the way in the case of his redefinition of Buddha's Dhamma, dalits will have to undertake this task, for giving themselves a powerful ideology. Their future as a social group almost hinges on this task.

There are enough clues left behind by Ambedkar himself that point to this need. There is no doubt that he was frustrated at the end of his life seeing the undesired aftermath of his lifelong struggle. He had to lament over the betrayal of the educated dalits in whom he had seen the crusaders of his mission. He had to weep with remorse that he could not do anything for his people in the villages. He had to disown the Constitution for working on which he had cut short his life at least by a few years. He had to swallow the frustration of not being able to pilot the Constitution of his conception (States and Minorities). He had to regret the anti-people State that emerged in republican India. He obviously lacked the analytical tools to see through the reasons for these happenings. His excessive religiosity and spirituality at the fag end of his life perhaps could be taken as the manifestation of this frustration.

The social engineer could only be busy with problems; he is unlikely to come to grip with the design defects in the system. Almost every thing that Ambedkar pinned his hopes on can be found today in antithetical shambles. His educational society, his vision of Buddhism, the political party of his conception, the social reforms could be some of the examples.

These tragic aftermaths also would denote the necessity of a critical review of Ambedkar's thoughts if they were to be used as the ideology to further the Dalit movement towards its logical end. If this process is sincerely followed, there cannot be any doubt that this 'redefined Ambedkar' would be a revolutionary icon, organically linking the Dalit struggle to the revolutionary struggle in the world. It will truly globalise the Dalit struggle. This paper is not an appraisal of his work. If it was one he is likely to still shine brightest among his contemporaries. It is an appraisal of his icons that came to be the beacon for the Dalit movement. It is the futuristic dimension that he represents which is called in question.

Dalits could be eternally indebted to a historical personality called Bhimrao Ramji Ambedkar for whatever he has done to them, but it does not mean that posterity should be bound by the parameters he operated within. For, he himself never meant it to be so. But then that precisely is the tragedy of Ambedkar, that his disciples always zealously acted exactly opposite to what he said or wrote, particularly what he meant to do. Plain talk of this nature is bound to hurt the sentiments of many people but when the disease crosses certain limits, the administration of bitter pills is inevitable. It is not blasphemy but true allegiance to Ambedkar, to his commitment to the cause of downtrodden that makes this introspective exercise a necessity.

8

POLITICS OF DALITISM—GANDHI AND AMBEDKAR

INTRODUCTION

The approach of Gandhi and Ambedkar for the removal of untouchability was diametrically opposite. Gandhiji firmly believed that untouchability should be removed by change of heart by Hindus. Ambedkar emphatically felt that it cannot be removed only by change of heart. He insisted on safeguards and political rights for his people.

Gandhiji felt that he was the natural guardian of the untouchables, whereas Ambedkar said that he was the natural leader of the untouchables. They criticised each other, but each was conscious of the other's necessary place in any final solution of the problems of the untouchables. The paths of Gandhiji and Ambedkar, while often diverged, ultimately converged, forcing on the Indian conscience the problem of untouchability as an issue of national importance.

Whatever the position the untouchables have today in Indian society, it is the result of the genuine efforts made by Gandhiji to change the Hindu heart and the constant attacks made by Ambedkar on Hindus and Hinduism. However the impact of Gandhiji was overriding which is evident from the fact that when the Constituent Assembly of Independent India made a legal provision on 29 November 1948, nine months after the assassination of Gandhiji, the house resounded with slogans of

"Mahatma Gandhi-ki-jai" right in the presence of Ambedkar who was present in his capacity as the Chairman of the Drafting Committee of the Constituent Assembly.

The irony of the moment was lost on those who were present-a legalistic measure was taken in the name of Gandhiji, who had no use for legalism. And only three years before, Ambedkar had ended his book, "What Congress and Gandhiji have done for untouchables", with the bitter comment that the untouchables have ground to say, "Good God, is this man Gandhiji our saviour"?

Justice V. R. Krishna Iyer says: "When we consider the stature and achievements of Ambedkar as an intrepid warrior for socioeconomic liberation of the lowliest, the lost and the last, especially the dalits and the exploited tribals there is no doubt that without diminishing the tremendous conscientisation of the Hindu community by Gandhiji vis-a-vis untouchability and Harijan debasement Bhim Ramji Ambedkar's ceaseless war on behalf of the Panchama proletariate, in its widest connotation is incomparable. And yet, the irony of history is that as the house passed the provision abolishing untouchability on 29 November 1948, the hallowed walls resounded with shouts of 'Mahatma Gandhi-ki-jai' although present at the session as Chairman of the Drafting Committee was Ambedkar, an untouchable himself and Commander-in-Chief of the Untouchable Army which waged a war against the reactionary system which sustained the Social Status-Quo Ante'.

"When the pre-independence saga of India comes to be written, only prejudice can assign a higher role in the liberation of the backward most brackets to anyone above Ambedkar. While both Gandhiji and Ambedkar were the symbols of the revolt against the caste, conscious oppressors within the Hindu fold, they chose different paths, strategies, and different ideologies. If Gandhiji was a deliverer of Indians including the weakest sector from the British Raj, Ambedkar was the spearhead of black power against the Varna front. There were many issues on which the two militant giants would not agree, the obvious reason being that Gandhiji wanted reforms to end injustice. While Ambedkar demanded rebellion for the annihilation of the caste system itself, Gandhiji was Vaishya and insisted on eradication of Sudrahood and untouchability.

"Ambedkar was mahar and indignantly insisted on the abolition of the Varna structure, thereby levelling up all castes into one oceanic unity or human sagar, Ambedkar was historic necessity, a dialectical demand if social democracy was to be India's desideratum. The fire of this mahar was rare in the Indian public life of his time." In his characteristic forceful manner, Justice Iyer adds to this appraisal a complementary sentence, "To go against Gandhiji, to fight the National Congress, to demand equal share of power for the depressed classes, to draft legislation for womanhood's equality needed the courage of an iconoclast, and Ambedkar was just that."

Gandhiji softened the Hindu heart, Ambedkar awakened self-respect and interest in politics among the untouchables.

During decades proceeding independence, the policies and programmes have been profoundly affected by the difference in views of Gandhiji and Ambedkar on the key questions like what is the ultimate goal-assimilation of the untouchable minority or the establishment of separate but equal status in a reformed version of the traditional social order? If change is in order who should change-the untouchable minority or Hindu majority? Given a commitment to change, how might it best be implemented-through voluntary means or government coercion? Gandhiji's answers to such questions were rooted in his belief that the caste Hindus were primarily responsible for writing the wrongs done to the untouchables. Meaningful change therefore must arise from a change of heart on the part of the Hindus. Gandhiji suggested that the real method of abolishing the distinction between caste Hindus and Harijans is by caste Hindus performing the purification ceremony of ridding themselves of untouchability and becoming Harijans themselves. He advised caste Hindus to declare themselves as such and to live also as such. This was according to him, the substantial and organic method of amalgamating the two into one body.

Gandhiji said: "I was wedded to the work of the extinction of untouchability long before I was wedded to my wife. There were two occasions in our joint life when there was a choice between working for the untouchables or remaining with my wife and I would have preferred the first. But thanks to my good wife, the crisis was averted. In my Ashram, which is my family, I have several untouchables and a sweet but naughty girl living as my own daughter."

During the last days of his life, Gandhiji declared, "I would rejoice to think that we had a sweeper girl of a stout heart incorruptible and of crystal purity to be our first president, assisted in the discharge of her duties by a person like Jawaharlal Nehru". Gandhiji directed his energies on the eradication of the sin of untouchability. Only the sinner could expiate the sin, he felt, and throughout his public life he exhorted the caste Hindus to do so. He did more than anyone else to make untouchability a public issue and to create public opinion against it.

Gandhiji pushed the issue to forefront of the Congress platform and did his best to keep it there for 25 years despite the objections of his colleagues that it sometimes diverted public energies away from the top priority goal of achieving independence.

POLITICS OF DALITISM: CREATING DALITS AMONG DALITS

The attempt of some of activists of Dalit movement in India to internationalise the issue in World Conference Against Racism (WCAR) concluded in the first week of September and follow up actions have created an impression that there is something basically wrong in the ideological orientation of the movement. The word Dalit was coined in post-colonial India by the disciples of Ambedkar. They did not accept the word Harijan (Men of

God) used by Gandhi for the untouchables in Hindu social order because of their aversion against him. The word Dalit therefore, became the vernacular terminology for the oppressed classes, with a wider connotation for electoral sociology in the democratic polity of the country.

Mahatma Gandhi & Dr. Ambedkar: If we look to the history of Dalit movement, it is as old as the birth of the concept of untouchability, which was the darkest spot in Hindu social structure. Though, Hindu reformists tried their best to fight against this social evil right from the days untouchability was born, the real concern over it came to surface during the freedom struggle, when Mahatma Gandhi and Dr. B. R. Ambedkar fought against it in their own way. While Gandhi wanted complete eradication of untouchability for emotional integration of Hindu society, Ambedkar was for abolition of Varnashram structure of the Hindu social order.

The conceptual difference between the two messiahs of untouchables continues to affect the Dalit movement even after their death. While the disciples rejected Mahatma Gandhi for the sake of power and fulfilment of their personal ambitions, Ambedkar became a symbol of Dalit movement. A clue to understanding Ambedkar lies in his hatred of Gandhi. The activists of Dalit movement adopted the same philosophy against the upper castes and are still found boiling in the anger generated by their messiah Ambedkar. Taking advantage of the violent landscape, which started emerging since the closing decades of twentieth century, the followers of Ambedkar adopted the sole agenda to create social disorder and capture power. In both the situations, the process of social transformation in Hindu society, which took off in positive direction just after independence got disturbed.

To understand the multi dimensional direction of the Dalit movement, we may briefly look into the difference between Gandhi and Ambedkar on this issue. During the first Round Table Conference, when Ambedkar favoured the move of the

British Government to provide separate electorate for the oppressed classes, Gandhi strongly opposed it on the plea that the move would disintegrate the Hindu society. He went for an indefinite hunger strike from September 20, 1932 against the decision of the then British Prime Minister J. Ramsay MacDonald granting communal award to the depressed classes in the constitution for governance of British India.

In view of the mass upsurge generated in the country to save the life of Gandhi, Ambedkar was compelled to soften his stand. A compromise between the leaders of caste Hindu and the depressed classes was reached on September 24, 1932, popularly known as Poona Pact. The resolution announced in a public meeting on September 25 in Bombay confirmed-" henceforth, amongst Hindus no one shall be regarded as an untouchable by reason of his birth and they will have the same rights in all the social institutions as the other Hindus have". This landmark resolution in the history of the Dalit movement in India subsequently formed the basis for giving due share to Dalits in the political empowerment of Indian people in a democratic Indian polity.

Even though Ambedkar was a party to Poona Pact, he was never reconciled to it. His contempt against Gandhi, which continued even after his assassination on January 30, 1948. On the death of Gandhi he expressed, "My real enemy has gone, thank goodness the eclipse is over". He equated the assassination of Gandhi with that of Caesar and the remark of Cicero to the messenger-"Tell the Romans, your hour of liberty has come". He further remarked, "While one regrets the assassination of Mahatma Gandhi, one cannot help finding in his heart the echo of the sentiments expressed by Cicero on the assassination of Caesar". Considering Gandhi as a "positive danger to this country", he quoted from Bible that "sometime good cometh out of evil, so also I think good will come out of the death of Mr. Gandhi" (Gandhi and Ambedkar-Saviours of Untouchables by Sheshrao Chavan. Bharatiya Vidya Bhavan publication 2001, page 263-64).

The reaction of Ambedkar over the death of Gandhi may be viewed as a politics of negation for vengeance against the caste Hindus and also for political power for Dalits. He felt, "the problem of depressed classes will never be solved unless they get political power in their own hand" (Thus spoke Ambedkar by Bhagwan Das). He however, did not clarify as to how in a democratic polity of pluralistic society, Dalits would be the sole custodians of power.

Post Ambedkar Dalit Movement: The post-Gandhian and post-Ambedkar Dalit activists re-invented the direction of their movement, which was by and large focused towards developing the negative ideas in a dark room. They are yet to take the next step to focus their negatives in light for positive prints. In the absence of a scientific endeavour their movement lags in its march towards social reform, as it has more or less become a platform for the political empowerment of some individuals for their personal ambitions and vested interests. This is not only against the concept of equalitarian Hindu sociology of Vedic India but also against the concept of democracy.

The present clash for Dalit leadership has confirmed the theory of C. Rajagopalachari that many Dalit leaders are interested for continuance of the undesirable status of Dalits for the fulfilment of their personal ambitions. Disagreeing with Ambedkar on Dalits issue he said, "...This is material explanation for the violent dislike of Gandhiji exhibited by Dr. Ambedkar, who looks upon this great and inspired reformer as the enemy of the untouchables, meaning thereby of the educated and ambitious among them who find that the depressed status furnishes short cut to position". ("Ambedkar Refuted" page 33, Hind Kitab Publishers: Bombay 1946)

It may be partially true that political empowerment is key to social and economic empowerment as suggested by Ambedkar but this cannot be the sole criteria for the social equality of Dalits. The representatives (122-76 SC and 46 ST in parliament against its strength of 543 and 1085-556 SC and 529 ST in state assemblies against their strength of 4370) of Dalits in parliament and state assemblies in sizeable strength have been sharing political power for last fifty years. But if they have failed to bring a desired social change and economic upliftment of Dalits, there is something wrong in the movement, which is yet to be identified. The students of the constituting history have therefore, a right to know from Dalit activists the reason behind the failure of their representatives sharing political power.

One may be amused to understand that how only 160 Dalit delegates under the umbrella of National Campaign on Dalit Human Rights in WCAR would have fought for the cause of Dalits in India if the representatives of Dalits sharing political power could not assert and agitate for the cause of their community? An objective analysis of the prevailing social condition and sentiments in India may corroborate the theory of C. Rajagopalachari that Dalit movement has become a vehicle to promote the personal interest of some individuals or groups.

The Dalits Despite Empowerment are not a Political Force-why?: In the absence of an All India mind with a cohesive and unified perspective, Dalit movement has also failed to emerge as a strong political force. Dalits are divided into hundreds of castes and sub-castes. About 56 percent of Dalit population belong to about 20 dominant castes among them. These dominant castes are presently grabbing all the privileges provided to the Dalits constitutionally. Even Dr. Ambedkar failed to give an intellectual explanation to unify them together, as a result, his political influence during his life time also remained confined to only Mahar caste of his community in the Maharashtra region.

Dalit activists, due to lack of actual ideological direction are not clear whether they are interested to ensure the material prosperity of Dalits or equal status in Hindu social order. Untouchability has almost disappeared, as touch of Dalit is no more considered to have any polluting affect on caste Hindus.

However, so long the Dalits enjoy the benefits of reservation in Government jobs and admission in academic institutions, they may have to bear the stigma of being considered unequal in merit to the caste Hindus. The objective of Dalit movements should be therefore, to erase such stigma, which is possible only if Dalits get a chance for their proper education befitting to the standard required for competitions.

Vested Interests in Command: Contrary to the objective of the movement discussed above, the managers of Dalit movement due to their vested interest do not want their people to be cleansed from the stigma of reservation and the agony of their past humiliation of being treated as untouchables. In stead of fighting for transformation of the Hindu social order, they are found more interested to promote themselves as Esperanto of United Nations politics. With weapon of hate, they are neither able to fight against the social inequality and injustice effectively nor in a position to contribute any significant social change.

In stead of looking on the growing consciousness among the educated caste Hindus against the social evil of caste discrimination against Dalits and appreciating this positive change, the Dalit activists ignore and understate the development. Their sole aim is now pointed towards personal ambitions at the cost of their community. This has created a new class of Brahmins among the Dalits, who are now exploiting the actual Dalits by grabbing the benefits meant for the latter. This may look like a paradox, but it is the hard reality.

The on going Dalit movement is gradually losing its track. Its multidimensional character based on the philosophy of love and hate is unfortunately turned into political theocracy, which is contrary to the basic concept of the total transformation of Hindu social order. Inciting the Dalits against the caste Hindus for historical agony without any honest effort for their emotional integration with rest of the Hindu social order is neither in the interest of this disadvantaged section of population nor in the interest of the nation.

The shrinking influence of the so called Brahmanism in electoral politics, social transformation, spiritual movement, or even other public affairs are enough indications of gradual changes in Hindu sociology. Dalit movements with a view to create social disorder by promoting caste hatred against the upper castes of ancient Varnashram system will simply ha t the process of the on going social transformation. With their political empowerment by occupying the post of President, Union Cabinet ministers, Chief ministers, and bureaucrats, Dalits are gradually getting more opportunities for achieving social empowerment under democratic process. By gaining more confidence, Dalits are now found to be quite assertive of their rights. This however, does not mean that they have been acceptable in community dining or inter-caste marriage, which is not even prevalent within the various Dalit castes.

The objective of any social reform movement is to ensure a peaceful, decent and dignified life for every body without any social confrontation. But, unfortunately the Dalit activists are so obsessed and possessive in their approach towards the historical agony of their community that they have made the latter as prisoners of Dalitism, which hardly has any constructive plan for creation of a just social order. Their slogan for abolition of Varnashram (professional units) system and total abolition of caste is an utopian concept, which will never take root in the diverse and pluralistic Indian society.

Casteism is the bane of Indian society but the Indian people accept caste as a hard reality. Even the Christians and Muslims boast themselves of their upper caste heritage. In South India even Christians are maintaining visible distance from the Dalit Christians as the latter continue to have separate church, separate burial ground and even separate places for social interactions. Similarly, even Muslims in India and Pakistan there is no inter-caste marriage among the Sheiks, Syed, Paithan and others because of their upper caste heritage before conversion.

The three Dalits groups and their separate agenda: As far as the present Dalit movement is concerned, it is in the hands of three vested interest groups of Dalit politicians, Dalit writers and Christian missionaries. Dalit political leaders like Kansi Ram and Ms. Mayawati of Bahujan Samaj Party and Ram Vilas Paswan of Lok Jana Shakti are having their influence exclusively among the members of their own community. They can never come to power on their own due to their limited influence among the voters. For coming to power they are compelled to join some other parties dominated by caste Hindus. They are therefore, hardly in a position to bring any social change.

The second group, which claims to be the champion for the cause of Dalits is of Dalit writers. Their personal ambition and ego have kept them away from the common Dalits, who are illiterate and poor. They are more interested in their self-promotion than serving the cause of their community. Their possessiveness is often mistaken as love for Dalits. Since they do not get enough space in media to spit venom against the caste Hindus and are hardly in a position to play an effective role in electoral politics, they are always in search of the forces through which they could get national and international recognition. They have therefore, joined hand with forces (third group) determined to disintegrate the Hindu society.

The interest of the third group in Dalit movement is to de-Hinduise the Dalits and promote their proselytisational endeavour. The argument of this group that Christian society does not have any caste discrimination is not based on ground reality. The Dalit Christians are facing the problem of caste discrimination even in Christian society. Such discrimination is prevalent in Kerala even after the death of Dalit Christians, whose corpses do not find any place in the cemetery meant for upper caste convert Christians. T. V. Rajshekhar, a Dalit writer, while speaking in a seminar (Church and Dalit) organised by Christian leaders in Madras on June 14, 1986 said that Dalit Christians form about 80 percent Christian population in India but contrary to what Jesus Christ preached, the Dalit Christians are also the victim of caste discrimination as they have separate burial ground, separate churches and separate dwelling places.

Ever since the promulgation of presidential order No 19 of 1950 debarring the Dalits of non-Hindu and non-Sikh community to be included in the list of Scheduled castes, the Christian missionaries have been facing difficulty in alluring the Hindu alits for their conversion. For this they have already launched a movement for constitutional privileges for Dalit Christians. If they succeed in alienating the Dalits from Hindu social order, the entire Dalit community will get the benefit of constitutional provisions and it will help them in their mission for proselytisation.

Indian Social Institute (ISI), a Roman Catholic Mission outfit organised a meeting on "Durban and Dalit Discourse: Post Durban Scenario" on September 20. The meeting was organised with a view to forming a "broad alliance of disadvantaged section of society to battle the status quo that would prefer to keep them on the periphery of the country's social structure" (Hindu dated September 24). The move of the institute is to internationalise the issue. Had it not been so, it should first cleanse the Christian society in Kerala. In fact the Christian missionaries are also facing a dilemma of the isolation of Dalits from the affluent sections of the community. Dr. Prakash Luis, Executive Director of ISI said, "There is a sense of vertical divide within the community between the socially mobile 'Brahmanical Dalits' and the real Dalits among Dalits".

Conclusion: In the backdrop of the dialectics of Dalit movements, it appears that the Dalits have now become the victims of the politics of Dalitism being played by various groups. Instead of fighting the evils of caste discrimination in Hindu society, the Dalit movement has given birth to neo-Dalitism, which hardly has any difference with the polluted Brahmanism.

The movement, which does not have the ingredients to bring about reconciliation among conflicting social groups and fails to accelerate the process of social harmony and human dignity, is bound to lose real direction. Dalits should therefore be very careful about the politics of Dalitism being played by vested interests not only at the cost of the disadvantaged community but also at the cost of social harmony, which is more dangerous for the nation.

Proposed Indian Round Table Conference 1922

Descriptions of what happened vary greatly (listed from the most to least probable)

a. Malaviya Proposed Round Table, The Viceroy Lord Reading Agrees, Mahatma Gandhi Sabotages the Idea Proudest p 194-5 (fully referenced).

"The Prince of Wales was due in Calcutta on 24 December, and any more violent disorder there had to be prevented at all costs. During the next two months over 30,000 people were arrested in India as a whole, and of the top leadership of the noncooperation movement, only Gandhi remained free. There was a very real danger for the government that its new wave of repression would drive the Liberals and Moderates back into the Congress camp, which would have been disastrous. Malaviya had been urging the viceroy for some time to call a round-table conference with Gandhi and the Moderates.

In mid-December, Reading agreed, promising at the same time to release the political prisoners, end the repressive measures, and even grant 'full provincial autonomy' if Gandhi would call off the noncooperation movement.... At first, Gandhi agreed. But he quickly changed his mind, wiring Malaviya: 'Noncooperation can cease only after satisfactory result conference. In no case have I authority to decide for Congress. ' His 'private notes' made at the time give a more complex, perhaps more revealing, reason for his decision: 'I am sorry, 'he wrote, 'that I suspect Lord Reading of complicity in the plot to human India for eternity.'

There is little doubt that if Gandhi had agreed to attend the conference, the Moderates would have joined forces with him to achieve substantial constitutional concessions. Reading was prepared to give full responsible government to the provinces, despite the doubts of London and most of the senior governors. He told Montagu: 'I was prepared to act on my own responsibility if the proper assurances had been forthcoming. ' This would have been not merely a step but a giant leap towards self-government, advancing the eventual transfer of power by a full 15 years.

But it was not to be.... at a stormy annual session of Congress in Ahmedabad, Gandhi came under attack both from those who wanted to seek an accommodation with the government and those who wanted more militant action immediately. But in the end, as always, Gandhi carried the day, His rejection of Reading's offer was confirmed, and he was given dictatorial powers over noncooperation. He announced that the postponed campaign of 'offensive civil disobedience' in Bardoli would go ahead.

"Although they had been upset by Gandhi's intransigence, some of the Moderates were still hoping to find some way of bringing Gandhi and Reading together, to achieve the positive constitutional advances they knew were possible. Jinnah and Malaviya called an all-parties conference in Bombay .... Gandhi attended 'informally', after Congress had agreed to postpone the start of civil disobedience until the end of the month. The motions calling for a round-table conference were passed unanimously, But then Gandhi threw another spanner in the, refusing to take part. Obsessed with putting full-scale Satyagraha to the test, he decided that a conference 'for devising a scheme of full Swaraj is premature. India has not yet incontestably proved her strength'."

b. Reading Proposed Round Table-Cabinet Vetoes Bridge p. 11 (Based on D. A. Low, "The Government of India and the first Noncooperation Movement, 1920-22", Journal of Asian Studies, XXV (1966), pp. 241-59)

"Lord Reading, the Liberal Viceroy (1921-6), had reached the end of his tether.... faced with massive demonstrations looming against the Prince of Wales in Calcutta, he wavered add asked for permission to convene a round table, conference and offer concessions-possibly full provincial autonomy. An emergency meeting of the Cabinet India Committee refused him outright and told him to arrest Gandhi, who was still at large, forthwith. Still smarting over the Irish Treaty of the previous week, they were not prepared to retreat again at the bidding of a nervous Viceroy whose character some of them doubted. Gandhi was arrested in March 1922 and jailed for six years (though he was out in two). Civil disobedience collapsed."

c. Reading Opposes the Proposed Round Table Reading 1945 p. 195

"The situation was in fact critical. The influence of the Government had so gravely declined that in various quarters both in India and in England it was suggested that the only course was for the Viceroy to call a Round Table Conference in an attempt to reach an agreed settlement of India's political problems. But Lord Reading set his face against all such hints and proposals, and not only declared his intention of refusing to take the initiative in summoning such a conference but also of rejecting the proposal if made by anybody else.

For he realized that there could be no compromise with the out-and-out extremists, who at this time were in full control of the noncooperation movement; as he himself wrote: 'The truth is, the more I consider the question of a Round Table Conference, the more I lean to the conclusion that unless the non-co-operationists make very material changes in their programme, it will not be possible to conciliate them.'"

THE CONCEPT OF AN ALL INDIA FEDERATION

The Montagu-Chelmsford Report (1918) foresaw the eventual need for an All-India federation ("Granted the announcement of August 20th, we cannot at the present time envisage its complete fulfilment in any form other than that of a congeries of self-governing Indian provinces associated for certain purposes under a responsible government of India; with possibly what are now the Native States of India finally embodied in the same whole, in some relation which we will not now attempt to define. ") The Simon Commission clearly foresaw the necessity for an All-India federation but saw it as a far off goal. It was not within the Commission's mandate to investigate this issue. The Report states (vol. 2 p. 13)

"That some of the leading Indian Princes envisage some such polity in the future is shown by the pronouncement made on 19th December, 1929, by H. H. the Maharaja of Bikaner to the Legislative Assembly of his State. "I look forward to the day when a United India will be enjoying Dominion Status under the aegis of the King-Emperor and the Princes and States will be in the fullest enjoyment of what is their due-as a solid federal body in a position of absolute equality with the federal provinces of British India." However distant that day may be, we desire in our proposals to do nothing to hinder but everything to help its arrival, for already there are emerging problems that can only be settled satisfactorily by cooperation between British India and the States."

THE GENESIS OF THE ROUND TABLE CONFERENCES

The Viceroy, Lord Irwin, convinced the new Labour government of Ramsay MacDonald to allow him to make the following public statement to still Indian suspicions on 31 October 1929 (see India, Gwyer & Appadorai pp. 225-227).

The Chairman of the (Indian Statutory) Commission has pointed out in correspondence with the Prime Minister ... that as their investigation has proceeded, he and his colleagues have been greatly impressed, in considering the direction which the future constitutional development of India is likely to take, with thc importance of bearing in mind the relations which may, at some future time, develop between British India and the Indian States.... He suggests that what might be required, after the Reports of the Statutory Commission and the Indian Central Committee have been made, considered and published, but before the stage is reached of the Joint Parliamentary Committee, would be the setting up of a Conference in which

His Majesty's Government should meet representatives both of British India and of the States, for the purpose of seeking the greatest possible measure of agreement for the final proposals which it would later be the duty of His Majesty's Government to submit to Parliament. With these views I understand that His Majesty's Government are in complete accord.

The goal of British policy was stated in the declaration of August 1917 to be that of providing for the gradual development of self-governing institutions, with a view to the progressive realization of responsible government in India as an integral part of the British Empire.... I am authorized on behalf of His Majesty's Government to state clearly that in their judgement it is implicit in the declaration of 1917 that the natural issue of India's constitutional progress, as there contemplated, is the attainment of Dominion Status.

In the full realization of this policy, it is evidently important that the Indian States should be afforded an opportunity of finding their place, and even if we cannot at present exactly foresee on what lines this development may be shaped, it is from every point of view desirable that whatever can be done should be done to ensure that action taken now is not inconsistent with the attainment of the ultimate purpose which those, whether in British India or the States, who look forward to some unity of all-India, have in view.

His Majesty's Government consider that both these objects, namely, that of finding the best approach to the British Indian side of the problem, and secondly, of ensuring that in this process the wider question of closer relations in the future between the two parts of Greater India is not overlooked, can best be achieved by the adoption of a procedure such as the Commission has outlined.

When, therefore, the Commission and the Indian Central Committee have submitted their Reports ... His Majesty's Government ... will propose to invite representatives of different parties and interests in British India and representatives of the

Indian States to meet them, separately or together, as circumstances may demand, for the purpose of conference and discussion in regard both to the British-Indian and the all-Indian problems. It will be their earnest hope that by this means it may subsequently prove possible on these grave issues to submit proposals to Parliament which may command a wide measure of general assent."

This statement was backed by Stanley Baldwin the leader of the Conservative Party but opposed by many Conservatives as well as by prominent Liberal Party leaders Lloyd George and Lord Reading and by Sir John Simon. The statement did have appositive impact in India at least until opposition pressure forced the government to declare that Irwin's announcement did not imply any change in established British policy toward India (Bridge 1986 pp. 37-37). According to Bridge (p. 34):

> *"There is little doubt that Lloyd George's interest in the declaration was purely strategic, but Reading's was not. His objection was that the declaration rested on two dangerous ambiguities. First, it could be read as constituting a departure from the 1919 policy of reform by stages. Second; it was not clear that Parliament, not the conference between the British government and Indian politicians, was the final arbitrator.... Perhaps there was a personal element too. As Viceroy, Reading had been denied a round table conference in 1921. Why should Irwin be allowed a declaration in 1929?"*

Were They Really Round Table Conferences-were they Honest Negotiations?

The Oxford dictionary defines "round table" as "An assembly where parties meet on equal terms for discussion." The Indian Round Table Conferences did not fit within this definition since the British Government issued the invitations, set the agenda and chaired the conferences. However, they were a big step forward from the extremely patronizing approach exemplified by the Simon Commission. In the event, the first conference was by far the closest to the ideal of a round table conference while the third, was really just a short and limited consultation exercise.

By inviting representatives of minor elements in Indian life *e.g.* Indian Christians, Eurasians, British commercial interests etc. the British diminished the role of the few elements that really did count *i.e.* Congress, Muslims, and the Sikhs in the Punjab.

The White Paper and the subsequent Government of India Act 1935 did not reflect an honest attempt to accommodate Indian opinion as reflected in the round table conferences-

> *"Among the divergent reasons for the condemnation of the (white paper) proposals there was, in the first place, a general agreement in regard to the failure of His Majesty's Government to respect the principle of negotiation. Every section of Indian opinion held the view that the Government had ignored the implications of the statement made by the Prime Minister on December 2, 1931, in, which he said that "the Government must carry on these negotiations until a point was reached when the proposed agreement was initialled-a very well-known stage in the negotiation of treaties." But the White Paper proposals did not bear even the semblance of an" initialled" agreement."*
> *(Gangulee p. 165)*

Agenda-Dominion Constitution?

If the British leadership really stood behind their pledge of eventual dominion status for India they would have asked the Indian delegates to frame their own dominion constitution and then met with them to broker compromises on issues on which they could not agree, negotiate temporary safeguards, perhaps with a treaty (as was done with Eire, Iraq and Egypt) to cover British responsibilities and interests. This would have enabled the British leadership to keep overall control for another generation while allowing more constructive cooperation with Indian politicians. A few quotes will illustrate this-

According to Bridge (p. 25)) Halifax thought:

The solution had to be daring or it would fail. He was proposing dyarchy at the Centre. This, he hoped, would, be enough to satisfy some Swarajists but also to keep control over essentials. He elaborated further in a letter to Lord Stonehaven, a fellow Conservative who was Governor-General of Australia:

I don't believe, with the right admixture of courage and prudence, this problem ought to be insoluble. Whatever you do is clearly a risk. I should seek to define very clearly-to myself what were the limits of risk you were entitled to run and what were the safeguards you must retain. And I don't believe that, on these principles, it is impossible to present the problem in such a form as would make the shop window look respectable from an Indian point of view„ which is really what they care about, while keeping your hand pretty firmly on the things that matter and on the gears that you may have to work if the engine races.

Irwin, in accordance with his commonsense Conservative philosophy, had found a solution above logic, based on personal judgement and tacit trust more than upon constitutional devices. The Indians would get the appearance and some of the substance of central responsibility, while Britain would keep ultimate control over the essentials of the army, States, foreign affairs, police and finance should things get out of hand. "

It is possible that this would have been acceptable, as a transition stage, with moderate nationalists. According to Gopal (pp. 50-51)-

The Government were now committed to consultation with Indian leaders and a precise ultimate objective. This statement, Irwin's first real initiative in India's constitutional problem, lost him friends in England.... In India, on the other true that the Viceroy had given no pledge that Dominion Status would be established soon, or even that it would be discussed at the conference; but few had expected it. Indeed it was believed that only joint discussions with the Princes, as envisaged in the statement, could form the prelude to even the first step towards Dominion Status. In the Congress, while Jawaharlal Nehru was inclined to suspect this 'ingeniously worded announcement, which could mean much or very little', Gandhi and his senior lieutenants were not prepared to reject it out of hand. The real test was whether the British meant what the Viceroy said.

I can wait for the Dominion Status constitution, if I can get the Dominion Status in action, if today there is a real change of heart, a real desire on the part of the British people to see India a free and self-respecting nation and on the part of the officials in India a true spirit of service.'

So the Congress, . In association with the Liberals, issued a manifesto offering to cooperate in drafting a Dominion constitution if certain acts were done and certain points clarified....

> *"We understand, however, (added the signatories), that the conference is to meet not to discuss when Dominion Status is to be established, but to frame a scheme of Dominion Constitution for India. We hope that we are not mistaken in thus interpreting the import and the implications of this weighty pronouncement of the Viceroy."*

In a speech at the Federal Structure meeting Nov. 25, 1931 Gandhi said-

> *"Yet, while I say that the safeguards are unsatisfactory as they have been presented, I have not hesitated to say, and I do not hesitate to repeat, that the Congress is pledged to giving safeguards, endorsing safeguards which may be demonstrated to be in the interests of India.*
>
> *"At one of the sittings of the Federal Structure Committee, I had no hesitation in amplifying the admission and saying that these safeguards must be also of benefit to*

> *Great Britain. I do not want safeguards which are merely beneficial to India and prejudicial to the real interests of Great Britain. The fancied interests of India will have to be sacrificed. The fancied interests of Great Britain will have to be sacrificed. The illegitimate interests of India will have to be sacrificed."*

If Labour were in power with a strong majority and Britain were not in extreme financial crisis, it is possible that Halifax and the Labour Government might have followed this path. However, the labour minority government was weak, unstable, transient and overwhelmingly focused on domestic issues. Labour Prime Minister Ramsay MacDonald was anxious to maintain India as a "non-party" issue which meant appeasing the Conservative and Liberal parties. The Conservative Party in turn wanted to appease its right wing diehard element. The leader of the diehards, Winston Churchill in a speech in Parliament on August 20, 1930 (James p. 4913-4914), stated-

> *"The original plan, on which all three British parties had agreed, was to send out the Simon Commission, to consider their Report in Parliament, to refer it to a Joint Committee of both Houses before whom Indian deputations could express their views, and then to pass a Bill carrying into law the Report as modified by Parliament, and to give orders to our officials and officers in India to put it strictly and firmly into effect. That was the adopted plan, and that was the constitutional procedure. But all this has now been swept aside in favour of a Round Table Conference, a sort of large lively circus in which 80 or 90 Indians, representing hundreds of races and religions, and 20 or 30 British politicians divided by an approaching General Election are to scrimmage about together on the chance of their coming to some agreement.*
>
> *"I wish to place on record my conviction that it is almost certain that the result of the Conference will be confusion worse confounded. I hope, indeed, it will not be disastrous. It is very wrong to encourage false hopes in*

the minds of the Indian political classes. They are only a handful compared to the vast Indian masses for whom we are responsible, but they are entitled to be treated with good faith and sincerity. It would be wrong to lure and coax them over here with vague phrases about Dominion status, when it is quite certain that these Indian politicians will not obtain Dominion status in their lifetime. We may not be able to win their agreement; let us make sure we do not lose their respect. In dealing with Indian problems and with earnest men it is far wiser and far safer to be blunt and plain. The Round Table Conference has no power to confer any Constitution upon India. Parliament alone can deal with that. No proposal for Dominion status would pass through, even the present House of Commons. We do not know what the next House of Commons will be like, but it seems certain that is will be less favourable to Dominion status for India than the present Parliament. Therefore I take this opportunity of stating these facts and truths simply and straightforwardly so as to prevent, so far as a private individual can prevent, the very grave dangers and reproaches of disappointed hopes.

"Let me, however, also reaffirm the inflexible resolve of Great Britain to aid the Indian people to fit themselves increasingly for the duties of self-government. Upon that course we have been embarked for many years, and we assign no limits to its ultimate fruition. But I thought the great merit of the Simon Report was in showing that our steps should be turned in a different direction from that followed in the Montagu-Chelmsford reforms. The experiment of magnifying the power of an All-India Assembly has failed. It has produced weakness and inefficiency in government, confusion in the minds of the masses, and has in no way satisfied even those political classes for whose benefit it was devised. It is in the building up of truly representative institutions in the great provinces of India, institutions which shall have their roots deep in the soil and in the life of the

Indian masses, that the path of practical progress now lies. Until these local organisms have been effectively developed and are seen to be working well and giving good government and justice to the Indian people, it would be unwise in any way to increase the responsibilities of the Central Assembly-that artificial abstraction of Indian nationalism which only ignorance and folly could identify with India."

It was clear that whatever its aim, the round table conference would not be framing an Indian constitution let alone a dominion constitution.

Why the Congress did not Attend

"As the Viceroy's House meeting wore on Jinnah and Sapru reasoned with Gandhi and Nehru, urging them to realize that the avowal of Dominion Status and the offer of a Conference were tangible advances in British policy. Gandhi then said that he did not want his people to go to the Conference in their weakness. While India was disunited as she was at present, and while there were these vast differences of opinion among his friends, there was no use in going to London.... For this lack of unity he blamed British rule and said that he had learned the lesson of divide and rule from the British.... Could the Round Table Conference bring about unity in England?... The only difficulty he saw was the lack of unity. If there were complete unity, His Majesty's Government could not refuse to admit the grant of Dominion Status.

"It is quite clear that Gandhi was not referring to the left and right wings of the Congress but to the Hindu-Muslim conflict. When Motilal wrote to Gandhi in complaint against the viceroy's secretary's transcript of the discussion, he was explicit about the thrust of Gandhi's remarks: that 'owing to (the) weakness in (the) communal position the British Cabinet's assurance of support was necessary'. There was 'no use going to

> *London while communal differences persisted', unless the Indian leaders knew that the viceroy and the Cabinet would support their claims. To go to a Conference divided and without assured British backing for Dominion Status would be to invite Britain to play off the communities against each other and to deny constitutional advance in view of their disunity....*
>
> *"Moonje wrote direct to Gandhi to urge him not to agree to any modification of the Nehru Report in order to placate the Muslims, and a group of Bombay Hindus proffered similar advice. ' Jayakar counselled him that no concession could possibly be made except at the stage when a Dominion constitution was being framed. Earlier concessions would be plucked from their context and become the basis for further demands. Clearly, Gandhi could foresee that he would have no room for manoeuvre on the communal question unless the government were prepared to back his demand for Dominion Status.*

It is scarcely surprising that Gandhi refused to attend a Conference in London without being assured of either Indian unity or government support for Indian freedom.

> *... Both Sapru and Jinnah believed that Indians must as a first priority solve the communal problem. If India could not achieve her own unity then she could scarcely expect to achieve dominionhood."*

All the Indian actors attended the first round table conference except Congress which was the only organized national party and the only organization that could justly claim to speak for a mass or supporters. It really was Hamlet without the prince of Denmark. Congress might well have attended a round table tasked with drafting a dominion constitution. However, even this would probably have split Congress as radicals, such as Nehru had rejected dominion status as a goal in favour of complete independence. "Like the rest of the Congress leadership, Gandhi knew that attendance at the London conference would be political suicide. Congressmen would be forced to follow an agenda set by the British and they were certain to return home with far less than they demanded. Moreover, and this galled, Congress would have to sit alongside other 'representatives' of India, most notably the princes. They were forthrightly denounced by Gandhi as 'pawns' created and used by the British." (Lawrence James p. 524).

First Round Table Conference (Nov. 1930-Jan. 1931)

All India Federalism Embraced and Lack of Hindu-Muslim Agreement Glossed Over: Three key points about this conference were:

- a weak Labour minority government was in power which increasingly sought support from the Conservatives and Liberals;
- the Congress boycotted the conference though "moderate Congress" positions were espoused by the Indian Liberals; and
- the huge economic crisis of the Depression was putting huge stresses on the British economic-social-political system.

The Round Table Conference was opened officially by the King on Thursday, 13 November 1930. Someone to everyone's surprise, the idea of an All India federation was unanimously moved from a likely necessity in the dim future to the centre of discussion. All the groups attending the conference supported the concept though for different reasons. The Conservative and Liberal leaderships saw this as a way of avoiding the demand of British India for a responsible national government. In the first place, the inclusion of the Indian Princely States would delay any transfer of responsibility at the Centre and secondly, providing the princely States with weightage, and ensuring that the princes themselves picked their representatives at the Centre could be used both to deny the Congress power, and to ensure a conservative and pro-British cast to the eventual federation. According to Bridge (pp. 55-57)-

Sir Samuel Hoare lost no time in acquainting himself with the implications of all-India federation. First, he saw Hailey, who was in London as a Government of India adviser at the Conference. The shrewd Hailey advised him to press MacDonald for "an undertaking that there will be no dyarchy at the Centre except on the basis of a central federal assembly". "Having begun with federalism", Hailey continued, "and arranged for a further enquiry into it", it might then be possible to go on with provincial autonomy.... the Conservatives and Liberals saw it as the "only chance of getting away" from the road to central responsibility for British India .... If it failed, it was still a useful delaying tactic.

If the Princes actually did federate, their presence would make central responsibility much more palatable from a British point of view.... On 12 December Hoare presented his thoughts to shadow cabinet in a document headed "Conservative Policy at the Round Table Conference".... None of the Conservative delegation had "the least intention of weakly surrendering our position in India", Hoare then related how the Conference had agreed to an all-India federal legislature and thereby taken the "remarkable step" of "eliminating the Legislative Assembly of British India". This had "made it possible to rescue British India from the morass into which the doctrinaire liberalism of Montagu had plunged it".... "It is possible to give a semblance of responsible government and yet retain in our hands the realities and varieties of British control", to "keep for ourselves the threads that really direct the system of government'

There could be "a very wide interpretation of the overriding powers of the Viceroy". The army, "the ultimate instrument of control", would be "completely in our hands".

As to finance, we could (so) tie it up with (1) a Statutory Currency Board for the control of exchange, (2) a Reserve Bank for managing reserves and many kindred financial questions, and (3) a permanent prior charge upon the Federal revenues for interest upon loans, salaries and pensions, the payment of the army etc. that the sphere of responsibility could be reduced to a minimum.... Like Irwin before him, Hoare unfolded a grand design for holding the commanding heights of the Raj while gaining important kudos for giving away unessentials.

It is clear that even Hoare, the most moderate of the Conservative leadership did not intend to honour Britain's commitment to give India dominion status if this could be avoided.

At a Conservative Party Council meeting on 30 June, he (Hoare) announced that Conservative participation in the session would be contingent upon "a clear and definite assurance from the Government" that "the essential safeguards must be real and permanent, and capable of being exercised in the interests of this country no less than in those of India" (p. 66)

- The Labour leadership saw the All India federation concept as one which could plausibly be portrayed as in keeping with Britain's liberal long-term Indian commitments while, gaining Conservative and Liberal support and allowing Britain to maintain control of India's finances to Britain's (and, in the British view, India's) benefit;
- The Princely States say the All India federation concept as a way of reducing the burden of British paramountcy and ensuring their future autonomy within a truly self-governing India if one should ever emerge; and
- Sapru, the leading Indian Liberal, worried about the inability of Indians to negotiate a communal agreement, saw an All India federation as a means of progress as a path to rapidly acquiring Dominion Status with safeguards while somehow brushing under the carpet the vital Hindu-Muslim disagreements.

There was little attention paid to the obvious contradictions-

- without the Congress no worthwhile deal was possible;
- without a major and immediate share of real power at the Centre and a clear path to a democratic, united,

dominion status India with a strong central government no deal with Congress or the Indian Liberals was possible;

- a democratic, united, dominion status India with a strong central government would be unacceptable to the Muslims and Princes;
- the essence of the Conservative party position was to deny Indian politicians power at the Centre for as long as possible and to prevent, if possible, the emergence of a dominion status or independent India controlled by Indian politicians.

These contradictions would doom all attempts to work out and acceptable Indian constitution before independence in 1947.

Second Round Table Conference (Sept. -Dec. 1931)

A Conservative Federation Scheme: Four major differences from the first round table:

- Congress Representation-The Gandhi-Irwin Pact opened the way for Congress participation in this conference. Gandhi attended as the sole official congress representative. Gandhi claimed that the Congress alone represented political India; that the Untouchables were Hindus and should not be treated as a "minority"; and that there should be no separate electorates or special safeguards for Muslims or other minorities. These claims were rejected by the other Indian participants.
- National Government-two weeks earlier the Labour government had fallen. Ramsay MacDonald now headed a National Government dominated by the Conservative Party.
- Financial Crisis-During the conference, Britain went off the Gold Standard, Cabinet tied the rupee to sterling thus using India gold to stabilize Britain's currency and the general election returned a large Conservative majority.

This conference proved again that the devil's in the details. In spite of serious efforts Ghandi was unable to reach agreement with the Muslims on Muslim representation and safeguards.

At the end of the conference Ramsay MacDonald undertook to produce a 'communal award' for minority representation with the proviso that any free agreement between the parties could be substituted for his award. "Mr. MacDonald announced the 'Communal Award' on August 16, 1932. According to the Award, the right of separate electorate was not only given to the Muslims of India but also to all the minority communities in the country. The Award also declared Untouchables as a minority and thus the Hindu depressed classes were given a number of special seats, to be filled from special depressed class electorates in the area where their voters were concentrated." (The Communal Award 1932).

Aiyer (pp. 346-347) justly commented-

> *... is any country in the world which has not had its own backward classes, or the problems created by their existence. The problems are generally more acute, where the backward classes are racially distinct from the other classes in the country. The treatment of the coloured races by their fellow subjects of European or American extraction is a far more heinous blot on the civilization of the latter and the governments of the countries where such treatment is tolerated. How solicitous the white races are at heart for the welfare and uplift of coloured races can be judged from the manner in which the negroes are treated in the southern states of America and the negroes and the Asiatic races are treated throughout Africa and elsewhere. The world knows how, after going to war with the Boers on the pretext inter alia of the ill-treatment of Indian settlers in South Africa, the British Government coolly handed over the destinies of its Indian subjects to the keeping of the white settlers and how the Imperial Government proposes*

> *to confer responsible government on a handful of white settlers in East Africa in disregard of the interests of the much larger numbers of Indian settlers. No one in India can believe in this effusive solicitude of the British Government for the depressed classes as a sincere answer to the political demands of the country. It is believed, not without justice, that the various reasons put forward as arguments against any large relaxation of Imperial control are not the real reasons which weigh with the Imperial Government. The true reason is that, though the British Government admits that they hold the country as trustees for the people, they are not wholly disinterested trustees. On the other hand, they are deeply interested in the maintenance of the status quo and in their own domination of India.*

Gandhi took particular exception to the treatment of untouchables as a minority separate from the rest of the Hindu community. To reverse this situation, he negotiated the Poona Pact with Dr. Ambedkar the untouchable leader.

Third Round Table Conference (Nov.-Dec. 1932)

From September 1931 until March 1933, under Hoare's supervision the proposed reforms took the form reflected in the Government of India Act 1935.

POONA PACT

Poona Pact, Agreed to by Leaders of Caste-Hindus and of Dalits, at Poona on 24-9-1932. The following is the text of the agreement arrived at between leaders acting on behalf of the Depressed Classes and of the rest of the community, regarding the representation of the Depressed Classes in the legislatures and certain other matters affecting their welfare:

1. There shall be seats reserved for the Depressed Classes out of general electorate seats in the provincial legislatures as follows:

Madras 30; Bombay with Sind 25; Punjab 8; Bihar and Orissa 18; Central Provinces 20; Assam 7; Bengal 30; United Provinces 20. Total 148. These figures are based on the Prime Minister's (British) decision.

2. Election to these seats shall be by joint electorates subject, however, to the following procedure:

   All members of the Depressed Classes registered in the general electoral roll of a constituency will form an electoral college which will elect a panel of tour candidates belonging to the Depressed Classes for each of such reserved seats by the method of the single vote and four persons getting the highest number of votes in such primary elections shall be the candidates for election by the general electorate.

3. The representation of the Depressed Classes in the Central Legislature shall likewise be on the principle of joint electorates and reserved seats by the method of primary election in the manner provided for in clause above for their representation in the provincial legislatures.

CENTRAL LEGISLATURE

1. In the Central Legislature 18 per cent of the seats allotted to the general electorate for British India in the said legislature shall he reserved for the Depressed Classes.
2. The system of primary election to a panel of candidates for election to the Central and Provincial Legislatures as i herein-before mentioned shall come to an end after the first ten years, unless terminated sooner by mutual agreement under the provision of clause 6 below.
3. The system of representation of Depressed Classes by reserved seats in the Provincial and Central Legislatures as provided for in clauses (1) and (4) shall continue until determined otherwise by mutual agreement between the communities concerned in this settlement.

4. The Franchise for the Central and Provincial Legislatures of the Depressed Classes shall be as indicated, in the Lothian Committee Report.
5. There shall be no disabilities attached to any one on the ground of his being a member of the Depressed Classes in regard to any election to local bodies or appointment to the public services. Every endeavour shall be made to secure a fair representation of the Depressed Classes in these respects, subject to such educational qualifications as may be laid down for appointment to the Public Services.

   (Adult franchise but reservation has been provided for Dalits on population basis, till 1960).
6. In every province out of the educational grant an adequate sum shall be earmarked for providing educational facilities to the members of Depressed Classes.

Introduction: Babasaheb Ambedkar has undoubtedly been the central figure in the epistemology of the Dalit universe. It is difficult to imagine anything serious or important in their collective life that is totally untouched by Ambedkar. For the Dalit masses he is everything together; a scholar par excellence in the realm of scholarship, a Moses or messiah who led his people out of bondage and ignominy on to the path of pride, and a Bodhisatva in the pantheon of Buddhism. He is always bedecked with superlatives, quite like God, whatever may be the context in Dalit circles.

It is not difficult to see the reason behind the obeisance and reverence that dalits have for Ambedkar. They see him as one who devoted every moment of his life thinking about and struggling for their emancipation, who took the might of the establishment head on in defence of their cause; who sacrificed all the comforts and conveniences of life that were quite within his reach to be on their side; who conclusively disproved the theory of caste based superiority by rising to be the tallest amongst the tall despite enormous odds, and finally as one who held forth the torch to illuminate the path of their future. Few in the history of millenniums of their suffering had so much as looked at them as humans and empathised with them as fellow beings. He was their own among these few. It was he, who forsook his high pedestal, climbed down to their level, gave them a helping hand and raised them to human stature. It is a commonplace occurrence to see dalits right from the humble landless labourer in villages to the highly placed bureaucrat in corridors of power, emotionally attributing their all to him. They all believe that but for him, they would still be living like their forefathers, with spittoons around their necks and broom sticks to their behind.

It is thus natural for dalits to place him at the centre as their beacon and conduct their collective affairs as directed by its beam. This beam however is not monochromatic like a laser beam, to use an analogy from physics, but is composed of many light frequencies, the filters for which are controlled not by the masses but by some others. They manipulate this beam as per their desire, sometimes letting some frequencies pass and some times some other. They could selectively amplify some part and de-amplify the other and present an entirely different spectrum. What reaches the masses, thus, is not the holistic and true picture of 'Ambedkar' but its part, sometimes a distorted part, carefully filtered out and amplified by the 'technicians'. This fragmented and false Ambedkar is what reaches the masses. For them, Ambedkar is no more a historical personality named Bhimrao Ramji Ambedkar. He is already metamorphosed into a symbol-a symbol for their collective aspiration, an icon for the thesis of their emancipation. Because for the masses icons come handy. They are sans complexity of the main body, practical useable artefacts. Iconisation of the great heroes and their ideas at the hands of masses is thus inevitable. Human history is replete with such icons; rather it is largely made of them. The Dalit politicians who never let the masses see the material aspects of their problems and kept them entangled in the cobweb of emotional issues have moreover promoted iconisation of Babasaheb Ambedkar.

This paper is premised on a hypothesis that the history of post-Ambedkar Dalit movement is largely influenced by the icons of Ambedkar that were produced by the sociopolitical dynamics of post-independence India. The process of iconisation, whatever be the motivations, has to have the basis, howsoever tenuous, in the material reality, in the facts about the subject. Being essentially a simplification of a complex reality, it involves the playing up of facts as per one's proclivities and propensities. The paper therefore attempts to trace out the bases for various Ambedkar-icons in Ambedkar himself and simultaneously highlights the motive force behind the underlying distortions that they embody. While it largely holds these icons responsible for the current sorry State of the Dalit movement based on the near-monotheistic devotion of dalits towards Babasaheb Ambedkar, it still considers that the conceptual framework that he reflects could be used, not only to further the emancipatory struggles of dalits to its logical end but also to promote a true democratic revolution in India, provided it is seen in a radical light.

The paper is divided into four parts. The first reviews the post-Ambedkar Dalit movement, essentially in relation to certain significant milestones or trends and attempts to trace the specific icon of Ambedkar that underscores each. The second part discusses the general limitations of transpositioning the ideologies, characterising specific episodes in the history across the historical periods and in specific reviews the predominant profiles of the Ambedkar-icons. It outlines the need to redefine Ambedkar, if he is to be the ideological icon to guide the Dalit movement to its logical end. The third part discusses certain predominant issues that will have to be essentially resolved in the redefinition project and gives clues for profiling 'Ambedkar' for the future Dalit movement. The fourth and final part sums it up, emphasising the relevance and validity of the basic framework implied in Ambedkar's work-to view the contradictions in the society from the standpoint of the worst victim and work for their resolution, to bring about a democratic revolution in India.

POST-AMBEDKAR DALIT MOVEMENT

A review of the significant events and episodes in the Dalit movement after the demise of Babasaheb Ambedkar is attempted here in order to identify the icons behind them and assess their characteristics.

Gaikwad vs. Others

After the death of Babasaheb Ambedkar, the mantle of leadership fell upon the shoulders of Dadasaheb Gaikwad. He appeared to be the natural choice, by virtue of his stature in the movement as well as his age. He had grown up to be Ambedkar's trusted lieutenant through frontline participation in all the battles, right from the days of Mahad. He represented a typical activist of the Ambedkarian movement and had a mass identity. He seemed to know the exact pulse of Dalit masses. It is interesting to note that the question of land that by and large constitutes the crux of the Dalit problem (as recognised by innumerable scholars even today) was and could only be taken up by Gaikwad.

It was the biggest and by far the most glorious event in the post-Ambedkar Dalit movement. Even during the days of Babasaheb Ambedkar, the mass struggle for land had never materialised in direct terms and at such a scale. At the most, it could be said to have materialised symbolically in the form of a struggle for abolition of 'Khoti'-a kind of landlordism that prevailed in the Konkan region of Maharashtra. At any rate, as a mass struggle for land at the national level, it did not have any parallel in Indian history. It was the first time that the economic dimension of the Dalit problem was effectively integrated with their social oppression. It had gained an overwhelming support from the masses all over the country. Scores of Dalit families went to jail and many Dalit hamlets remained deserted for days.

However, although it had caught the fancy of Dalit masses, the rest of the Dalit leadership thought otherwise. They disproved Gaikwad's struggle as being communist and declared that it had no place in Ambedkarian agenda. They highlighted Ambedkar's statement that mass struggles were the grammar of anarchy in the constitutional regime and should not have any place in a parliamentary democracy. They argued that if the land question was at all important, it could have been taken up judicially in the Supreme Court of India. Fortunately, none suggested parliamentary solution. It was perhaps considered infeasible as none could muster requisite majority to effect the people oriented fundamental changes after the Poona Pact. In tacit terms, the other leaders were accusing Gaikwad of being intellectually incapable of comprehending the subtleties of Ambedkar's ideology and hence unsuitable to step into his shoes.

Gaikwad, a rustic in the common man's Dhoti-Kurta attire, and not embellished with university degrees, could not be accepted by these people. They considered themselves the true heirs to the leadership after Ambedkar on the sole criterion that they fitted the Ambedkarian mould (as they conceived it) better than Gaikwad. This mould was based on the contemporary middle class cultural norms that Ambedkar displayed in his attire and general demeanour. They would conveniently forget that his western attire was basically a counter to Gandhi's belaboured austerity and a representation of modernity as against Gandhi's anti-modern views. Instead, they aped him in all appearances. They wore trousers and shirts, were suited and booted, had university degrees and could command better sophistry than Gaikwad. They would exhibit their law books as the key to the treasure left behind by Ambedkar. They could thus project themselves as better clones of Ambedkar to the gullible Dalit masses. Gaikwad and the people of his ilk could be activists but not the leaders!

The first attempt to iconise Babasaheb Ambedkar and considerably successfully so, as the later times proved, is apparent in this early post-Ambedkar episode. That was the icon of a 'saheb' the epitaph used for an Englishman but later used as an honorific for natives, who were educated, westernised and placed in bureaucratic authority. It denoted someone far above the masses, one who was endowed with authority and power. It was the icon of a saviour. It projected leader as the saviour incarnate who would liberate them from their bondage and lead them to prosperity. All that masses had to do was to stand solidly behind him. They did not have any specific role in the project of their own emancipation other than being meek followers of the leader.

This particular icon distanced the Dalit leadership from the masses in every way in terms of physical attributes like appearance, clothes, language and lifestyle. It promoted blind following and servile notions. The leaders were to be treated as their quasi-monarch (a la Bhim Raja). They could not be questioned on equal terms. They bestowed favours by their very existence. Without leaders the masses could not exist. It obfuscated, mystified and externalised the problems of dalits, if not their very existence. The saheb syndrome that curiously settled among dalits as the general honorific, almost devoid of any attribute association, got significant reinforcement by this icon. Moreover, in so far as this syndrome reflected middle class aspirations and value associations, this icon helped petty-bourgeoisize the entire Dalit movement.

Although, later the Dalit Panthers brought in a change in this leadership model, certainly in its physical attributes and so made it more people friendly, it approximately recoiled back to the old RPI (Republican Party of India) model with the demise of the spirit behind Panthers. This leadership model was certainly regressive as it reproduced the decadent feudal structure that dalits were so familiar with in real life; perhaps it was both, its cause as well as its effect. Paradoxically, its protagonists and promoters were the very people who seemed to claim a larger share of modernity. Gaikwad's equation with the masses and his charisma would not be easily swept away by their attempts but it is a fact that he could not take up mass based struggles thereafter and rather chose to fall prey to the enticements of power and pelf form Congress circle. Thus, this early icon of Ambedkar certainly blocked the emerging mass orientation of the Dalit movement.

Tailist Pursuit of Power

The importance of dalits in the scheme of post-1947 politics was duly recognised by the ruling classes, then predominantly represented by the Congress party. It was vital for them to tie dalits to the parliamentary alternative. Hypothetically speaking, if the latent alienation and the proletarian consciousness of dalits were allowed to grow in an unhindered manner, revolutionary prospects for India would have been closer than in any other conceivable place in the world.

However, no ruling class would allow this to happen, much less the Indian one, which had impeccable credentials in its adeptness at keeping its victims within the institutional bondage for millenniums with mere soft strategies. Whatever the other motivations, there was certainly this element of strategy at work in making Ambedkar the chairman of the drafting committee for the Indian Constitution. It is said that it was done at the instance of none other than Mahatma Gandhi.

For Gandhi-the super-strategist of the Congress, the Poona Pact with which he effectively blocked the political voice of dalits within the parliamentary framework, it was necessary to commit them to the latter for a long period. Could there be a better method to achieve this than getting Ambedkar-the undisputed leader of dalits, who had come to regard him as their Messiah, to author the Constitution! It is a tribute to Gandhi's farsightedness and cunning that he prompted Nehru to make it happen. Gandhi and Nehru knew that the composition of the Constituent Assembly, surfeit with representation of the propertied classes by design, provided enough fortification not to let Ambedkar's ideology penetrate the Constitutional draft. But, at the same time, Ambedkar could be eulogised as its maker.

The strategy killed several birds with one stone. It won the Dalit commitment to the Constitution; it projected a progressive facet of the Indian ruling class to the world and planted false consciousness among dalits. Thus, although the content of the

Constitution was decided by the ruling classes, the ruled ones were made to own it up. It was a feat of strategy certainly comparable in its import to that behind the caste institution. Behind its generosity and progressive veneer was hidden the trap which would effectively incapacitate the dalits for a long time to come. Once trapped they would stay in perpetual fragmentation in the turbulence of electoral game played by various sections of the ruling classes. Dalits constituting over 15 per cent of the total population are a significant factor in the number game of electoral politics. Their spread prevented them from winning any election on their own steam but at the same time none other could possibly win it without their support. Every ruling class political party would vie with each other to get them as a vote block on its side and still collectively prevent their coalescence into a class.

The mass struggle that materialised under the leadership of Gaikwad certainly shook the ruling classes. They had to devise special strategies to contain the threat of the emerging Dalit challenge. It was a challenge indeed, although inadequately articulated, that had exactly touched the most sensitive nerve of the feudal structure, which still lay at the base of everything that mattered to dalits. The implementation of this strategy was soon seen in Gaikwad being befriended by Yashavantrao Chawhan, the then chief minister of Maharashtra and later the Deputy Prime Minister of the country. It culminated in the first alliance between the RPI and the Congress, which helped Gaikwad, and a few others reach the Parliament and Legislative Assemblies. The inauguration of the era of unprincipled alliances could be discerned right here. The Congress was undisputedly a representative party of the Indian ruling classes comprising the high caste capitalists and landlords. The alliance between this party and the party of the most exploited in the land, to say the least, could only be termed unholy.

In the face of it, it appears difficult to associate this phenomenon with Ambedkar who for the best part of his life had fought the Congress tooth and nail, criticised it ruthlessly above-indicated icons. The leaders were always seen endowed with an uncommon wisdom that was really beyond the reach of masses. Leaders thus could do whatever they wanted without any scruples and they did it even breaking away from the party.

As a result, the so-called giants who claimed the legacy of Ambedkar became contented with the identity of the parenthesised alphabets of their names after the RPI. They did not even worry about the fact that the formations represented by these parenthesised identities were basically a mere coagulation of their own sub-castes, in their respective geographical areas. It was a qualitative leap backwards for the ones who had proudly launched upon the annihilation of castes as their mission. Every one claimed to be a better follower of Ambedkar than the other is, and in the process, proliferated his icons by projecting one's proprietary models.

❑❑❑